Rel~'

Nayantara Sahgal is a noveli   ⹁no
has published nine novels and   ⹁tion. One
of the first Indian writers in t   ⹁e a mark on an
international readership, she w⹁   ⹁ommonwealth Prize
(Eurasia) in 1986 for *Plans for Departure*. Born into the 'first
family' of Indian politics – the Nehrus – Sahgal saw at first
hand India's emergence as an independent nation under the
prime-ministership of her maternal uncle, Jawaharlal Nehru,
and her cousin Indira Gandhi's rise to power. She was a
member of the Sahitya Akademi's Advisory Board for English,
till she resigned during the Emergency, she was a Fellow of
the Woodrow Wilson International Center for Scholars, the
National Humanities Center and the Bunting Insitute, USA;
she has also served on the jury of the Commonwealh Writers'
Prize in 1990 and 1991. In 1990 she was elected Fellow of
the American Academy of Arts and Sciences. In 1997 she
was awarded an Honorary Doctorate for Literature by the
University of Leeds.

Born of non-conformist parents and the essence of non-
conformism himself, E.N. Mangat Rai (1915-2003) looks on his
world with unusual sensitivity, combined with an irreverent
eye and a singular lack of dogma. E.N. Mangat Rai worked
in the Indian Civil Service for over three decades, of choice
almost exclusively in the states, mostly the Punjab, where
he was Chief Secretary for the bulk of Pratap Singh Kairon's
tenure. He resigned from the Petroleum Ministry and from
the ICS in 1971.

Publications

by Nayantara Sahgal

Prison and Chocolate Cake, 1954
A Time to Be Happy, 1958
From Fear Set Free, 1962
This Time of Morning, 1965
Storm in Chandigarh, 1969
The Freedom Movement in India, 1970
The Day in Shadow, 1971-72
A Situation in New Delhi, 1977
A Voice for Freedom, 1977
Indira Gandhi: Her Road to Power, 1982
Rich Like Us, 1985
Plans for Departure, 1987
Mistaken Identity, 1988
Lesser Breeds, 2003
Before Freedom: Nehru's Letters to His Sister, 1909-1947

by E.N. Mangat Rai

Famine in the Southeast Punjab, 1946
Civil Administration in the Punjab, 1963
'Indian Federalism at Work' 1964, an essay included in *Public Policy*
The Lalru Murders, 1973
Commitment My Style: A Career in the Indian Civil Service, 1973
Patterns of Administrative Development in Independent India, 1976
Afterword to *The British Conquest and Dominion of India* by Sir Penderel Moon, 1989

Relationship

Nayantara Sahgal
&
E.N. Mangat Rai

HarperCollins *Publishers* India
a joint venture with

New Delhi

Published in India in 2008 by
HarperCollins *Publishers* India
a joint venture with
The India Today Group

First published by
Kali for Women in 1994

ISBN: 978-81-7223-682-3

2 4 6 8 10 9 7 5 3 1

HarperCollins *Publishers*
A-53, Sector 57, Noida 201301, India
77-85 Fulham Palace Road, London W6 8JB, United Kingdom
Hazelton Lanes, 55 Avenue Road, Suite 2900, Toronto, Ontario M5R 3L2
and 1995 Markham Road, Scarborough, Ontario M1B 5M8, Canada
25 Ryde Road, Pymble, Sydney, NSW 2073, Australia
31 View Road, Glenfield, Auckland 10, New Zealand
10 East 53rd Street, New York NY 10022, USA

Typeset in 10/13 Plantin Linotype
Mindway Design

Printed and bound at
Thomson Press (India) Ltd.

Contents

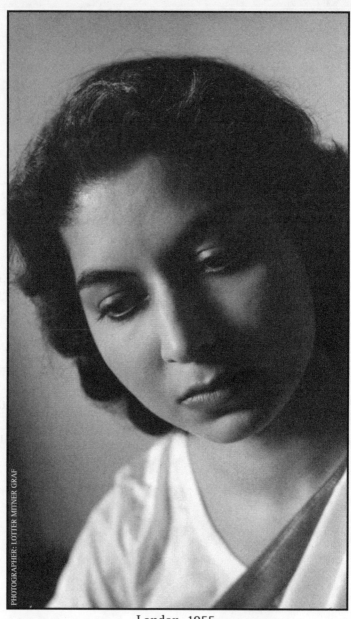

London, 1955.

Preface to the Second Edition

Relationship was originally published in 1994. The only change in this edition is the 'Chandigarh Diary' in place of the essay 'The Secretariat-Field Relationship' by E.N. Mangat Rai. I made these brief jottings during the winters of 1963-65, describing the experience of settling into the new house at Chandigarh, referred to in the letters, and from where many of them were written. Part III of the diary becomes the prelude to the marital crisis discussed in *Relationship*.

I am also including here two letters I received, one from Padmaja Naidu and the other from my mother, both offering support at a difficult time.

Nayantara Sahgal
August 2008

~

Raj Bhavan, Darjeeling
May 5, 1966

Tara darling

For many months now I have been wanting to write to you, yet I could never complete any of the letters I started because each time I was overcome by a sense of the utter futility of human speech.

Though you yourself have never said a word to me about it—and I have admired your reticence—to whom it has been a

viii • NAYANTARA SAHGAL

bitter sorrow—I have watched with pride and affection your gallant efforts for the sake of the children to save a marriage that I always feared who doomed from its very start—and now that you have taken the brave decision to make a clean break and lead your own life in peace and freedom, what is there I can say? I have always hesitated to intrude upon the sanctity of another's life but you have been so dear to me since your childhood that whatever touches your life is of importance to me. You have been so constantly in my thoughts of late that since the beginning of the year I have re-read every one of your books in the desire to understand your better.

May the New Year of your life bring you joy and peace and whatever is your heart's desire. I wish could have spent your birthday with you but I resisted the temptation to press you to come and stay with me because I felt that you still need a little time to settle under your own roof. But I hope you will come something during the year and spend a few days with me.

Do you known that according to the Buddhist calendar today is the anniversary of Mamu's death? The Buddha Purnima–the day he was born, attained Buddhahood, and died, is calculated from midday to midday. It was on the 26th of May in 1964, and he died on the 27th, about the time the Buddha Purnima ended.

Did Mamu ever recite to you a poem on the Buddha that he loved? He had come across it is a magazine and did not know who wrote it. I shall copy it out for you.

I have sent you a little birthday gift through the Talyarkhans who were here. Hope you will find it useful.

All my love to you, darling,
Yours as always,

Padmasi

~

In the train, going from Delhi to Dehra Dun
September 16, 1974

Darling Tara

There are so many things that I who have such a facility with words, never seem able to express. One of them is love. My love for you has been an enriching experience—the fact that you are what you are and that I have had the supreme good fortune of having given you birth, has always been a big factor in my life, and yet when I think of you it is not your achievements that I see but all the sorrow that has come into your life and against which you have fought so gallantly, with supreme courage. To say that I admire you would be very trite. My feelings for you are a combination of many things, but above all a deep abiding love with which I try to surround you, but which, alas, has not been able to project you. How I wish, and how I have prayed, to be able to share your burdens even if I could not carry them for you, but life is not like that and perhaps some unkind fate has ordained that I should suffer through you. In the final analysis how little love can really achieve. But because it is there, firmly embedded in the faith one has in the loved one, perhaps it does convey *some little comfort* when it is needed.

I am writing at Hardwar. It is pouring with rain and the train is late.

My thoughts are with you—

Mummie

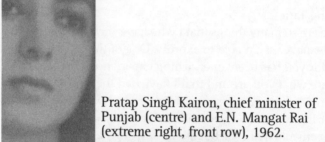

Pratap Singh Kairon, chief minister of
Punjab (centre) and E.N. Mangat Rai
(extreme right, front row), 1962.

Introduction

These are extracts taken from a collection of letters written over about three years. Rereading them, I am glad we did not destroy them as I, at least, had wanted to at the time. The story they tell may be of some interest to others: those caught up in a similar human situation; those in such a situation who have hidden it out of sight of their domestic and working lives, in a sealed compartment where it did not offend the proprieties and they need not account for it; and even those who have chosen to forget they ever had such thoughts and feelings, or took part in such events, for societies are built as much on what people choose to forget as what they remember, and conventions are so much easier to maintain by a deliberate forgetfulness that erases whatever may be inconvenient to their smooth observance. From this point of view it is best, of course, to bury the subversive, jeopardizing example. One can then safely and righteously condemn the deviant and the non-conformist. Enchanted gardens there may be, but so long as they are cultivated in secret, no one can point to them, no one say what happend there, and in due course even the two who planted one can disown it, swear no garden existed, nothing happened at all, for there is not a telltale petal nor a blade of grass to prove it did.

Fortunately oblivion was not the fate of these letters. Wiping out the past does nothing to advance our knowledge of ourselves or others. For those who wonder why people behave as they do, or what circumstances bring about that behaviour, letters are more personal and more revealing, especially of the immediacy of raw emotion, than perhaps any other form of writing, written as they are with the complete confidence of privacy. These may appeal, also, to those who enjoy a turn of phrase or a light on character, or are attracted by ideas, and above all to those who have ever questioned the foundation of what convention considers moral and respectable, though there may be the reader who decides honesty is a fool's policy and pen is best not put to paper.

Most of these are love letters, read, absorbed, and possessed repeatedly and lingeringly when they were received. Nearly everybody has written a love letter, or wishes he or she had, and the predicament and expressions contained in these may strike a universal chord. But what struck me at the time these were being written, and again now as I reread them, was what the two people concerned made of their encounter: 'Faith and belief and confidence were not what I created, but what we created between us. It would be difficult to unravel my contribution from yours; they are inextricably one.' (Mangat Rai, p. 257) It was this 'we' and 'us' that gave the encounter a terrifying strength and compulsion which neither letter-writer alone possessed. Starting as an invitation to transparent truth-telling between them, it grew in the process of writing—for meetings were rare and hard to arrange—into a relationship with a life and integrity of its own, a 'higher morality' both writers took as their first allegiance, although they were well aware that conventional morality is quite differently assessed.

Neither of them was insensitive to social conventions. Both were acutely aware of their respective homes and responsibilities, even of each others', and of all the human beings involved, which gave their dilemma a painful poignance. It had its public side too. The man was a well-known civil servant at the height of his career who, when the correspondence began, had just been appointed Chief Secretary to the Government of Jammu & Kashmir after serving as Chief Secretary, Punjab. His reputation for incorruptibility, including a disinterest in the scramble for position, favour and profit, were as well-known, as were the distinctly individual values he lived by. Yet a career that steps out of line becomes a target for attack, and there is a price to pay.

The woman, a writer, sought no advantage from a family in power, and was soon to become, as a political commentator, a forthright critic of its misuses of power. But as a woman she was vulnerable to publicity, particularly any that adversely affected her marriage. A childhood of upheavals and partings during the national struggle for freedom, when her parents were never certain what tomorrow would bring, had given her a craving for continuity and permanence, and she believed this was what marriage should mean. Fun, laughter and affection had been her experience, as of nature and of right, in her parents' home, regardless of national upheaval or personal disagreement. When she found the health of her marriage seemed to depend on the woman's devotion, submission and nurture, she gave it all these, not only because she had a natural propensity for devotion, and submfssion in the cause of a structure built to last seemed worthwhile, but because this was what women were expected to do, and she had a woman's instinct to cherish and preserve. And if submissiveness was at odds with her own upbringing, it had, in any case, been the men of her family who were feminists, the women fulfilling their potential and achieving personal, social and (in this family) political stature as a result of the atmosphere and opportunities at home. In her own very different circumstances, she, on the contrary, went out of her way to compensate for the openness of her upbringing and her American college education, by accepting the traditional male-dominated culture which her marital environment took for granted. So this relationship, as it developed, became a testing ground of courage, and a battleground of value.

Such situations are always harder on women. All but a few societies make a ruthless cult of male honour and female virtue. Down the ages the halo of virtue has extracted an awesome range of self-denial in return, from the sacrifice of life, as in sati, to the sacrifice of personality, expression and ambition, depending on the times, and more crucially, the culture of the home, especially of its males. The concept of an equal partnership between' husband and wife is not unknown, but it is unusual. Religious mythlogy has carried virtue into fantasy in the worship of a woman who, though it was conceded had conceived, become pregnant, and given actual birth, was pronounced an immaculate virgin in order, apparently, to remain worthy of worship. What is virtue in a woman? Is it compliance with society's laws, or should it be judged by a larger vision and standards? These were questions 'we' of the correspondence discussed.

The word 'society' covers a multitude of attitudes. And whatever 'society' decrees, it is people who decide. Even in our tradition-bound country the marriage bond has survived all kinds of turmoil and turbulence. Husbands have respected their wives' separate identities through marital crises and conflicts, including affairs both open and covert. Wives have exercised varying levels of freedom with no destruction to their marriages or themselves, and in this respect the village culture has shown far more tolerance than that of the more rigid urban middle class. Looking back I still can hardly believe or accept that the virtue/honour contract need have prevailed in mine, that mine was judged and broken on these terms. The true meaning of union between a man and a woman in marriage surely consisted of far more than this. Curiously, no other marriage among our friends and acquaintances—whether modern or old-fashioned—in similar, or far more radical circumstances, was judged by this yardstick. No husband or wife exacted the extreme penalty of divorce. The pound of flesh in this case was not society's demand but of a husband's individual temperament.

Afterwards I greatly desired some form of healing contact with Gautam and his new wife to help repair the ravages of divorce. This he never allowed. But the family whose daughter-in-law I was for seventeen years stayed lovingly in touch. In this uprooted, post-partition family—my first experience of Punjabis, and of the riotous humour, ardour, vigour and impetuosity of the Punjab—I remained warmly and generously welcome. My two sisters-in-law and their children have showered me with their affection; my brother-in-law and his wife have been unfailingly courteous, considerate and kind; even my orthodox mother-in-law, whatever her views, treated me gently as long as she lived, whenever I had occasion to meet her. These continuing bonds, along with my own family's support, provided a ballast which eased the transition to a new life.

The women of my next two novels limped their bewildered way to a new definition of virtue, one that meant leaving home. They had no idea there were human equations that did not extort obedience as the price of love and shelter, but they chose to take risks rather than settle for the shaky security only obedience would ensure. Like myself they had a tendency to grieve over broken bonds, and a longing for ordinary, uninterrupted living. Like myself, too, they were undramatic creatures on whom drama had insisted on descending, to beckon or goad them to decision and action. My rupture with tradition seems to have had a subduing, even inhibiting effect on my fiction for some years, preoccupied as I was with the rigours of earning a living and the well-being of three minor children. Possibly it was too difficult to fight on two fronts, both in life and fiction, and soon a third front of political confrontation with my flesh and blood on the throne at Delhi. Possibly my sort of woman, possessed by an ache for

virtue, takes years to square her account with a tearing break.
But the women in my fiction did finally emerge, and so now
can these letters.

How one woman reacted under stress, what she thought,
felt, did, may interest other women in what is still a man's
world. But ultimately sharing these letters is a celebration of
the relationship they brought to birth.

Nayantara Sahgal
Dehra Dun
1994

Part One

Nayantara Sahgal with her children: Ranjit (top), Gita (left) and Nonika (right), 1969.

E-8 Mafatlal Park, Bombay
February 9, 1964

Dear Bunchi[1]

The dispute, or the no-dispute, seems to arise out of the fact
that I am essentially a secret person. Reserve is natural to
me even with those I know best. This may be, as you once
suggested, a desire to keep from being hurt, but also to keep
from hurting—which frank expression, often ignores. It has
another aspect. My rewards stem from solitariness, and
perhaps this is vital to many of those who 'write books and
dabble in the human substance' Haven't you noticed such
people give and share less easily in everyday life, and at great
cost when they do? I agree that this creates barriers, but being
so constituted, it is difficult to be anything else. I cannot share
myself indiscriminately, and this is what lends enchantment
to the special encounters that do take place from time to time.
If such a possibility does exist between two people, I think it
comes through the barrier in time. Are there really shortcuts
to the high points of living ?

You said at Hardev's,[2] 'You have been coming here for
four years and we still don't know you.' And that night I
realised with a shock how appallingly forbidding a creature I
must appear. I realized, too, that I had never lived in a society
that had demanded more of me than I in my reticence was
prepared to give. Inch by inch had always been enough before.
But suppose you are right and it is not enough, in all honesty

---

[1]Nickname of E.N. Mangat Rai.
[2]Hardev Singh China, a friend of the authors'.

I do not know how to project that 'wholeness of impact' you talk about, if whatever I have projected has been so little as not to be evident at all.

I'm glad you remembered it was not I who used the word immoral. I do not see things clearly in terms of moral or immoral, right or wrong, and this may be why I choose compassion and consideration as guides. I envy you your certainty, but I am less and less certain. This dreadful detachment is probably the fate of all those who cannot fully involve themselves with their fellow human beings. If one cannot, the next best thing is to know such a person. So, without realizing it, you do me a service.

Love
Tara

~

E-8 Mafatlal Park, Bombay
March 26, 1964

Dear Bunchi

I was relieved to get your letter. I am full of anxiety every time I open a newspaper… There must be some reason why Pakistan is carrying on the way it is, but it is hard to understand how any government can be so wildly irresponsible in its utterances and behaviour. It was somehow reassuring to know you could drink a quiet cup of tea in a garden. I suppose since they had to set someone down in the middle of a crisis, it is as well it was you, though the news came as a bit of a disappointment as I had hoped to see you here this month. I can imagine the difficulties of the set-up, but perhaps its very strangeness for you qualifies you all the better to cope with it. Certainly the fact that you are working with men whom you consider outstanding is a great redeeming feature. This happens rarely enough in one's working life.

It is getting hot here and I am up to my ears in children, household, school and pointless comings and goings. I wonder what it feels like to be quite unencumbered. I have been wanting to go to Delhi for a few days to see Mamu,[3] sometime towards the end of April, but this is almost certain not to happen. Something invariably comes up to prevent my leaving, so I am sure to be stuck fast here till our Chandigarh trip in winter. I shall envy you in May when you move to Srinagar.

Love
Tara

~

Raj Bhavan, Bombay
April 19, 1964

Dear Bunchi

I moved here to Raj Bhavan on Friday with the girls. Their holidays have begun and Mummie[4] has given us this guest cottage right on the sea so that we can have a change from the flat and use the nearby beach every day. The sea is so close here, a huge shining expanse, so beautiful and terrifying. In ten years of proximity to the sea I am still not used to the sight and the power of it.

I am intensely interested in what you have to say about Kashmir. Sadiq's[5] speech, reported today, is so confident and courageous. One feels also that the Kashmir government acts

---

[3]Jawaharlal Nehru, Nayantara Sahgal's uncle, then Prime Minister of India.
[4]Vijayalakshmi Pandit, then Governor of Maharashtra.
[5]Chief Minister of Kashmir.

as a team, a feeling so lacking in so many other states. I was unhappy about the Sheikh[6] being released before the Security Council meeting, and just before Id, but perhaps this was the psychological moment.

I wonder if Delhi is the best place to meet you, since you must be fully occupied when you are there. On the other hand, what other place *is* there? Rather a dim conclusion considering it's such a big world.

There are about ten thousand other things I'd like to write about. One cure for this malady is complete silence.

Love
Tara

~

Prime Minister's House, New Delhi
June 3, 1964

Dear Bunchi

Your letter about Mamu was forwarded to me by Gautam. I feel an utter desolation. For years I have dreaded this event[7]

---

[6]Sheikh Abdullah, former Chief Minister of Kashmir (then known as Prime Minister) who had been in detention since April 29, 1958, charged with conspiracy in the Kashmir Conspiracy case. The case was withdrawn on April 8, 1964 following consultations between Ghulam Mohammed Sadiq, the head of the J&K government, and Jawaharlal Nehru.
[7]The death of Jawaharlal Nehru.

Note: The denominations 'Prime Minister' and 'Sadr-i-Riyasat' were changed to 'Chief Minister' and 'Governor' through an amendment to the J&K Constitution with effect from May 30, 1965.

and since last January I have tried to steel myself to accept the possibility. How little I have succeeded is apparent to me now. I have never been as passionately devoted to anyone as I was to him. He was a rare and wonderful human being. There will not be another like him in a thousand years. He would have hated to be mourned with tears and yet I cannot help myself, and sit here crying. I know that I shall miss him till I die, and the thought of returning to Bombay and living my ordinary life again is somehow unbearable. We are taking his ashes to Allahabad on the 7th. It will be the last time, too, that I will see my childhood home since it will now become a memorial to him. This is right and proper, but it will sever the last link with my childhood. All thoughts of a trip to Kashmir or anywhere else are very far from my mind at the moment.

Love
Tara

~

E-8 Mafatlal Park, Bombay
July 23, 1964

Dear Bunchi

We are flying to Srinagar on the 7th from Delhi for the weekend. Gautam has work in Chandigarh, and a magnolia to plant at Anokha which he brought from Switzerland, and this is why we are going there for a couple of days. I don't generally make these short trips with him but I have been wanting a break for a long time. I feel a deadly detachment though life goes on and there is plenty to do, plenty one must do. My difficulty is partly finding my sort of people. I must admit I have not looked too hard since I am happy enough to be alone, but there are moments when one yearns for true companionship, whatever that might be. What exactly is it? I have had such satisfactory relationships with my sisters, my parents, and my uncle that I have not made a real effort to look beyond. My college days were spent abroad and I haven't been able to establish a similar closeness with anyone here. It has taken me years to find myself in the smallest way, because I tried too hard to adapt to a new sort of life and erased too much of myself in the process. Only within the last few years I've traced my painful way back to a point where I can, in a sense, start again from the real me. And now at last I have the confidence to be myself.

Love
Tara

~

1 Church Road, Srinagar
August 10, 1964

My dear Tara

I have returned from office a few minutes ago (6:10 pm now) and would much prefer writing when I was fresher, but I see a long day stretching before me tomorrow, and wish to write. I have much to say, but the thoughts are disjointed, and may not come with any ease or vigour.

The enclosed chit was handed to me at the Cabinet meeting about 12 noon from my PA, whom I had asked to ring up to find out about the Viscount. So the clouds did not help to keep you here as I had wished they would. I am sorry you have left, and I am sorry I did not get a chance to talk to you, or be with you, adequately. I wanted both, and am presumptuous enough to believe that you did also. Did you? Always say No to me when that is so, as I can understand and take it.

You talked of greed—was that the word? I am glad you were greedy. So was I. I wanted you to know, as soon after I met you as possible, what had happened and was happening to me. I decided I may not get the opportunity and even if I did, it may be difficult to talk about it, and so decided on the letter, which puts the facts fairly chronologically and clearly, and included some of the feelings. So I wanted to thrust on you knowledge of me as soon as I could possibly do so. Was that not greed?

And if you were also greedy, as you said you were, I am glad of it, for to me it means you wanted me to have knowledge of what you felt and were. And greed I value, for I think it is the only way people give something of themselves to each other. Unless you want, the processes of giving and taking do not even start, and we remain indifferent and closed up within our wretched or 'disciplined' independence and isolation. I hope you will continue to be greedy; I hope we both will. It may be a different, or difficult matter later as to what we do with our greed, in taking or growing. But let us be grateful at the moment that we were both, after many years of acquaintance, able to talk with each other, though only, for lack of time and opportunity, only a bit.

And you say in the brief note you left with me that you would like to do something for me. But don't you see you have done something for me already, made me anxious to know you, anxious to make myself known to you. You have touched me, and I want to have more, and I hope I have touched you, and you want to have more. Could we not leave it at that for the present, accept the mutual greed, practise it when we get the chance? And you must accept from me the responsibility of deciding whether this will do you damage.

I hope you will come here in October. Please let me know as far in advance as you can, as I am to visit Leh sometime before the government goes down to Jammu,[8] and would like to make my plans so that they did not clash in any way.

Bunchi

~

1 Church Road, Srinagar
August 12, 1964

Lovely Tara

Forgive the effusion, but that's how I thought of you at Dachigam, as you lay on the durrie mid the shine and shadow of hills and trees. Why should I not say it, and add that I cast a glance at the pale hue of that loveliness. I looked where I should, and where I should not, and I'm afraid mostly could not, for you were hidden (by clothes) from view. And I hoped I'd have a word from you today, from Delhi. Greedy?

Bunchi

~

1 Church Road, Srinagar
August 13, 1964

I have ventured to make a few (minor) modifications in your Kashmir article,[9] for your consideration. Can you make more

---

[8]The government of J&K remained in Srinagar, May-November, in Jammu, November-May.
[9]No Shadows in Kashmir' an article that appeared in the *Indian Express*. Reproduced at the end of the book.

comment on lack of communal feeling? For example, it is well understood practice that persons who hate each others' politics, socially and otherwise are friends. There are few inhibitions about food—even the Dachigam bear is supposed to eat meat. All leaders of whatever views in the Valley—I regret not Jammu—have even through the gravest provocation of the '47 massacres, not only stuck to, but been able to enforce, that there shall be no communal killing. All this sounds trite and obvious perhaps, but I think some amplification of what is a unique point about this place, seems called for. In fact it is my belief that communalism (and of course at political levels it does exist today) is an injection by India and Pakistan.

Could you work in somewhere, though it may abhor your soul to indulge in propaganda, the almost duty of Indians to visit this place, as not only a need for Kashmir's tourist trade but for their own understanding and enjoyment of Kashmir, both as a state, and as one of India's biggest international problems. I do believe the attitude has been cowardly this year particularly. There is no danger whatever to any tourist. The Kashmiri well understands that his politics are his own, as far as the future of Kashmir goes, and has never bothered (or inflicted these in any way on) the visitor, unless the visitor himself is a politician.

And now briefly what I think of you:

a)   Somewhat of a cheat—big fat envelope sealed with scotch tape and inside no Tara, only an article. I liked getting the article, but surely something from you was needed (by me).

b)   Somewhat of a cold fish—reasons same as above.

E.N. Mangat Rai

E-8 Mafatlal Park, Bombay
August 15, 1964

It pours and pours all the time and Srinagar seems so remote in all its loveliness.

I am in the rather peculiar state of carrying on a perpetual conversation with you while I go about my work, so bad for discipline (which I highly prize) and peace of mind and routine, and it is hard to be a good wife. I have been thinking about the type of relationship I would like to 'invest' in with you. There are as it happens countless difficulties in the way of what I personally want. It remains to discover what I can actually have. What is important is that I should keep whatever I can of it rather than lose it altogether. I know how delicate and uncertain the ground is beneath this relationship, not between you and me, but because of the other people concerned.

What makes this different from anything else? I'm not sure, except that it is different in quality. What do I want from you? I don't know, but I do want you to recognize the person I am, good or bad, however I may be. Now this, if you knew me, is a strange thing. My purpose so far has been to shield myself from any possible onslaught. I don't particularly want to protect myself now. Do you think I am exaggerating? I wonder, too. I am not familiar with this feeling. Have never had it before, despite a lifetime of meeting many sorts of people, and travelling and being on my own since I was about fifteen. Will this last? I don't know.

India is a very big country. Hundreds of miles between here and Chandigarh, for example. What are you doing this afternoon, I wonder? Do I really want to be with you, or am I imagining it? Am I really feeling different, or am I imagining it? But then, what an imagination this is—and what it wants is a sense of belonging at last.

I am not ashamed of writing to you or of what I say. I am not overburdened with a sense of shame about anything.

Gautam considers this a serious lack in my character, an amorality, a not knowing right from wrong. And it is true I am frequently confused about the distinction. I have done some—from his point of view—horrifying things because I couldn't (still can't) see that they were 'wrong'. So I have to not do what *he* considers wrong, which is why I live in a fairly constricted atmosphere, associated in my mind with marriage and the need to consider and accommodate the other person. He did not, you remember, agree to leave me in Srinagar an extra day, and having me back here seems to signify safety, or at least an out-of-harm's-way attitude for the present.

I do not agree with your 'open' philosophy. It's a luxury few people can afford. Most have too many ties and commitments. I consider my many duties almost sacred. I give them all I've got and I'm something of a perfectionist. But there is a side of me I could never share or involve with any human being, and this side is free and amoral, and perhaps deceitful if that is what I must call the pursuit of many hungers. I found out very early in my marriage that Gautam must be protected from the truth if the truth concerns me. I must enter his world and stay there with him. Then I am free intellectually. Any other kind of freedom he is not prepared to tolerate or discuss.

I have been asked to write an article on Mamu for a special issue of the *Illustrated Weekly*, but I won't get down to that just yet. First I must deal with my Minister[10] and get all the untidy ends of the book tied up. Then, if Fate is kind, I shall be allowed to polish the manuscript in Kashmir in October, and send it off.

Tara

~

---

[10]Kalyan Sinha, a character in *This Time of Morning* which Nayantara Sahgal was working on at the time.

74/Sector 9-A, Chandigarh
August 18, 1964

My dear Tara

I cannot write with any ease. The house is full, including four children. I am not good with children, but these have adopted me, and I believe I am the only person they have no fear of whatever.

You ask me if I have anything 'special' for you. Surely that is obvious. Long before this debacle, it was I more than you who wanted to contact you. It was I who wrote to you when you left here, in an attempt to get hold of you, to make you put down some of the barriers. I also told you, when you asked, about Kaval.[11]

You are somewhat right, and yet wrong, when you say that I give so much to 'everyone, anyone'. I do not think I was indiscriminate. I was very choosy and had few friends, even at Chandigarh where I have lived so long. You and Gautam, in your short visits, established a greater variety of relationships than I have in over a decade. I had a kind of influence (or so I imagine) but few real contacts. Of course you are special, and have been for a long time. How difficult you have been in fact—never relaxing, never allowing me near, till I had almost to quarrel with you. It was I who quarrelled, not you. You merely accepted the quarrel.

But as to the rest, you are quite right, I do not know. I do not know what will happen to me, where I will go, how long it will take. For I was breaking the laws of man. I would still break them. I am not penitent. I do not repent. In fact one thing that comes through these days almost as a conviction is that I must break the laws whenever the opportunity comes, in

---

[11]Kaval Khushwant Singh.

work, in life, these laws which make it difficult for people to even talk to each other, make them guilty and fearful, these must be broken and destroyed.

Bunchi

~

74/Sector 9-A, Chandigarh
August 19, 1964

My dear Tara

I don't know exactly how I can define my statement about damage to you. Personally, damage has never occurred to me and I do not believe I have kept away from anything because of the possible damage. But how could I accept it for anyone else? How could I accept it for you? I should, in fact, fight its possibility for you. But obviously I am not doing so, and therefore asked you to help.

Chandigarh is very sociable and except Sunday, when I arrived, I am dining out every day. Conversation is one-track—Punjab services and politics. They are full of it, nothing else is mentioned, an occasional half-hearted reference to Kashmir, in deference to me. The Punjab still is an obsession. And I wade through it all, live the moment, let time pass, not try to piece things together to achieve a pattern for the future or an understanding of the past. I wait.

And of course I think of you. Is that not obvious? If not, why do I snatch these moments to write to anonymous Tara?

Bunchi

~

1 Church Road, Srinagar
August 24, 1964

My dear Tara

If you are coming up with the children, you should stay here in October. It's a large house and you can run it (which would help me) while you are here. I am busy almost 6 am to 6 pm so that you will be able to work undisturbed. It would be quite wrong and expensive to stay at the Palace. In 1964, would it be socially unacceptable to stay, with your children, or even otherwise, at my house? Surely that is quite absurd. So please consider.

Children, was accidental, not deliberate. Not that I wanted any. I definitely did not, but Champa did, and I would have accepted that, and I believe, them also. I do not regret that they did not come, but it was not planned.

Please write.

Bunchi

~

E-8 Mafatlal Park, Bombay
August 27, 1964

It's funny you should say I belong to the 'upper upper crust' since my entire upbringing has been contrary to all that this represents, and it sounds odd to me to be associated with it. But marriage has set me down in a very different world from the one I grew up in, so you may be right. I like comfort and beauty and the good things of life, but I do not feel entitled to these on account of my birth or background. I just enjoy them and don't like to pretend I don't.

I don't know how to talk about myself. How does one go about it? What I knew I was missing did not come my way and the rest made little difference emotionally. If out of curiosity or interest you wanted to know more, I would tell you, but otherwise need I? Anything which smacks of the confessional or of unburdening myself is difficult for me to do. And yet I would like you to know me and whatever helped towards it.

I am really not in a very well state. And I know no release is possible. This is not a question of what you or I decide to do or not to do. I have a feeling of fatality and finality about this and the reason might well be that I was in need of you long before I knew of your existence, and this is why no one has reached or touched me before. Perhaps I am speaking too soon and this high tension will not continue. I know myself for a changeable creature with a horror of being trapped in any way. It becomes a necessity for me to demonstrate my freedom from time to time. But I don't see any sign of this happening. So I will not run away. There would be no point. I can't very well run away from myself, can I?

What to do about all this is again a problem. Between Gautam and me there is an unspoken dialogue about this matter, and I want to keep you for both of us. But the fact is the even tenor of my life is disturbed and likely to remain so. Perhaps at some point there will be a transformation to 'wellness', but this condition is at least something for me to wonder at, turn over in my mind, explore, even the discomfort of it. It's rather like the nine months of carrying a baby, every minute of which I have enjoyed, though it is comfortable and uncomfortable by turns. And for that matter giving birth is the incomparable experience, the only time of stark no-pretence. And perhaps love is like that too?

Tara

~

1 Church Road, Srinagar
August 29, 1964

You are in luck. I was going to inflict a long letter on you today but have got up late, a Cabinet meeting at 9:30, so time is very short, and I will only be able to write half of what I wanted.

I am not confident of where I am going and taken aback that I have lapped you up, as it were, and liked and wanted this association in its latest manifestation; a little afraid for you also—the 'bombarding' as you call it—don't know exactly what that may lead to. And I could add to these.

You are right about much that you say about me. My 'openness' is intellectual to a large extent, and deals with matters in the abstract rather than personal, though these may be based on personal experience or individual problems. But that intellectual openness stops or changes when I accept a person, or they accept me. And then I can almost use your words, I am 'demanding' and 'do not let well alone' and 'there are no safe corners' or 'hiding places', and there is a 'relentlessness about it'. All that is true and I'm afraid you are in it now and I will not let you go, unless you make it very clear to me that you wish to go. I am going to know you better, unless you run away, which you'd have every right to do.

So you will not, cannot, stay with me in spite of this big house. In fact you could stay upstairs and banish me downstairs. Anyway, if you cannot, I do not argue. Why not then stay in a houseboat, which could be stationed on the bund just behind the house, and you could have your meals here and use the house as an extension of the houseboat? Perhaps you don't like houseboats?

You are careful about not mentioning that you write or hear from me. So am I. But people somehow get to know, and at Chandigarh Kaka[12] said to me that I had 'progressed' with you, and referred to a correspondence, not specifically, but the implication was clearly there. I said nothing and have no idea how he knows that I have written to you since you left Chandigarh. People do.

What are you working at? You tell me so little of yourself, what you do. 'Demanding?' Poor Tara.

Bunchi

~

1 Church Road, Srinagar
August 30, 1964

Lovely Tara

I'm afraid I'm not content with 'the miles and weeks between us' and would much prefer it if you were here. I've hesitated much before saying this but it is a fact nevertheless. And thinking and trying to analyse the reasons, I see no clarity, so you must let me leave it at that, except that I want the opportunity, which only you can give, to know you, the whole person. And it seems we both want the same thing.

Why can't your mother seriously think of Kashmir, or is it too small a canvas? I do not know enough about politics to see exactly where she'd fit in, and that may be a difficult problem, but surely not insoluble. Kashmir needs a few really dedicated people. And what is badly needed here is cohesion in objectives, lack of too much compromise in methods and means. I think there is a world here which India has somehow missed, and which it must get if the Kashmiri's loyalty, which

---

[12]Dr H.B.N. Swift, who retired as Principal of Medical College and Hospital, Amritsar.

is the only worthwhile basis for a state while we practise democracy, is to be ours.

Perhaps your amorality is like mine, but unlike you I raise it to the convenience of a principle, a passion, an ideal. In fact perhaps I should call it immoral, for I do have an attitude, an emphasis about these matters, which does not accept the moral structure. If I were to define some of its ingredients briefly, I'd say these include, first, that the only sin is a broken relationship. There is no other sin. A relationship may be with God, and some have it, and it is then defined by religious tradition or religious personal experience; and a sin would be going against this tradition or experience. At the other end it may even be with a dog, where there is a certain undefined acceptance of terms of treatment, and if you break these, you may well have sinned. It may be with a servant, and you treat him, and he expects from you, behaviour of a certain type. And so to the most difficult and delicate equations, like friendship, parents-children, husband and wife, where there is a unique unwritten equation, and it is that equation that must be lived up to, and departure from it may be sin—not the accepted structure. So, for example, I have no sense of sin about my relationship with Champa, for I have always told her of my feelings for Kaval. I had a sense of responsibility, of fear of practical consequences, but no feeling of sin, even though I was contemplating something generally assessed as unusual.

Second, I believe morality is not to be judged by whether you hurt or do not hurt. Of course it is important not to hurt, if that is possible, and I'd make no bones about lying or deceit, to an extent if it saves hurt. But if the thing you fight for is important enough, and of public interest, it is not only *not* immoral to hurt, but it is moral to do so. That is the law of human progress and the way to discover truth. An absurd and simple example may help, for extremes make things clear. The

Muslim woman who got some education and stepped out of the mohalla without a veil may irretrievably hurt her parents, uncles, equals, but obviously unless she did it, there'd be no progress for that type of woman. She must hurt if she can. The problem, and it is one, that presents itself in more subtle and difficult form to most people is really the basic problem of freedom: practical (which is easy to see), and social and moral (which are more difficult). And on each occasion the actor must of course search his heart and knowledge that he is acting for something really worthwhile, either aesthetically or socially, or even in terms of human happiness.

So my immorality or amorality would hold that there are endless patterns of morality between God and man, man and woman, even man and animal, and in each case the moral is to honour the terms of the particular equation, the unwritten law that is peculiar to that relationship. Where you don't, you sin. And where equations clash, and moralities clash, do not be afraid to accept the principle of hurt, but with it also the responsibility that what you seek is an advance of the human good, general or particular, or an advance of truth both of which, along with freedom, are achieved only through long processes of suffering and of hurt.

Reading through this I recall, though I cannot now state chapter and verse, an idea from your Mamu's autobiography which I read in the 1930s and has always remained with me, a difficult and true test. Nothing can be moral (though I don't think that is the word he used) unless you can talk about it, put it in the marketplace, the testing ground for truth and untruth. I have been a recent victim of the process, for while the relationship between Kaval and me was hidden, it flourished, luxuriantly. I personally never hid it from anyone in my circle who was concerned with it, Champa chiefly. I accepted the test of the marketplace and never hid behind bushes, or in clandestine rest houses or the like. Kaval did not, and I accepted her morality because of the children. I could understand that and appreciate it, and be loyal to it. But when she came to the marketplace it collapsed in 72 hours, or perhaps less, and I pick up, for understanding, the debris that remains. So I do not know if your Mamu was right; aesthetically and morally he is, I am certain, but it is a test that most of us would fail.

Bunchi

~

1 Church Road, Srinagar
September 2, 1964

My dear Tara

Can only write a line to say hello today as I have long meetings on my hands. The clouds gathered yesterday and neither of the two planes arrived, so no newspapers or letters. In any event I doubt if there was one from you, as you stick to the rule of letter for letter, which today I am breaking.

Got your article in the *Indian Express* of August 29th and read it more than once. Liked it but did not like the heading they gave it. Met Sadiq for dinner 31st and he had read it and liked it. Dhar is in Delhi so I do not have his reaction.

Bunchi

~

1 Church Road, Srinagar
September 3, 1964

My dear Tara

I have climbed the hill (Shankaracharya), an hour and a half from door to door, and am sitting down to write to you 8 pm. I did not write this morning because I had an unexpected official visitor whom I could not shake off.

No, I will not say that 'no one knows about the future, what may happen a month or six months hence'. I have never used that as a basis for living. I think it is always our business to try and find out, though in fact we may never know with absolute certainty. You talk of the October trip and its difficulties. I know it will be difficult. I have two contradictory suggestions to offer: 1) I want you here without reservation, in fact this morning I was rather shamelessly counting the days to October 10th. And yet I'd say you should not push it to the point of a defined difference, and give it up if necessary; and 2) which you will think very theoretical. Why not tell Gautam quite frankly that you see the possibilities of a worthwhile friendship with me and I have urged you, when you left, to visit again? There is often a misunderstanding we carry with us, that people are smaller than they in fact are. They are frequently made smaller because we do not give them a chance. I feel he may well accept the position and respond to it. Of this you are the best judge and I may be quite wrong.

'Nothing did affect me', you say, but that could not be true. Gautam did, for example. Your uncle did, your children must. If I get the chance, which I may not, I will make you talk to me. You enjoy writing so why not start an autobiography for me, for I'd like to know you, where it started, what happened, who came, who went, what they did to you, how they influenced you.

Are the children with you at Poona? I shall think of you tommorrow in the Deccan Queen, or are you flying? I don't know. I should. That's how demanding I am.

Bunchi

~

1 Church Road, Srinagar
September 4, 1964

My dear Nayantara

You are Nayantara today because I have been to the two Kashmiri bookshops asking for your books and drawn a blank. So you'd better send them to me VPP. Don't try and send them as a gift. I will collect all my gifts from you in kind and not in books or the like.

I have imagined you arriving in Poona. How? With whom? Tell me what you do, the people you meet—like them? hate them? who are they?

What does Nayantara mean? You might educate me.

Bunchi

~

1 Church Road, Srinagar
September 6, 1964

My dear Tara

I am at Chashmashahi again and at a little table in the broad landing on the first floor, in front of me a screen formed by the open end overlooking water, valley and fields beyond, today in a haze of autumn warmth. I am engaged today in 'clearing the decks'. I wrote at some length to Champa, telling her of the Kaval business, requesting that I be allowed time and aloneness to discover my resources. I said I knew this was hard on her these many years (on me also, though I bore it in silence and more manfully), that I could not ask forgiveness for I was not penitent. I would do it again, for these were the lights I knew. For the future, though I was confused today, I had to live my truth, whatever it may emerge, more rather than less blatantly.

How was Poona? Did you enjoy it? I heard from you a long time ago and would like to hear more.

Bunchi

~

Raj Bhavan, Poona
September 7, 1964

This has been a wonderful change from Bombay. The garden is full of flowers and old trees and at night an overpowering scent of jasmine. The rain is light and silvery and not the deluge it is in Bombay. I have felt almost too languid to make the effort to write, as if I had had about half a glass of wine at eleven o'clock in the morning of a medium-warm day. Since you demand detail, it is now 11:30 pm, and the girls are asleep in the bedroom. I am writing in the dressing room before I go to the veranda to sleep.

I don't know if the October trip will be possible. Imagine a simple instance of a few years ago when I wanted very much to have lunch (in a restaurant) with someone, and said so. Gautam's reaction was so wounded, suspicious, and finally enraged (because the incident grew) that no such thing was possible. Things are better now. I could not have gone on a lecture tour to America last year otherwise, but there is still no such thing as freedom. And at all times I would rather keep things pleasant. If this is hypocrisy, I have been through an inquisition on account of the truth, so what way out is there?

Goodness, what a lot you want to know, more and more. In Poona there is an aliveness about the people, a mental activity and awareness of the world. I was impressed by the women at Mummie's tea yesterday, who were informed and hard-working. In Bombay I meet only society ladies, not women. There is a coldness about the Maharashtrian, an inability to be forthcoming, an aridness of response. But there is intellectual alertness and great respect for learning. The Maharashtrian in me responds to this, and maybe my reserve, too, is my Maharashtrian inheritance, though my father certainly did not possess it. I also admire what I know of the South. It is sure of itself. The Northerner is a kind of unsteady transplant.

My children are close to me and friends with me. Now that Gita is eight and impatient of cuddling, I miss the cuddling. What more do you want to know? I don't like bores. I absolutely dread bores. Going to parties is an ordeal because so many people are bores and since I don't drink, beyond the one or possibly two drinks, there are long hours of boredom. I also hate the Swatantra[13] mentality I encounter in Bombay. Women like to exchange confidences and this I can't do, so I have no close women friends.

There are all kinds of relationships but even the most rationed kind has a value so let's occupy the area we do at present. I wish I could stay with you in Srinagar. It would be comforting and companionable to be under the same roof, but I have not broached the subject of the trip again. It may be the twentieth century for you. For me it's still the Dark Ages and men and women are still in caves. It is true that Gautam has

---

[13]The reference is to the Swatantra Party, formed by C. Rajagopalachari.

stayed with Eulie when Jugal[14] has been away, and Kikook[15] has stayed with him in my absence, and frankly I have never given a thought to these things, but Gautam says he does not look upon any other woman as a woman. None of this can make any sense to you unless you have the background, which I have attempted to give you in the 'truth' I wrote two days ago but did not post.

How dangerous this situation is for me, as for a bird caged too long that can't fly properly again. I think some part of me actually prays for blindness and deafness again, for solitary confinement, for not being able to think or feel. It goes against my grain, too, but I can submit to it, as I have done. Frankly, I wonder what's left of me. I would like to go on writing but it is late and I am cramped now, sitting on the floor. There are mosquitoes annoying me too.

Tara

~

1 Church Road, Srinagar
September 8, 1964

My dear Tara

D.P.[16] Dhar returned from Delhi and I met him in Cabinet on the 5th and asked him if he had read your article. He said, 'I blushed in the plane reading it on my way out to Delhi' and seemed pleased. But one criticism also, in a letter from Delhi: 'Tara wrote an article of her visit to Srinagar and of how relaxed and cordial had been the atmosphere, how friendly and uninhibited the ministers, especially over beer. It

---

[14]Eulie and Jugal Chowdhury, architects.
[15] Kikook is a nickname for Jaya Thadani.
[16]D.P. Dhar, Home Minister, J&K.

appeared in the *Indian Express,* and I did not see it, but was told by somebody who did, "So she thinks they're all wonderful because they drink!"' So, young thing you should have taken my advice and cut out the beer. The great Indian mind reacts unimaginatively, and invariably in the same key, to this kind of thing. And talking of liquor, as I read your description of the visit to the Collector's office I was a little put out that you were going to get a drink permit.[17] Somehow did not like that you should; seemed wrong for some reason. And then it all changed towards the end when you told the Collector you were not ill, and why you wanted it, and I was quite proud of you.

I shall be disappointed if you do not come to Kashmir in October. And the more I think of it, the more I feel it is quite absurd that with this large house you should stay anywhere else. After all, you'll have the children with you, and in any case in the mid-sixties to have these inhibitions about staying seems absurd. But let me not try to persuade you against your better judgment. I am just having my say.

We do not know each other adequately, leave alone fully, and we should remedy that as soon as we can There is a vacuum between us, of things fructifying before they grew, and growth takes time, opportunity, patience. Both of us must accept it that way, that we must fill the vacuum with knowledge and experience, with time spent together, something to feed on. Good fellowship between us may well be like childbirth, which you describe as 'the only time of stark no-pretence'. Childbirth between human beings, each an individual, is a more difficult and delicate process, but

---

[17]Because of prohibition, liquor was not openly available in Bombay at the time and people had to have permits in order to serve alcohol and enter what were known as 'permit rooms' in hotels if they wanted to entertain or be entertained there. Permits were more easily granted on the plea of illness. Nayantara Sahgal had never had a permit before.

of supreme worth. So we must be patient, and cultivate the habit and practice of truth, however uncomfortable, however unpractised. So let me have your truth and I will try and give you mine. For it is only when you are determined to put the cards on the table—all the cards—that you can gamble for the big things. And why be afraid? At least somewhere, anywhere, with one person, do not be afraid. It may become a touchstone for a whole attitude—or a dastardly failure if it does not work. That risk you must take. I know I want to, and you want to. That in itself is a big thing for the moment, the iron in the soul which will not accept good manners merely, but will demand more. So give me that time, and even if it becomes impractical to visit here, give me that time on paper—pen and ink—by just being yourself, saying what time you feel, contradictory and difficult though it may be, not sorting it out into logic and clarity where it is not clear—just giving it to me as it came. Difficult for Tara, but surely not impossible.

Bunchi

~

1 Church Road, Srinagar
September 10, 1964

My dear Tara

I received an unexpected summons to Delhi, where Sadiq is at the moment, and have to leave at short notice, tomorrow by Viscount.

Will be there till Sunday morning and will probably not be able to write till Monday or Tuesday. It's hard not to know where you are and why you have not written. Some love,

Bunchi

~

Claridges Hotel, New Delhi
September 16, 1964

The cocktail party is making a loud buzzing noise and I have
retreated into the bathroom to write this hurried note. We had
nearly forty people to cocktails yesterday and this evening
there are sixty. To match this suite I had to bring finery to wear,
and jewellery, which I dislike and never wear ordinarily. These
two days have made me feel suspended in time. I don't like the
atmosphere of Delhi, at least not in the circles I know. There
is a kind of violent ambition in evidence. I have mentioned to
Jugal about stopping here the night of October 9th with them
on my way to Kashmir. I must go now or I will be missed.

Love
Tara

~

1 Church Road, Srinagar
September 16, 1964

My dear Tara

These unexpected journeys of yours and mine have put me in
a queer position with you. I have as many as six unanswered
letters with me, and now I may not write to you till you are
back at Bombay. Surely I could have dropped you a line at
Claridges, but you seemed to think it inappropriate. Anyway I
have not done so. I would have liked to have written something
about each one of your letters over a period of days for you
have said a great deal to me, and I am grateful and pleased
that you have. On the other hand I also feel, in spite of these
accumulated communications, somewhat out of touch, as if
nothing from me had got to you for days. The mutuality of the
contact seems to be marching on one leg instead of two.

This debacle with Kaval has brought me, almost simultaneously, two relationships, Kikook and yourself. I hardly knew Kikook before this, had talked to her at social occasions over 12-14 years, never anything of consequence. But since this debacle we have corresponded, originally at her initiative, perhaps twice a week or so. It probably started with her as a mercy occupation, but we have found much to write about. She has, I believe, an intense and vivid relationship with God: religion means a great deal to her. I think somewhere, somehow, she has also had an intense experience of suffering—personal suffering. And there is an intellectual and aesthetic, perhaps even a moral understanding between us of these matters. It is of these that we mostly have written, and to begin with of Kaval and Khushwant; she knows the latter well. And I have got a good bit of understanding from her of what I have faced, which was beyond my mental comprehension. With her it has been a process of discussion that has given me knowledge of a person who knows suffering and who believes in God. With you, it is very different, and I come near you with a need to love, a need to give and take emotionally—the 'alchemy' is there. It is as if something filled this being almost to bursting, and needed to be touched, and to give. I do not know what it is, and why it should be, and indeed even how it can be. And yet I have this need to get nearer you, and have perhaps overdone the communication with you, albeit mostly by letters.

You haven't sent me your books. I do want them. And I wanted to read them before you arrived here. So do not argue any more. I want the books as one other means of knowing you better.

In your letter of the 10th you refer to my swearing at you at Hardev's in Chandigarh, calling you 'aloof and arrogant', and that had I not written you would have withdrawn and closed up. May I explain that those words were a compliment, a statement to you that I was willing to take truth and equality from you. If I accept a person, I must draw them to the level with me, and I will even instinctively provoke or goad them to come out with themselves to me, to be naked with me as it were, for I can only deal with those I want to be near in terms of nakedness. And strangely enough, whether it was that encounter at Hardev's, or what came later, you accepted my demand on you. I do not propose to leave you for you are valuable to me. I do not propose to start with accepting limitations, for they do not come easy to me. Look at the way I am talking, as if I were laying down the law. Surely, as between us, that cannot be. Whatever this is, and wherever it takes us, limited or otherwise, we do it together.

I have had to deal rather briefly with many things of which I could, over some days, have said more, but it is one of the tragedies of a working man's life that he gets little exclusive leisure, in office in the day, and even at home in his study the family is around, a presence felt.

I shall think of you returning from Delhi today. I hope it went well.

Bunchi

~

1 Church Road, Srinagar
September 18, 1964

My dearest Tara

Two letters, short ones, one in pencil from the bathroom, today, and both were welcome. About accommodation, I think the Tourist Centre will be best (though it is not spick and span). Nedous may have more privacy, but this will be much cheaper. So please decide. Is it not good that you are coming here at all, which seemed so impossible even a few days ago. And I miss you, too, ever since you left here, (even while you were here) and my PA sent the chit to say the plane had gone, in spite of the hopeful clouds.

Delhi *never* attracted me, though I have been offered jobs there since 1944. I sometimes came near accepting, but at the end always said No. When I came from America last year[18] they twice rang up to ask me to come as Additional Secretary, Home, a key job in ambition—'may end up as a Governor'—and it never even occurred to me to say Yes, not for one minute. Yet I was asked to see Shastri on the 28th of February, met him on the 29th, and agreed to come here on the 1st of March, without even consulting Champa. It was in the blood, drew me like fate. I am surprised you should feel that way about Delhi also. But come here and we will talk about you and me.

And now, 'star of the eyes', I am really much too late and must rush.

Bunchi

~

1 Church Road, Srinagar
September 18, 1964

I did not realize till I got your letter of the 15th that you were coming here alone, and had assumed the children would be with you. If you are alone, then staying in a houseboat, or as far away as Chashmashahi, is not appropriate at all. Nothing clinches as just correct, except of course that you stay here with me, but that, you say, is impossible. So please let me know what you finally feel. I could speak to Sadiq and

---

[18]E. N. Mangat Rai had spent the previous year as a fellow, Center for International Affairs, Harvard University Cambridge Mass., USA.

I think he would readily agree to the guest house. Gautam's attitude about where you stay does not sound strange to me. I have come across it, or aspects of it, repeatedly. But I think such attitudes should be resisted, and not allowed to become a habit. However, obviously this is not, in your estimate, a suitable occasion, and your judgement would be soundest about this.

About our relationship you say 'it is a little frightening because it may be growing artificially and a little too fast, and will it stand up to the fresh air?' I had had the same thought before you wrote it, but like you, I am certain I want to see you and be with you. But you must not allow me to bully you, and provided you said you would not like to talk about this or that, I'd take it.

Bunchi

~

1 Church Road, Srinagar
September 20, 1964

My dear Tara

I sit somewhat uncomfortably and write to you, squatting cross-legged in the shade of half-forest, just above a path that goes round Shankaracharya, about halfway to the top. I have discovered it today and must bring you here. The Bible says Christ used to go up a hill 'apart from the others' to pray. I come up the hill to escape possible callers, not to pray. A little way up I discovered a path going round, undulating, and I have followed it. It is built by the Forest Department to operate on the meagre forests of Shankaracharya, and winding gently up and down you go through trees and get glimpses of the lake below, the Palace Hotel, Chashmashahi. And now I have turned the corner and below me and beyond is the hill with the fort, rows of houseboats opposite the boulevard, and the thick cluster of Srinagar town. Beyond that, fields now turning to yellow and still beyond the outline of hills, and the unfortunate knowledge that somewhere beyond, perhaps even in sight, is Pakistan, and turmoil for this valley and its indescribable beauty, and what could be its unbeatable peace, if man had peace in his soul.

And I said to myself if Tara can write to me from bathrooms, and sitting on the floor of a Poona dressing room, with mosquitoes biting her beautiful body, why can't I write to her from the hill, in a very real sense my hill, for I must have climbed it during these last eight weeks on an average four times a week, till it has become a joke with Nasir Ahmed[19] and Mahmuda,[20] who call me a 'dedicated walker'. I hope to show you this spot where I sit and have you sit here a while to see the ever renewed wonders of this land.

A few yards away I could see Sadiq's house, and just behind it Mir Quasim's,[21] and to the left, Mahmuda's. And these are friends. If you happen to drop in at Mahmuda's, at least four times a week you'll find Sadiq there, and Nasir, often Mir Quasim. It is rather queer that I have been allowed to enter this circle of old comradeship, for I am often asked, and it is invariably these people, may be one or two more. Not that I 'belong' — I am too new — but I am accepted, and there are few reserves, and I am even sought. So I do imagine sometimes a fate brought me to Kashmir, not my will, but the beginning of a pattern which has to work itself out. Here it was I received the unexpected death blow of an association of over two decades. Here also I met you on the 7th of August, and I don't think I

---

[19]A doctor.
[20]Mahmuda Ahmed Ali, Principal, Government College for Women, Srinagar.
[21]Revenue Minister, J&K.

could have met you in quite the same way anywhere else, in Chandigarh or Delhi or Bombay. And that also must have some meaning. And why should I look forward to, and count the days to meeting you again. As I climbed the hill I said, 'Exactly three weeks from today, Tara will be climbing this hill with me,' also 'It will be the day after she arrives, and she probably will resent disturbance in her work' — and I began wondering when you do most of your work, at what time or part of the day. Do not change your mind about coming here.

Bunchi

~

1 Church Road, Srinagar
September 22, 1964

My dear Tara

Your letter that sticks out at the moment is that of the 18th night where you put so clearly and vividly the relentless way I pursue you, and that it has a strength and compulsion that impels you, even frightens you. In the morning I had a letter from Khushwant from England, in which he also says I 'brainwashed' his wife, substituted my own values for her essentially religious and conventional ones. As I read your letter I had to recognize that what you say is true. I cannot quarrel with it. What Khushwant says is untrue.

I was aware I was pursuing a correspondence with you, that I wanted to know you, see more of you. But I was not quite aware that I would not let you go, and that I put this burden on you. I am sorry I have done so and yet I am glad. I can only ask for assistance from you, about what I should or shouldn't do, write less, more casually, about impersonal problems that occur to me, my work and politics here?

Perhaps you would not like me to comment on 'the truth' you sent me. I should not till I have really imbibed it. But I do want to say two things. I am very glad you sent it, and could trust me, and I accept it with a degree of humility. The second is that I felt as I read it, and reread it, that I understood every sentence not only with my mind, but with feeling, with the association of similar, though not identical experience and observation within me.

I have arranged that you have a portable typewriter while you are here. And now I must stop. It's about eight and there have been some unfortunate arrests this morning which worry me greatly.

Bunchi

~

E-8 Mafatlal Park, Bombay
September 14, 1964

My dear Bunchi

Here is some truth for you.

I suppose that freedom was the operative word all through my childhood—freedom in the larger sense, for India, and the individual sense for each one of us in the home. A happy childhood is not unusual and mine was certainly happy in a soul-satisfying way. I adored my parents and my uncle in whose home we lived. It was a household of which every member, young and old, master and servant, children, dogs, guests and strangers, everyone was a respected member. I now realize I took all this so much for granted; I did not know another sort of atmosphere existed—one in which there might be less than complete freedom, and complete acceptance of the person one was. I was never made to feel ashamed in that climate, and I was always and solely responsible for my actions, though there was love and sympathy when I sought it, and understanding when I made mistakes. This, then, was my take-off point into the world, and if I had remained faithful to it, obeyed my 'inner voice', I would not have entered the marriage I did. Partly I did so because, as I said, I didn't know a world so alien to mine existed. I never suspected it. And partly, because I did not think things through and allowed myself to be persuaded that all would be well. It never would and never could be, and I had warnings of this all the time within me, but I pretended it would. So Gautam and I got engaged.

I had just returned from college in America. Towards the end of that four-year period I had become entangled, as they say, with a man, an artist, much older than myself. Seduction is a silly-sounding word. It also puts all the responsibility on him, and I certainly would not have accepted this interpretation of the event at the time, or for a long time afterwards. I thought, in fact, I had done part of the seducing myself. I know now how small that part was, and that no young girl as unsophisticated as I was in the ways of the world, is a match in this respect for a much older and experienced man. Seduction included wooing me with ideas, with the people he knew, the whole world he introduced me to. I was too young not to be impressed by his courtship or his feelings for me, which were wholehearted and genuine. He belonged to a society that does not place a high value on virginity and he did not think he was doing me any harm. Nor was he, in my opinion. He fell in love with me and could not understand why I didn't with him. He felt the experience should have meant more to me. It didn't. Two months after I left him, I got engaged.

It seemed to me I should tell Gautam about this man. It didn't occur to me not to. I was still living with my childhood values. I told him there had been this episode, a part of my growing up. He said in reply, 'I wouldn't care if you had had

50 affairs and 60 children.' Fifty affairs and sixty children. I turned that over in my mind and thought I had had the good fortune to meet a remarkable man with whom I could live in the sun. The matter rested there, but I was uneasy in my engagement. I seemed unable to establish a closeness, except physical, with Gautam. There were conversations and attitudes that filled me with doubt. It was a troubled time and I tried to disengage myself but never hard enough, I now realize, and never honestly enough, for fear of the blow to him. I was unhappy and uncertain for reasons I could not explain. Gautam was madly impatient to get married and told me over and over again that none of my uncertainties would remain so once we were married. He was so confident, I thought my fears were foolish. I did make one desperate attempt to postpone the wedding—not to call it off—to give myself time to think things over but this he would not allow, and with some justice, since I was so vague about my reasons and this vagueness could not stand up to his definiteness and his confidence. And so we got married.

And then Gautam could not endure the knowledge of the other man and the long torture began. It became a sort of inquisition for me. Day and night I was a prisoner on trial. The questions never stopped. Why? Where? How? And above all, why, why. I could feel his torment through them and I tried to atone by giving him everything I could, assuring him, of course, that nothing like it could ever happen again, that I had been young and unthinking, had never realized there might be consequences for the future. But he couldn't stop torturing himself or me. There were days on end when he could not speak to me, when the sight of me repelled him, and the deathly stillness was terrible. At such times I could not help him because he rejected me completely and sat for hours fighting his battle alone. And then the coma would lift and he would come out of it like a man out of a long illness, and things would be nearly normal for a while until it began again, the questions, the accusations, the horrible re-creation of scenes and conversations. Anything could start it off, a picture we would go to, a story someone told, a hotel we stayed in, some trivial passing remark by someone. I began to live in dread of those moods and I began to be confused by the questions, because I no longer remembered how or why anything had happened, or what exactly I had said or done. What I could not assure him of was repentance because I didn't feel repentant. I did not think I had committed a crime. I was sorry, really deeply sorry for the grief I was causing Gautam, and I told him so time and again, but I could not ask his pardon. Pardon for what? I did not feel guilty. I still don't. And this inflamed him and he said I was not fit to be the mother of children. I had no morals, I was not clean. There is no point in enumerating all he said. He developed a suspicion and hatred of anyone I had known before I met him.

He conceived a loathing for America, which he has not quite got over yet. All the while I knew he was crying out in his own agony and my one desire was to comfort him. I tried and tried. But I couldn't because I couldn't concede what he wanted. I tried to enlarge the scope of our marriage, to discuss things with him, talk to him, but talking became a problem because there were things, I now realized, that I mustn't speak of. He mustn't know I even thought these things. I was no longer free. I was in a room about two feet square, and the only light and air were from a little grating far above my head, far beyond my reach. But I tried to be happy in that room. After all, I had chosen it. No one had forced me there.

I cut myself off from my old contacts and isolated myself from everything I had known and thought and felt. I devoted myself to being Gautam's wife. Someone who had known me before my marriage was aghast at the change in me and said he could not recognize the person I had become, so devoid of joy and gaiety. I did not acknowledge this to my friend, and pushed it to the back of my mind. Gautam did not see this happening to me because he was happiest when I was docile, obedient, when my life revolved around him. And things went on in this fashion for ten years, ten years of inquisition with intervals of normalcy, ten years of a slow divorce from myself. Ten years was perhaps the limit of what the mind could take in this respect because that was when the explosion came. Even during this period I sometimes tried to tell Gautam how dissatisfied I was with our relationship, how I felt I was carrying a burden alone—not only of our marriage, but of our children, of everything big and small that had to do with a household. We were not building anything together. There was no meeting of our minds. He said that was nonsense. He didn't feel any emptiness. He actually did not realize anything was wrong, and he continued to take refuge in our physical relationship. To him what was wrong was that I had known another man before him. That was the poison in our marriage and what corroded him constantly. I know during those ten years something died in me. I was no longer spontaneous. I became guarded because I knew he distrusted the spontaneity in me. It produced a side of me that made him nervous. Perhaps he thought I might be unfaithful to him. He minded my going anywhere, and yet the only fun and gaiety I had was away from him on occasional trips to Delhi. With him I could only watch his gay moments, be glad he was happy whenever he was, but I could never share those moments. I stood apart and watched. I was two different people, his wife on the one hand, and myself on the other. And I tried to fill both roles to the best of my ability, but myself suffered. I took my responsibility as his wife seriously. It became a job. I knew the standard he demanded and I gave it to him. And he was happy. He relaxed more. His moods became less frequent. I thought we were beginning to achieve something.

Suddenly I realized how cramped I had been, how stunted. And when in '59 I met a man who seemed to me interesting, someone I could talk to, I wanted to see more of him. I wanted to have lunch with him. Gautam did not see the need for this. Why did I want to see any man alone? Why alone? If I wanted to talk, why couldn't I talk in his presence? How could I explain that I was not myself in his presence? Till then I had always given in for the sake of peace in the home, but now I couldn't. I saw something slipping away which was a chink in my darkness, something innocent to hold on to, and I became rebellious. I had no idea of the explosion we were building up to, or I might, even then, have let the man go. Or I might not have. I can't be sure. In the middle of this strained state of affairs I had got tickets to take the children to a pantomime, an annual feature in Bombay, with this man and his wife and daughter. When we bought the tickets, Gautam had been willing to go. On that evening his mood came upon him again—and it used to happen just like this, with last-minute cancellations and excuses—and he said he was not going. Ordinarily this would have finished the evening for both of us, as I would always rather have stayed home than endure scenes on my return. But this time I went and stayed out all night. Because after the pantomime and after dropping the children home I met Kjeld at a friend's flat and we sat and talked till about 3 am. I was starved for adult companionship, for give-and-take, for naturalness, and our talk was personal, and friendly. Given time it could have become much more. Gautam found me there. He was incensed and in a terrible state and came near to hitting my friend. I told him I would not go home with him, but would come on my own, and he left. And I was actually afraid that early morning to go to my own home. But I went, and we talked, and I assured Gautam there was nothing between this man and me. I was trembling and exhausted. So was he. I don't know what sense our talking made in that state. But afterwards, in the next few days, I did tell him I wanted to see Kjeld again, only to talk to him. Gautam was wounded and suspicious. Why alone? And I held myself away from him for once and was determined not to nurse his wounds, but to force my own view. I finally persuaded him we should ask Kjeld to a party we were having on our tenth anniversary a few days later. It was a disaster and a nightmare. It never should have taken place. I should have known this. Kjeld stayed on after the others had left. He and Gautam had both drunk too much. I hope I shall never live to see such a quarrel again. The horror and violence of it are still with me. I could not in the days that followed bear my burden alone any longer. I had kept my married life a close secret, but now I had to write to my mother. I had to in any case because Gautam phoned her in London and told her my behaviour had outraged him and he was divorcing me. For two days after this he lay drunk and unshaven on his bed with a bottle beside him, and somehow the days passed, and somehow I appeared normal in front of the children, and sent them to school and received them home, and around it the nightmare revolved.

It was then that Mamu, whom my mother cabled, rang up from Delhi, and his gentleness dissolved me into tears. He asked why, if Gautam and I had been so unhappy, we had not come to him. He said he was leaving for Nagpur for the Congress session (January '59) and we should meet him there. We did. He spoke to us singly and together and things began to look less nightmarish. Mamu then suggested I should spend some time with him in Delhi, away from my own home, to think things over. He did not shrink from the idea of a divorce or separation, but he did not like haste. He wanted us to be sure, and he wanted me, above all, to be happy. So I spent a month in Delhi and returned home nearly whole, at least prepared to make a fresh start. And so was Gautam. But we were like two invalids, both shaky on our feet, frightened of the wreck we had made of our relationship, uncertain if it could ever be worthwhile. But we carried on. Gautam still doubted me, and for me this was not a complete solution. But I felt, nevertheless, that in our sadness we were closer than we had ever been, and that from this, at least, something would emerge. I didn't know Gautam did not feel quite this way. His vanity had been cruelly wounded. This burned deeply into him, and he is not the man to forget. I didn't realize he was not prepared to put all this in the past and go on from there. He was haunted by it. He had been humiliated and I was responsible. And I found this out when we went to Simla that summer.

We had been planning to go to Kashmir but the question of building a house in Chandigarh[22] came up and we decided to go to Simla so that Gautam could go to Chandigarh as often as required to make arrangements. And in Simla, with his family around us, he launched his delayed vengeance. It began when I told Gautam I had written to Kjeld because I had without warning cut him off completely, and had not been allowed even a telephone conversation with him to explain what had happened. The letter I wrote, and the one I received in reply, contained nothing Gautam could not have read. I cannot explain my fear of what followed except that hostility built up around me and I lived in the terror that only an atmosphere of unreason can bring about. I could talk to no one. No one spoke my language. This was the time I had hoped we would start our new relationship, and this was the time when I saw every door close one by one, until there was blankness around me. And there was evil. I couldn't get away from it. I took to my bed and stared at the wall. I could hardly get up except when Gautam demanded it, to meet anyone who came. I felt very

---

[22]A brief diary written during 1963-65, descibes the experience of setting into the new house named Anokha by Jawaharlal Nehru. Part 3 of the diary becomes the prelude to the marital crisis discussed in *Relationship*.

ill. I tried to plan my escape, to leave Simla. I could have, but I could not abandon my children to this sense of evil, to this hostility in the house. Ill or well I had to be near them. But I was conscious of being of no use to them, to anyone, not even to myself. Gautam's brother-in-law, Anantan Menon, was also there at the time, and would sit by my bed and do what he could for me. And sometimes he would sit by me in the garden and I would beg him not to leave my side because for the first time in my life I was really afraid. I could not understand why this was happening, or what crime I had committed to deserve it. And Anantan stayed by me until Gautam in an outburst of fury told Anantan one night to leave the house and take me with him. Finally this came to an end when we came back to Bombay and at least to the relief of my own home. But I knew I had to get away to understand all this. Gautam had suddenly without warning, in the heart of his family, turned against me and started to punish me.

I wrote and told my mother I would come to her, also told my uncle and he agreed. In London I slowly recovered. I wrote Gautam several long searching letters. He replied curtly never answering my questions. I had gone to London without the children. I had to go back to settle my affairs and decide my future. I decided if Gautam would not talk, if he would not understand, then we must part. And I went back with this decision made. I had no idea what I would do for a living or how I would arrange to have the children with me—for Gautam had said he would resist me in this respect. Children could not be brought up by an immoral woman, and he would not give me anything resembling a living allowance.

I went home, and there, to my amazement, found him happy to receive me, but still not willing to talk, only to cling to me physically as before. I distrusted this and said nothing could go on unless there was a basis of self-respect for it. He agreed to this and said we would work things out if we tried. Perhaps when it came to the actual break, Gautam did not want it. He began to believe me more, doubt me less. I expected nothing to come of this new effort, but something began to come of it. The atmosphere cleared and I could talk to him more. His work began to make more demands on him, he was given greater responsibility, and all this combined to make him happier and give him purpose. And then the house in Chandigarh started a new phase for us too. Gautam found honest friendship and fun of a kind he had missed all the years in Bombay. He renewed old contacts and felt at home as he can only feel in the Punjab. A change came over him and the children noticed it and profited by it. And of course it made a world of difference to me. But I arrived in Chandigarh encased in armour. I had been too shattered to ever expose myself again. I wanted to be left alone in my privacy. I didn't want to expose myself at all. I couldn't, in fact. To whom? I was Gautam's wife instead, and my own life, as always, continued hidden. I never talked about my feelings. I couldn't. I could take no risk again. But I enjoyed seeing Gautam happy with his friends, at his beer parties, on his walks. He was coming to life and it was what I had long wished for him. For myself I had decided to fill my life with work, write more, do whatever I could to make a life for myself. He did not become less jealous or possessive. Sometimes I feel he is more watchful now because he values me more.

I have been conscious ever since our reconciliation of the need for greater independence for myself—of thought and action. I have felt urgently that I must assert myself more in every way without striking any mortal blow at Gautam's love or trust. I must be more and more myself, but gently so that I don't injure him. Because I must, if the rest of my life is to have any meaning, go back to the values I once held so confidently, or forward to a new understanding of them. I am not the person I once was. I am surrounded by a stone wall. I built it myself for my protection. Nothing can be as it once was. But it can be better than it has been. I owe it to myself to try honestly and uprightly for that betterness—and that is something I have yet to figure out, how to be myself, yet honest.

And this is how you find me.

Tara

~

E-8 Mafatlal Park, Bombay
September 23, 1964

About my trip—I don't feel I can give it up, and I am grateful Gautam has agreed to my staying with you in view of all the accommodation difficulties. To me it seems reasonable and natural to go away for a while, not too much to ask. I hope he will not change his mind. I live constantly on the edge of a volcano, never knowing, never sure of the change of mood and temperature in this house. If I have been determined to come it is because I have struggled against paralysis at various stages, known it was wrong to live like that, known also that it needed more than the strength I had to lift me out of it. Most people live like that, and look at most people.

There has been an unbelievable amount of 'politics' involved in deciding who should get the Phulpur seat[23] once my cousin Indira refused it. She could have been elected from there with ease if she had agreed to do so soon after Mamu's death. The atmosphere was emotional enough for her to have perhaps been returned uncontested. But she said she couldn't face the electorate at that time, also that she was (is) frightened of the Opposition there. Understandable, since there is no dirtier Opposition than in UP and elections there have always been

---

[23]The constituency vacated by the death of Jawaharlal Nehru.

fought on a below the belt level. It happened to my mother in 1937 when a court case was brought against her on the grounds that her marriage wasn't legal. The UP mind is in a class by itself where matters of sex, especially, are concerned. Mummie asked for this seat as soon as Mamu died, saying she did not know whether she would win but she would put up a better fight than anyone else and would give them the time of their lives. But she still has not been given a decision. My cousin has put forward a candidate of her own and opposed Mummie's candidature, though not outright. So things have become complicated.

Last night Kaval and Rahul[24] came to dinner. It was my first real meeting with her because those few times in Chandigarh at the end of our holiday hardly count. I found her very animated, full of talk. She and Gautam started an argument about Shiv Shastri — the reason why he had not visited us last year in Chandigarh. It went on a good half hour and they went at it hammer and tongs, battering the issue to absolute pulp, and at the end of it, which came because Rahul was fed up and insisted they change the subject, neither one had yielded an inch to the other. This fascinated me immensely. Each had an absolute disregard for the other's knowledge and background of the situation, each was pursuing a point singlemindedly and deaf to the other. It could easily have gone on all night. I felt that in such a situation, at some point, you would have conceded that the other party had the possibility of a case, but neither of them did. I felt a primitive core in both of them, also a civilization in you that neither of them has. Which is why I am so surprised that Khushwant should have used the word 'brainwashing' in connection with her. I cannot see how this word would apply.

Things are somewhat tense here. Do you wonder I hold people at arm's length and don't allow them near, because to be

---

[24]Rahul Khushwant Singh.

near me is to enter this unsavouriness, be under suspicion and doubt. It has always been so with anyone who has befriended me, and Gautam's struggle to isolate me is always instant and intense. It is the reason why for years I have not ventured out of my isolation, but I don't believe giving in to him all the time can be the answer, and at this stage of our lives it would actually be wrong.

Tara

~

1 Church Road, Srinagar
September 26, 1964

My dear Tara

Guests in the house, much conferencing in office, and I feel surrounded. I got both your letters of the 23rd yesterday. I *am* glad you are staying here, and you must tell me what you like to eat as I am unimaginative, and my cook Ganesh, who is a youngster, ditto. He can make new things if told how. I am glad the crisis of the 24th passed and that the tickets and bookings are done and you will be here as planned. I somehow keep doubting you will arrive here in October. I will meet you at the airport on the 10th unless there is some unavoidable work, and if I cannot, will send the car.

I was interested to hear you would go to Allahabad to help with your mother's election. What would that involve? And where do you stay now when you go to Allahabad? I believe the family home is no longer available. I can almost hear you saying 'too many questions'.

Bunchi

~

White House, Gamadia Road, Bombay
October 1, 1964

My dear Bunchi

Apart from writing to you from bathrooms and dressing rooms I seem to have started using all kinds of paper—this is the only thing I can find on top of my very cluttered desk in our new flat. But at least the move is nearly completed. Gitu is home. Noni comes later after her French lesson. She quarrelled with Gautam this morning as she wants to see a film called 'Honeymoon Hotel' which he forbade. He is terribly, needlessly rigid about these things, which breeds defiance in her. Personally I'd have let her go—it's a silly picture with glamorous looking females and people jumping in and out of a swimming pool and everybody very gay, just the kind kids enjoy at her age. We saw the trailer the other day. I feel sorry for Noni, remembering the understanding I had from both my parents at fourteen. You have given your sore throat and cold to Gitu—the vibrations in the air, or something. I had to keep her in bed a couple of days.

What an untidy letter—blotchy, uneven, interrupted, but I don't even hesitate to send it. Am I progressing toward spontaneity?

It has been a difficult weekend, beginning with dinner with the couple I wrote to you about who are not married. They talked a good deal about their situation, how it had developed, and that they were now able to live together for some months every year because her husband agreed to it. Gautam said when we came home that he was gravely disturbed about the views I had expressed, which were that since everyone concerned had accepted the situation, I couldn't see what there was to worry about. I realized I had treated the subject a little facetiously from his point of view. But I didn't enter into a discussion because it is never a quiet or rational one. He wanted to know if he met an attractive woman, would I have any objection if he slept with her. I never know how to answer this kind of question. All I could say was if he wanted to, how could anyone stop him, and why *should* anyone stop him? And this was the wrong answer.

~

1 Church Road, Srinagar
October 8, 1964

My dear Tara

I suppose it is silly of me to write to you when I hope you will be here in about 48 hours and this will get to you after you arrive. And will you arrive? I will not believe it till you are here, and even before your letters telling me of your argument with Gautam, I have said to myself continually that I must expect this may be called off suddenly. For I have known it would be difficult, and may in the end become impossible.

I know exactly what you have been through in this terrible argument, every bit of it. For I too have lived in a kind of paralysis where everything you do or say is just the wrong thing and does not help—though my circumstances and its manifestations were very different, not only intellectually, but really. It is perhaps trite to say that nevertheless you must win through, try and try again, when there is the slightest opportunity. I do not mean necessarily about seeing me, or anything of that kind, but about achieving freedom of being, which is essential. Love may be a doubtful commodity, bound up with persons and with some degree of greed, and must be tested again and again as to whether it is genuine and worthwhile. But truth is never doubtful, and without freedom you may not have it, except in ways that twist and distort it. So you have to go on trying for truth and beauty, and for love if and when you are certain it has come your way. And you have to go on trying that Noni can see her cinema, and have a chance to discover and discriminate, taste, and reject or accept, now she is growing up. For look at the world you are landing her in. She will surely not go just from the shelter of her parents' home to the shelter and tradition of her husband's, as so many women used to do. We have abandoned that way of life and must be prepared for the consequences, and the only way to prepare is to be strong within oneself. So you have no option but to achieve freedom in however small a way, and however slowly, and with whatever despair and heartbreak, not only for your own sake, but for that of others whose lives you influence and affect.

I did not like 'But none of this is your problem ...' Not that I can help you in any concrete way. I know I can't. But there is something in sharing a thought, sharing a hurt, in even sharing sullage. Perhaps there is something in not being too practical—'my problem', 'your problem'—for what does friendship, or affection, or trust, or faith, or whatever we have between us, or may achieve between us, mean? So I do not accept what you say—not today—I may some day when you have made me wiser. I may have to, but I shall do so with regret, that we could not open a particular door between us, could not read a particular chapter.

Bunchi

1 Church Road, Srinagar
October 23, 1964

Dearest BD[25]

This is just to say hello to you at Bombay as soon after your arrival as I can get to you. It is difficult to write to you today when I am alternately aware that you *are* still here and I will be with you this evening, and that you who seem to belong here so naturally, almost casually, leave tomorrow, and will leave a big vacuum in Bunchi's daily life. I shall miss you and want to catch up with you, the sooner the better. I have loved having you here with me and loved everything we did together, and I found everything you were or said or did lovable, almost as if waiting for me, and to be known by me, as if I were recognizing and confirming my own. It was as natural and easy as that, almost as if it did not happen, merely emerged. And all the thinking and defining ('I came and quacked beside you in the wood') also seemed to emerge simultaneously, and not in analysis or by plan.

And now go away, and let me do some work.

With love,
Bunchi

~

1 Church Road, Srinagar
October 24, 1964

I should like to give you something before you leave, and thought of it (quite hard) yesterday. But no bright idea came. And I am seeing you off empty-handed, and feel rather greedy,

---

[25]Beautiful Diversion, a name for Tara used by Kikook in a letter to E.N. Mangat Rai.

but somehow not guilty, doing so, as if I had fed of food and gentle nourishment and known I was so fed, but returned little, except words. But I have been grateful for you, quietly and fully grateful, and that is why I have no guilt at sending you empty-handed from Bunchi.

~

In the plane
October 24, 1964

Bunchi

I felt sick as I got onto the plane, something like a child going away to school, because being with you was home and all the rest from now on will be school. How effortless it has all been. For the first time I feel wholly natural, and under no obligation, or desire, to hide or pretend. You will say this must be considered every day on its own merit, but for today it is true.

You have given me an interest in the present, forced me to focus on today, not live in the past, but the present I am focusing on is strangely unconnected with the life around me that I must live. I have to live this life and fulfil its many obligations. At any rate I must not complain because at least there is a window open that was shut before, and some fresh air to be grateful for. How did all this happen?

I have been thinking of what you said about the difficulties in 'our' way, not mine alone, though there are far more in mine. I will not say I am full of courage, but it is simply not in me to go back. Apart from you and me, Bunchi, this is the road to freedom, and every step of it is more real than my whole life till now.

With love
Tara

~

1 Church Road, Srinagar
October 25, 1964

Dear BD

When your plane started I drove just out of the airport and saw it take off, rise and turn towards Banihal and the plains of Delhi, and it seemed the endless distance to Bombay. I came home for a late lunch and into Baramulla, and all through what turned out a long evening I missed you and occasionally looked at my watch to ascertain where you were. For we lingered through the sports and prize-giving to the sound of the last post played by a band of 85, resounding and echoing back from the hills almost as if the echo was another band in the hills. Drinks at the mess and a huge dinner and 1¼ hour's drive back to Srinagar, getting to sleep at 1:30 a.m. I was glad of the late hour for that made me less aware of the peace and warmth I had so much loved for so many days. Whatever we did or said was homecoming, without pretence or effort. And now you have confirmed the fatality and finality for me, as if this, between us, was of the ages, not of the fury and passion of feeling only, but of the substance of being, the substance of life and friendship, all the many things between people from which love emerges, grows and envelops them. It had none of the flare up of an affair, none of the high fever merely of sexual attraction, but has been the fullest sharing. And yesterday I thought I had also found another love in 1964—Kashmir—and never doubted from the moment it was mooted that I had to take this offer of work here. And I have loved every minute of it.

I can see bits and pieces of you, even today, in the letter Pearl Buck wrote about you to your mother, and was jealous that I did not know you then: 'No one thing or person will satisfy her complexity... she cannot be happy with simplicity' and 'indeed she is very beautiful'. I thought that even a year ago I did not see this, and now that I know you, I am sorry I was such a fool before. It was obvious even in 1947 that you were going to be a difficult person for she says '... do hasten to get her married, even if later she changes her mind! She will need more than marriage anyway.' Yet I do not see all the intricacies and complexities, except those of the life you have made, and what it has coiled round you, through which you will have to struggle for freedom and the light of the sun. All that I can see, but I can also see you very clearly now as a whole person, a whole beautiful woman within this, certain of your idealism and values, confused only occasionally by practical ties.

Let us accept in future that there will be no barriers between us. Will you? And let us accept the terms on which this will be possible. I have for years believed in and talked of the concept of a 'higher morality'. One can talk perhaps to one person only of things one normally just could not mention—things that involve fundamental and basic loyalties, like the relationship between husband and wife, for example. It can only be done rarely, and only in an exclusive relationship. But once that happens, it is the very law and instinct of that relationship that all is told without inhibition and restraint. Where it is not, there is not only a barrier, but a burden. The 'higher morality' involves a complete discipline—which is the base on which it can be built—in regard to such information being absolutely and entirely exclusive, and not usable unless that is acceptable to both persons. Do I put this badly? But as I write I have felt it is hardly necessary for me to put it, as you understand it and know it. Do you? And will you accept it between us?

I said my interim farewell to Sadiq last night at Mahmuda's dinner, so all is well with my plans. I will be in Chandigarh on the 2nd and at Palam airport on the 5th at 7:30. Let me have your Allahabad address (or is Anand Bhawan adequate?) and think whether I should pay a short visit to Allahabad on my way back from Jaipur, or whether that would create too many questions all round. We can discuss this at Delhi.

With love
Bunchi

~

Wazarat Road, Jammu
November 11, 1964

And you will say, as you have already said in a different context, that when one loves one gets caught up in an exaggeration of reality, one feels and imagines more than the facts, and envelops them in a halo as it were. I would like to deny that for myself as far as you are concerned, for though I am suspicious of feeling—always looking at it again and again—with you I have not had to do this. It has been so easy, I do not quite understand how it could be, as if I was renewing knowledge of the familiar, of what I had known for years. Also, I believe some projection of feeling, some imagination, some fantasy even, is part of reality, and as real as the human experience. It is what urges and encourages discovery, this catching up with what you have seen. So, my dear Tara, I not only see and love you as you are, I also see and love you as I believe you will be, as *we* may well be. It is no longer, for the future, only individuals, but individuals who will matter to each other, and contribute to a further fullness, or at least a different fullness than we have alone.

Are you frightened? Don't be, for one of the rules of this game is that you can always withdraw, and indeed the game does not work unless you know you can withdraw, and yet every day, or week, or year, discover with refreshing certainty that you are still there.

~

Wazarat Road, Jammu
November 18, 1964

Dearest Tara

I left the airport at Allahabad with a distinct vision and feeling
of you. I could see you in your white sari, standing alone, before
the aircraft moved and felt I could feel your thoughts, wistful
and yet of truth and strength, like the breeze on transparent
waters, and yet irrevocably helpless, wondering.

And I enjoyed every bit of my time at Allahabad, from
the impatient looking out of the corridor of the train when
I arrived, to you at the gate of the airport as I left. I enjoyed
everything, the atmosphere of the house, the verandas, the
garden, the roof where we sat, the small table for meals, the
occasional chat with Lekha,[26] the occasional presence of your
mother (when I was never quite sure whether I should keep
sitting or stand up or what I should say), even, oddly enough,
Miss Kashyap,[27] who seems a very whole character. Also the
atmosphere of the roads and stately trees, the mixture of old
houses and new, the warmth of the Shervani[28] family and their
acceptance of a total stranger.

A disjointed scribble on my pad — 'You are not and should
not be my equal. You are too precious, you must get on to
your destiny, but let me be part of it. Let the journey of your
spirit be mine.' That is how I feel and love you. Everything
about you glows, as indeed it should, your face, your skin,
your concern with cleanliness, even the impossible suitcase
you carry around. But it is not only the physical, it is the

---

[26]Chandralekha Mehta, Nayantara Sahgal's sister.
[27]Nishtha Kashyap, Secretary to Vijayalakshmi Pandit.
[28]The Shervani family were old friends of Mrs Pandit, with whom
E.N. Mangat Rai stayed.

soul, the spirit, whatever you like to call it. You say you enter your house at Anand Bhawan and for the first time you don't go back to the past because I enter it with you. For the first time you feel a fullness of life and wait for it rather than do anything about it. Yours is a life sprouting, in abundance, in endless possibilities. And my saying so has nothing to do with any assumed humility on my part—I am not a humble person—but a lot to do with a sense of the apt. Shouldn't I just 'go home'? Yet you make me intensely afraid of losing you, intensely determined not to.

Much love
Bunchi

~

Anand Bhawan, Allahabad
November 17, 1964

I noticed a visible increase in election[29] tempo after my 3-day absence from it while you were here. There was much enthusiasm and jubilation all the way and wherever we went we got the impression all would be well, though dubious reports continue to come in from some workers. I prepared the press release on my return at 8:30 pm, then had a bath and dinner, and now, 10 pm, feel ready to fall asleep.

I looked up the *Encyclopaedia Britannica* and found the following information about Circe: In Greek mythology a beautiful sorceress who is represented by Homer as having converted the companions of Ulysses into swine by means of an enchanted beverage. Circean: pertaining to Circe, hence fascinating, but brutifying, infatuating and depraving.

---

[29]The election to the Lok Sabha from Phulpur, Jawaharlal Nehru's constituency which had been vacated as a result of his death. Vijayalakshmi Pandit was the Congress candidate from Phulpur.

I continue to be awed by the experience of seeing myself as others see me! Kindly treat me with respect so that some similar hideous fate does not befall you as did Ulysses' men and Gautam. Don't let the spells I am supposed to weave overwhelm you!

I have to assemble my thoughts and peace of mind to start another book. I feel restless without a job to do. And yet, how to get it going, and how to protect its conception and growth from being shaken and damaged by the atmosphere around me?

~

White House, Gamadia Road, Bombay
November 24, 1964

Lekha rang up from Allahabad a little while ago to say that last night when the results were announced, Mummie was taken out in a triumphal procession, with several bands each playing a different tune, from the High Court to Anand Bhawan. I'm sorry I missed all that, and this exciting news has dispelled much of the tension of the weekend, though it is there in the background.

Too much has happened too suddenly since my return and I am still trying to sort my way through what once again has become an impenetrable jungle. We are back to 'I will not share you with anyone'. Also, 'I am seeing my lawyer tomorrow. I want you to come down to my office for a talk.' I said I could not live in chains and was tired of being punished for my spontaneity.

I could so easily have lied under interrogation and given our relationship no significance. But I wanted to share something with Gautam, make him see me as I am, not behave as if anything of joy to me should be regarded by him as his enemy. I've always given in when it came to a struggle, but no longer.

Why should you feel responsible for me? I am, like you, essentially independent. Left to myself I would try and build a life for myself, one that would leave me free, for I have had enough of marriage and do not believe it is possible for people to grow in freedom through it. Mentally, I've shed it. Spiritually, it was never mine. And all of this is a process that has developed in me, regardless of you, but which now draws strength from your presence. No physical or legal separation can make more apparent what to me is already a complete separation. I had thought things were greatly improved since 1959, but it does not seem so. This is a chronic state of affairs.

If I have deliberately dragged this whole thing before Gautam, made him an unhappy and unwilling listener, it is because I feel the health of my marriage depends at least to a small extent on some little clarity in this regard—while he wants the safety, the unnatural safety of the womb where all is dark and warm and secure, and reality need not be grappled with. I have no desire to force any issue between him and me, though it may seem that way. I am not even struggling to free myself from this marriage, only from the constraints within it. I want to be reasonable. But we never talk about anything personal until it becomes a crisis, and then in a highly charged atmosphere.

How wasted he and I are on each other. He thinks a woman should go to her husband a virgin. I don't understand the double standard, and I have no sense of guilt about sex. Another sort of man might understand my desire for freedom. Another sort of woman might cherish his attitudes. Instead I strain at my bonds and feel terribly confused and hedged in. As things are, I must cooperate in this marriage in every way I can, and yet find freedom for myself. I shall not abandon you now or at any time. We must somehow have time with each

other, without any 'slaughter', and while we do our best in
our separate lives.

~

Wazarat Road, Jammu
November 29, 1964

My darling

You drag this effusion out of me, and ever since I got your
letter of the 19th I have wanted to hold both your hands, take
you in my arms, put my fingers through your much washed
hair, and keep you close to me. You write, 'I have had nothing
but goodness and gentleness from you.' If I have given any
of these, it is because you have compelled my being, my
body, my feelings like that. It has happened, not of me, but
between us.

In all your last three letters you mention the destruction
of our letters. I am sorry this is on your mind and that I do
not give you immediate relief from an avoidable anxiety. But
I do not agree. I think it is a risk we should take, of keeping
them, for they are more than just an exchange of news and
moods. One does not often have this kind of experience to
share and define. The written word of the time does capture
an aspiration, at times beauty, often intensity, an idea seen in
a particular way. But surely I do not need to debate this with
you, who are fond of writing, and write even for audiences.
Let us keep these between us and not destroy them. It is only
a small risk really, considering what else you, particularly,
are risking in the tempestuous jealousy of your husband. So
please consider this again. I do not want you in anxiety, and
if in spite of what I say you decide that they should go, I will
perform the murder and send you a certificate of death. But I

do regard it as some sort of murder and would hate doing it. I know we will not be writing like this again. We may be writing as much, but the subjects will change, the emphasis will change, we will grow to another phase—I hope, as important and worthwhile to us both—but necessarily different. So think about it and don't make me feel I cling selfishly to something that causes you anxiety.

Yes, Karan Singh[30] is, in the sense you put it, a Hindu. And yet somehow I do not think he is just that. I think there is striving in him, and he has been largely friendless. I think no one has come really close to him, perhaps after school, opened up his essential possibilities. They are there and could be tapped to refreshment of his spirit and being. He clings to tradition, for no one has been able to give him confidence in anything bigger. But he has the mental equipment, and I think, the emotional equipment, for it.

I recognize the Hindu in myself, a great deal of it; possibly I have more of it than you. You are, more than me, emancipated from the backlog of the heritage of the Hindu cultural-religious tradition. Perhaps because I do not belong by label, I have a kind of nostalgia in the soul. I provoke talk about Hinduism because I believe it should rethink its way to the modern world, give India something big that will churn it and produce constructive action. As it is, people like you, and Gautam, and hundreds of others, disassociate themselves from the tradition so that it continually loses its natural intelligentsia, and is left to the hocus-pocus of people with little education or opportunity.

In modern historical times, only Shivaji and Gandhi loved it from within and both of them worked wonders in transformation. There are no doubt others, more strictly within the religious fold, who did similarly, but these two stand out in my mind. Nehru basically abandoned Hinduism. So there

---

[30]Sadr-i-Riyasat, Head of State in J&K.

is, I believe, a problem, and you and I must talk about it when we meet. And tell me, when that will be.

Perhaps you have met your match in me, my dear Circe. We are, in very different ways, inheritors of a precious obligation to rebellion. Your forbears who, unlike mine, were very much in the public eye, were political rebels for liberty, and you are rightly proud of that tradition which indeed is part of the Indian tradition. My forbears, in much smaller places, and on more debateable ground—where I do not know whether they chose truth or heresy—were rebels against spiritual and religious acceptance. My father left home and hearth to become a Christian at 18, and there was no material inducement, as he came from affluent people. My maternal grandfather, Kali Charan Chatterji, did similarly at a more advanced age. Whether they were right or wrong, I am proud of this tradition. So perhaps somewhere rebellion is in our blood, though we are mild rebels, accepting much, but there may be a yearning in us for some kind of freedom, some assertion that human beings shall be free, and shall choose from the best lights they can see, not necessarily the accepted light. And that urge is heady wine. But we must take thought together and do the right thing so that you are not landed, as your letter of the 26th shows, in a prolonged, senseless ache and frittering away of spirit and of life.

No, your letter was not confusing. I lived through it all, saw and felt the horror and drama of it, and exactly what you had been through. It is so complete in itself, Gautam's reaction and its manifestations, its deep roots of unreasonable, almost demonic strength, that very little I can say could be of any help in what you bear. But surely you have made some progress. He did not, for example, ring up your mother straight away, and even got the hang of your statement that he forced you into a prison, did not allow you to share anything outside with him. You have to go on hoping, though admittedly in a forlorn way, that he will have glimmerings of the 'worthwhileness in me, which whether he approves of it or not, should be given a chance'. But I have understood what you face, the helpless tragedy, even cruel waste that it involves.

There is vigour, clarity, beauty in what you write, a strength and transparent honesty. I clasp that to me to judge of my responsibility, and because of it I have no guilt either, no remorse, no retraction. I have fears for you, for your person, and that life should not become a daily cross for you to bear, but no sense of responsibility, and none of immorality. Yet surely there is a responsibility between adults, not one of contract, not forced or extracted, nor recognized by law or obligation, but nevertheless there, of freedom and affection. In practical terms this may mean nothing. In terms of being with or without support, surely it already means something.

This morning, reading *The Shoes of the Fisherman*, I came across: 'If Creation and Redemption meant anything at all, they meant an affair of love between the Maker and His creatures.' And I think when love settles into your being, is part of the air you breathe, then there is an affair of love between you and every person you are near. That, according to me, is when men walk with God, when they can have an affair of love with their fellow men. Apart from the socialism of things material, there is a socialism of the spirit, and its passport and sanction is love. Love cannot remain just something between two people — an eccentricity, an alchemy of chance. It must always be that, but if it builds, it touches other people also, is an instrument of awareness. Lest you think I talk too much, think of your Mamu, of whom everybody who knew him said he was transformed from tiredness to life, even in his latter days, when he met the people, even in their thousands. Surely that was an exercise of some form of love, aware of itself and of others. So you have to go out with a message, be yourself with people whoever they are, wherever you meet them. There are tremendous depths of strength in you; start expending them now and they will come back to you in greater strength. I cannot bear to hear you say indifferent things of yourself.

And now, my darling again, time presses and I must rush.

Bunchi

~

Wazarat Road, Jammu
December 3, 1964

Dearest Child

You have made me feel very, and consciously inadequate when you write you have 'spilled over too much'. I want all the spillovers—I want them intensely—everything that you will give me matters to me. And it frightens me when you say you may have spilled over too much. I want to know all that happens to you, and within you, not as a matter of curious knowledge or morbid data collecting, but because of the warmth of being with a whole person. There can be too little spillover, not too much, in anything about you, whether it's laughter and fun (as I hope there will be) or this torture that you and Gautam seem to have between you.

Neither you nor I thought this crisis would take this extreme form, raking up 1947 and 1959, and the whole business of suspicion and torment as if these dates were yesterday. You seem to have spoken very fully and bluntly to Gautam, and surely that is, to an extent, a relief to you.

You are so terribly hemmed in by rules, dates, regulations, that I do not know when I will get this letter to you, keep it for days, I suppose, and then hand it over to you at Chandigarh. Are you always going to be as difficult as this? Tell me, wise thing, what one does in these circumstances. It has all been rather a rush these past few months since August 7th and all mounted up so quickly that I need some time with you to take you in, and understand ourselves. It is so long since I have seen you, and was thinking yesterday that I remember distinctly the look and touch of your hair as I put my fingers through it, and wondered how often and where you get it cut. I had my hair cut yesterday and am looking improved; But I've not forgotten a crack one of my teachers, named Anand, had at me at St. Stephen's when I was having a haircut in the hostel: 'Don't do that. We'll now have to see more of your face!'

I have been a little conscience-stricken about you. Is it really natural and easy for you to write to me every day almost? Do you really want to, or do you think you will disappoint me if you don't? Have I made you slip into this process? I do not want you to conform against your instinct, or even sheerly absent-mindedly.

As for me I want to live with you and it is painful not to have you here. But I draw consolation from small things, that I could not in any case keep you in the way you are used to, on my finances. You'd have to shrink considerably, and as I do not want you to shrink in any way, that is a negative and dissatisfying sort of consolation.

I am hopeful of your arrival at Chandigarh, and mine.

Meanwhile
Much love

Bunchi

~

White House, Gamadia Road, Bombay
December 9, 1964

You can't want to know where or how often I get my hair cut!
But since you ask, about every two months, by a man called
Ronnie. He's Anglo-Indian and has a Sicilian grandmother,
a cross old woman who keeps the cash box and bosses
everybody about.

I suppose you *are* very unorthodox in relation to the
general set-up around us, but as far as I'm concerned what
you say and do, your most 'fantastic' and 'preposterous'
suggestions sound perfectly sensible and natural.

I find the Circe business about me a bit depressing. I don't
object to the reference to men, because it is nice to be attractive
to men and I've never had any objection to this, but I do to the
idea that my influence on a man should be depraving, drag
him down to the level of an animal, because I'd rather fancied
myself as having an uplifting influence!

~

Anokha, 32/Sector 5-A, Chandigarh
December 14, 1964

Darling Valuable Scalp

Really, as long as I'm a Beautiful Diversion, I don't see why you
shouldn't be a Valuable Scalp, I felt our closeness through all
the disapproval and social chill, and felt you were as solid as
rock with me. You say you feel no guilt as your independence
(mutual) has been agreed on since the start, and Champa has
on occasion exercised hers fully. My guilt is purely that of
making another person unhappy, but I seem to do that just
by being myself. Would things really be better between you

and Champa if I were not in the picture, and can I forever efface myself with regard to Gautam to make him happy and secure?

At twelve Kaka came to fetch me to take me to your house. Your mother-in-law was up on the roof attending to a vigorous spring cleaning. We joined her there and she began to talk of morals. I didn't know if this was intended as general conversation or in the nature of a polite rebuke. She said anyone brought up in Christianity should know that self-abnegation was better than self-assertion. (I said Hinduism also preached this but she brushed that aside!) She said, 'Men who know better should not run after strange women and build temples to them.' I thought that a lovely way of putting it. It seemed such a specific pointed subject, and she spoke with such conviction, I couldn't believe she was just chatting. I came back home to lunch feeling happy, having been in your house.

I went to bed last night with an indefinable feeling of security and confidence, and woke up sometime later—I don't know what time, I didn't turn my head to look at the clock—to find that something I had been aware of for a long time had shifted minutely and come into exact focus, and I was standing in a place both sheltered and immense, and I felt both the shelter and immensity of it, and this was the meaning of this relationship between you and me.

Instead of my walk around the lake this evening I took Gitu for a short stroll and listened to her wise little comments, then came home. The children put on some music and did the twist in which I joined.

~

Wazarat Road, Jammu
December 15, 1964

My dearest Child

As I came up the lift this morning to the third floor where
I work, I thought, 'How well I am feeling. That's what my
contact with Tara does to me.' Could this be immoral and ugly?
And it is so incongruous that Champa, or Gautam, or Kaka,
or the rest should think of it as unhappy or ugly for them.
Even when you are separated from me like this, I am able to
think about you with confidence and knowledge and warmth,
and would be wretched if I could not. It was lovely to be with
you at Chandigarh, and I was caught up and involved, and I
simply do not understand the suspicions and hostilities, which
were there, and of which you were so much more aware, and
apparently more the subject of, than I was. I could not tell
you, though I wanted to at the time, that you looked serenely
beautiful at the party on the 13th. And I thought more than
once, this woman is mine if she looks like that when she is as
aware of me, and I of her, as we are today. And contradictorily
also, that I cannot and must not touch her, but must enjoy
her at a distance, for she is so obviously a thing apart, to be
respected and loved as an individual. I should watch her, be
with her, and not try to take her to me.

And you still do not understand why I call you child. It
has nothing to do with what you say or do, for you say and do
sensible things on the whole. It is because I imagine I can see
what motivates you. There is aspiration in you, a stretching
out, like a child puts its arms out for the moon, or a sweet, or
the electric switch, not quite certain, hopeful, waiting. There
is also another aspect to it, the one you wrote to me about
months ago, that your epitaph should be that you were a

'disciplined' person. While I have always seen the discipline, and can still see it in you, I now also see the potential laughter and effervescence, the joy and heartbreak, and the many years gone by in discipline with all these others there but covered up by it, put in their place, kept where they did not obtrude. And I wonder whether and how they will flower—not in an orgy or excess, but like I imagined you were that night of the 13th, quiet and radiant, yourself from the top of your head to the tread in your toes. This is somewhat how one sees a child one knows, its possibilities, the turn these could take, the difficulties of that turn, and the hope that it will arrive. I have said to myself, I want this girl on a strong, long-term basis, not any flimsy basis, and tried to be deliberate about that, not to do anything that would shock or bruise you in any way.

But you talk, my darling guinea pig, as if you were really just that, as if all this happened to you, as if you were hardly a party to it, hardly a participant; whereas it has been my distinct assessment, and my great joy, that you have been very much there, the whole time, in every way, in every act and feeling. If this has been an experiment, you have been a contributor, not merely the recipient.

I can quite see you have never been in need of endeavouring to collect scalps, and that they must have come your way in profusion, so I simply don't see what Champa means by the 'valuable scalp' you are now collecting. Anyway, it *is* in your bag, without any kind of doubt, and happy to be there, so do not on any account abandon it. I have loved being collected if you are the collector. And you yourself, BD, are one hell of a scalp for collection, but I will not go into that as it may not be good for you—'adulation' and all that!

My love will be yours these days in Chandigarh till I return. And this, my darling, will be a journey to you, so I hope you are duly impressed with your importance and will talk to me and be with me whatever the odds. And be happy, if possible a little of it because of me, and let me see it in your eyes and in your face.

My love
Bunchi

~

Anokha, 32/Sector 5-A, Chandigarh
December 16, 1964

Darling VS

The whole day has been quiet and beautiful because there has been no wind, only stillness and warmth. I am trying to count my blessings but missing you instead. How selfish one is, never happy with a little, always wanting more. I feel I'm treading new ground every step of the way for nothing like it has ever happened before. And every step is a consummation in a sense. I am happy to pause just there, look around, assimilate and enjoy, and go no further for as long as we both like. I wonder at myself. For I've been an impatient person, a creature of hurry and haste, driving things on to climax and conclusion, believing that was the way life was, despairing that it was so, until you showed me otherwise. Now I feel the luxury of every unfolding moment, all of time ahead of us. I used to be overwhelmed by a sense of loneliness, despite the 'adulation' I am supposed to thrive on. I never dreamed I would find what I sought. But it has happened.

December 23 – You three have just arrived for dinner and I am going down. I have had a bad time, a repetition, only worse, of the blowup in Bombay, but have persuaded Gautam to declare a truce for the duration of his vacation. He says he will never allow me to go anywhere you are, unless he is there too. He had no dinner last night, only drank, and no breakfast or lunch today.

~

74/Sector 9-A, Chandigarh
December 21, 1964

There is no peace at home and none within me and I have come for a few minutes to Rajinder Park. I have been in anguish through these days, not knowing what I could do with myself, unable to think or feel or take in anything unless in some way it brought the hope or possibility of being nearer you, and with you. It is a bad state to be in, and quite disgraceful for me, this almost stomach ache of need for you. And in spite of your little note of yesterday, I will expect you to tell me daily that you love me, to look at me as if you did, to know that I do, and to feel that you wanted and cherished my love. So I cannot let you off your pact. Is there any chance of even half an hour's quiet with you one of these days?

I can see so much that is simple and easy and joyful in you, just awaiting the nurture to blossom. I can see your need for tenderness, and how you would respond to it and give it back in zest and joy a hundred fold. And I can see it all held back. I saw all that painfully yesterday and could bear it with difficulty. Why can't I help you? I wish I could do something for you, and not merely love you, in your terrible, cruel, meaningless prison.

Bunchi

~

Anokha, 32/Sector 5-A, Chandigarh
December 25, 1964

Gautam did not eat yesterday or today, only drank. Spent all last night out, I don't know where. This morning turned up at nine, ill and bloodshot, and said he has decided to sell the house and is going to negotiate the sale today. He has also made it abundandy evident to everybody that he is suffering and I am responsible. I feel helpless to cope with this extraordinary situation. He won't even discuss the immediate future. I want to go back with the children to Bombay if he will make the arrangements. At the moment I'm not sure he will. I am beginning to feel like a criminal, accused of I don't know what crime. Life for me, with Gautam, is three steps forward and two back. No stability or certainty of any kind. And now it has been rocked to its foundations for the second time in a few years. I feel afraid of this terrible mood of his. I know there is more trouble ahead. I must just wait and let it catch up with me as and when it will. This marriage is tragic, and tragic for Gautam if I leave him, for the way he reacts to this, and always has to this type of situation, makes me afraid for his sanity, even for his life. And this is the pattern.

Thank you for your note, your love, for everything you have been and done these past days.

Tara

~

74/Sector 9-A, Chandigarh,
New Year's Day, 1965

I can only write a line to give you all my love for 1965 and to hope that it will be worth something. I do love you and now know it is for always, even if I wished it otherwise. We must, I am certain, stand together, even if continually parted as we will be, even if parted forever, as we may be. I love you with all I have and it is, in the event, so little, so very little, that I am ashamed of my poverty, and yet cannot give it up, knowing I also carry the burden of what I would give you and take from you, if only we could. You must believe it is we—not I or you, no longer that—in 1965.

Bunchi

~

Anokha, 32/Sector 5-A, Chandigarh
January 2, 1965

Last evening things simmered down a bit, I think because Gautam got a lot out of his system by hitting me as he did, not only in front of you but before that. Some of the fury left him and he became calmer though far from normal still. I told him the hitting did not matter. What mattered was his unwillingness to face the real issue and make way for my differences from him. He created quite a storm yesterday, talking to my mother after lunch (after you left) and she was upset. I am sorry she has been dragged into this because she was tired and deserved relaxation in the sun. However she is used to these upheavals in my marriage and she has been calm and wonderful. I am exhausted and drained. I still would work out an acceptable compromise for the children's sake, though it would be a dim and unrewarding one for me personally. My world has been rocked in an insane and ghastly fashion and I don't know if I can live in it again.

Thank you for your letters. The New Year one gives me heart and hope. You've given me so much, and offered me everything. Is that poverty? I've never felt so rich.

With love
Tara

~

January 6 – Since December 22nd, everything has revolved in confusion and misery, and you have seen now at close quarters how things are. On the 3rd night Gautam in a rage said I must move to a hotel. I said I would do nothing to shock the children, and went straight to bed and thought about whose assistance I could ask in the morning to get to Delhi, but in the morning he was talking to me again. I have kept a sort of blank self-possession through all that has happened since the 22nd, but now it is over I want to lie down and cry—and cannot.

Why are we alike, and why should we have met, and why remain apart? I miss our daily contact, the comfortable peaceful routine I have grown so accustomed to, and shall be glad to get back to Bombay to re-establish it again. And we are on the same planet after all. When all the dust and ashes have settled, we are still there, and still together. Now you know why I said I seem to bring about chaos, attract it. And you know so much else, the situation from the inside as you never would have known it otherwise.

It is a beautiful day, and night before last you must have seen the sliver of the new moon in the sky.

All my love
Tara

~

Wazarat Road, Jammu
January 6, 1965

My dearest love

I have fought temptation ever since I left you on the 2nd to get in touch with you, and back to you, drove past your house on the 3rd at least three times, and since returning home have wanted to sit down and write even though it may well be days or weeks before I can post or give you this letter.

You mentioned in one of your notes that you may get some light from me. I do not seem to have any in this terrible, bruising shock you have been through these many days now. I have been aware of them in a ghastly, lit-up sort of manner, where each bit of what I saw and experienced was only a part of what I knew, and could almost see the reality and the whole. I have been appalled, and bewildered and helpless—none of which helps you one bit. So that all I can say is that I have been with you every waking minute of your anguish, I have partaken of it, though I know I cannot take any of it from you.

On that terrible 1st of January I was acting in the dark for I did not know what you may have said to Gautam when he tackled you. I am only sorry that I should allow you to be hit like that before me—I had a premonition it was coming and decided not to intervene except to beg him not to as it would make matters worse if I intervened. As for you, what can I say? That I am proud of you—that would not be good enough. That I loved you—that would be true. That you did not do a single thing that was shaky, or doubtful, or in any way afraid or weak—that would also be true. I was there, and fully there, as if I held you within me, and every single thing you did, my darling, was good and whole. And again, I was proud of you, blessed that I had come across you, and knew and loved you.

I have been thinking that 'my journey to you' which is how I described the Christmas visit to Chandigarh, did not turn out a very constructive business. Yet I do not regret it. In spite of your misery and the awful experience you went through, my love for you took a sharp, clear, palpable outline, as if it was a thing of itself, stronger, clearer than before. It almost fed itself in this terror, as if it had to become stronger to face it, for itself, for you, and for us. This is how it emerged for me, with a life of its own, certain not only of its existence but its rightness, and in spite of the devastation, even of its joy and happiness. But it became so clear that we were pitted against the impossible, that this would never, never be accepted, in any ordinary easy way; it would always be a fight, and under fire in one way or another. I saw no compromise in Gautam, and in a queer way, no give in Champa, though they react so differently. The latter creates a running sore of non-acceptance, the former the barbaric gash of violence. And the last rags of my affair with Kaval dropped from me, as if of themselves, without effort, thought or feeling. It was as if the elemental strength of your situation, which became mine also, cleansed and swept it from me. Your turmoil and cruel torment, my own, even Gautam's, of which I am very much aware, did something within me, wiped the slate clean and left only Tara on it. Suddenly and wholly, you were my love for always, albeit my difficult, impossible love. And I knew I would always love you. I will not only accept (which seems the wrong word) but shall cherish the 'bleeding victory' you have achieved. I know what it has meant for I have been on the inside of it and seen what happened. This shall be the dedication between us, our bond, our marriage.

I was glad you had been able to get back to a rapport with the children, and can well imagine how everything must have become paralysed those Xmas days when each hour must have had to be watched to be got through. I had imagined my visit to Chandigarh might give me an opportunity to know the children, and I wanted to, as I do not really know you as a mother, and wish to, in every way. Anyway, in retrospect it was rather futile to hope I would get to know them at Chandigarh.

About 'quality'—I felt about you that day as 'quality gasping for expression'. I suppose by quality I mean what you mean by the word 'evolved', but also somewhat different. Quality, as I see it, is an awareness of a situation for the people in it, not only of your own point of view but that of others, as it were internal to them. Even with such awareness, it is an ability and determination to find the practical or possible course of action, to stick by the essentials in the best way possible, not to slur over the contradictions or lapse into the predominant fear or urge till some other issue appears. I put this poorly but I felt it clearly, and saw that in this horrible experience with Gautam, you seemed at the time to stay true to both needs—an understanding of him and what it meant for him, and a determination that you would not give in, *if anything* practical could be found and worked, even for a short while, a breathing space to the next point. Most people, especially women, in such situations tend to let the issue just slip, not be clear about it, cry about it, or wrap it up in some kind of slush and sentiment so that it gets blurred. I could see you keeping the matter quite clear in its principles and implications, and yet fighting to be fair and truthful about how Gautam felt and what *he* needed.

But that was not all. I could see there was a difference of kind between his attitude and values, and yours. He gets that almost demonic strength for his point of view from the fact that he believes so completely in the traditional marriage contract, and complete possession of the wife. Your point of view comprehends a much bigger canvas of possibilities—of life and freedom—indeed that possession is not possible, or of any value, unless you possess what is of itself, of its own nature, given in freedom. It seemed almost as if two cultures were at battle, and between husband and wife usually the lower culture (if I may call it that) wins, because of its very narrowness, which gives it a crude immediate strength. The more complex and subtle culture, because much of what it demands and needs is on the fringes of the uncertain, the untried, and often even suspected to be immoral, tends always to lose. I could not have seen it as a struggle for quality, had I felt you were unaware or crude about Gautam's feelings. You were gentle with them, and so, in a peculiar sense, you were fighting not only for yourself, but for him—for a desperate gamble that a possibility in him may open, and see, and relax.

January 13 – Champa got bits and pieces of the fury at Chandigarh—knew what was happening, though not the details. Driving to Jammu she said though the question was not fair in regard to someone I so obviously liked, but did I think Tara is rather a tart? I said I did not see how anyone could think so, since in the years we knew you at Chandigarh, not once had anybody associated you with any man in that, or indeed any other way. She said she meant you were very aware of yourself as a woman with the men you had anything to do with. And she said look at the way Kaka and Jugal and the like eat out of her hand, and she enjoys it. And added that I also had now succumbed to her charm.

January 20 – A clear sky, a cold breeze, and as I came out of the bedroom the moon was still visible, and the outline of the low hills. And I wondered where you were, sleeping with your face buried under your hair, and flat on yourself—in Claridges. And the journey back to Chandigarh before you. What time do you leave? How? You give me so little detail. I know you have a party on the 21st, two Swiss and perhaps Lekha, and that's all.

I seem to have travelled a long way since I started this letter. There has hardly been a waking hour that I have not thought and felt about you, and you have come upon me in the midst of a Cabinet discussion, while out for a walk, on waking up between 2 and 4 am, and going off to sleep again, in all sorts of places, at all sorts of times. When I came back from Chandigarh, thoughts and ideas of this problem that enwraps and envelops us were plentiful, like a deck strewn with chaos. You are dealing with such an inflammable, uncontrollable person, that you must realize, as has become clear to me, there is near terror around you. One must be conscious of its possibilities and not just hope for the best. We must not put you in a position of risk to your person. We must bring this correspondence to safe proportions. We should try to meet but you should not, at present, take it to the point of a fight. These suggestions are drastic and will cut us off much from each other, but it is the only choice with safety for you, my beloved, and some chance of your being able to live in some degree of security and peace in your daily routine, my precious, beloved and lovely child. Much love, and may all go well with you.

Bunchi

~

> Claridges Hotel, New Delhi
> January 17, 1965

Darling

Life has been hectic since arrival as we have taken Dr Keppeli (the Chairman of Ciba), his daughter, and Mr and Mrs Rohner sightseeing and have had to be with them all the time. The children are here too and I've taken them to the Red Fort, the Qutab Minar and Shantivan where Mamu was cremated. Must join Gautam and party at the Club for lunch and more sightseeing in the afternoon. Yesterday Gautam told Dr Kappeli in a goodhumoured way, 'My wife is a very stubborn woman. When she makes up her mind, nothing can budge her.' And Dr K., who is very Swiss, and the lord-and-master type, looked a bit taken aback and said docile women were preferable.

All my efforts at discipline so far, anything I have achieved in this line, will now be put to the test, and will have to stand me in good stead now. It is strange, too, to live a 'double' life which I am now doing. It needs qualities I've never possessed. It is a strain. My mother has always felt I create melodrama about myself and it may be true in her eyes. That is, she sees the drama, but doesn't realize I didn't create it. It builds up around me and catches me in it. I don't want it. I long for something quite different, for calmness, for life without hysteria, for the great, unimaginable luxury of being myself, being accepted as myself, liked for myself. I had all this for two weeks in Srinagar with you. Yet even this situation, so right for us, has somehow become entangled in grim unreason and melodrama, because of me.

One thing I'm sure of is that I will go on with it, but as to how, I don't know. I miss our 'daily business'. This thing cannot be carved up or shrunk to suit anybody. Nor can my painful need of freedom, something it is not in my power to deny. Through all the dreadful scenes in Chandigarh I clung to my point of view not out of obstinacy, but of real need, out of the conviction that I cannot let go something that has become a lifeline to me. I want to convince Gautam I should like to be myself without destroying anything between him and me. In the end his rigidity must relax a little, not only on this subject, but toward life in general. He has always—as a spoilt young man—been able to lay down the law merely by clenching his fist and thumping the table and raising his voice. People have taken this behaviour from him, and I have seen my friends and acquaintances melt away rather than face his absolute rigidity. I am the first person, perhaps the only one, who has stood firm before him without any theatricals, without temper, or buckling under to bullying. And I have come a long way with him, and have hopes of helping him in whatever way I can.

Lekha and I called on the President yesterday since he hadn't been well, and enjoyed the visit. He said it was time I did something besides look after my children. Why not stand for Parliament? I said politics, as a participant, did not interest me. I have missed Mamu very much. Could not bear to go to the 'Nehru Museum'.

January 19 – My darling, you must be terribly busy with the Bakshi case coming up, and 'surrounded' at home. I can't picture you in Jammu at all, home or office, and the only comforting factor is Ganesh. It is quite comforting to think of Ganesh![31]

We leave for Chandigarh tomorrow with two Swiss guests. I will also have to put away warm clothes and close the house. Have been immersed in Ciba the last few days.

Love
Tara

~

Anokha, 32/Sector 5-A, Chandigarh
January 20, 1965

I love being back here though the house is empty without the children and their friends and all their noisy goings-on. This Ciba interlude[32] has made things more or less serene. It is cloudy today, the sky shadowy and dark, but at last the roses are in bloom. You remember they weren't when you were here. This morning I picked some for the drawing room, and gave a rosebud to each of our guests, who are visiting the PGI[33] and the university till 4 pm.

Isn't Chandigarh beautiful, especially the view I have from my bedroom window—the garden and the hills beyond—but for me it has never been a peaceful place. Too much always to do, organizing the house for children and guests, never any time to myself. Yet walking has made up for this and in snatched moments it has been peaceful and isolated despite

---

[31]E.N. Mangat Rai's cook.
[32]Refers to the visit of the Ciba company executives.
[33]The Post Graduate Institute, a medical centre and hospital in Chandigarh.

my being surrounded. I am filled with foreboding about the future, wonder even if this is my last winter here, and what the, next months will hold. There have been no more upsets since we left here for Delhi on January 15th though last night Gautam said with a violent determination that I would never get from him the sort of freedom I sought.

I wonder sometimes if I am corrupt, and you too, and everyone else is right. Perhaps what we do—this higher morality as you call it—is a terrible thing. Perhaps people like me *should* be stoned in the marketplace. No one, when it comes down to actually taking sides, would support me in my stand. They would think me mad.

We have a drink party this evening and there are two bottles of champagne in the fridge to have with dinner. And champagne in Chandigarh now reminds me of New Year's Day and the sunshine in the garden, and lots of lighthearted, good-natured conversation—most of it on Mummie's part— and suddenly the day erupting into violence and ugliness. It reminds me, too, of your New Year's Day letter in my pocket, and you and Champa and her mother leaving after lunch, and myself stumbling along the road to get away from the house. Gautam caught up with me and I was dazed and stunned with his blows across my face. I hardly realized his hitting me again and again till I fell down.

I kept telling myself that I must get up and go on, but it was quite comfortable to be there with the sun beating down on my face. I felt that as long as I stayed there I wouldn't have to think about what to do and where to go next. But one or two people passed by and looked at me curiously, so I got up and went on across the road and along the path we take to go on the lake walk. And just below where you and Gautam afterwards sat, and where I saw you, I found a kind of niche in the hillside and sat down in it. There was a breeze and the grass was blowing. The ground was hard and caked. And everything looked warm and dry and lovely, even through my dullness. I remember thinking, 'I'm not going back. I'm never going back.' Which was stupid since I knew even then I would in a little while, because the children had asked their friends to tea. And Mummie was at the house too. And there were things to be done. So eventually I got up and came up the path and saw you and Gautam sitting there, and that seemed to rouse Gautam again and he came at me. And that was when he got it all out of his system because afterwards he was much calmer. And we all went to the house for tea.

January 22 – It is a bright, beautiful day and I am having a hamburger barbecue in the garden. Our guests leave after lunch. At our drink party last night Serla[34] took me aside to ask whether I thought it would be a setback to family planning in the state if she had another baby! I said she was in charge of family planning, not family elimination. Kaka gave me many long and soulful looks and said he understood everything, whatever that might mean.

I want to get back to Bombay and routine again, yet leaving Chandigarh is a wrench, and I feel I'm going further from you. And I want to tell you again how much I appreciate (how formal that sounds!) all that you did for me here. I know from experience how people have reacted to Gautam's outbursts in the past, simply fled or faded away, never tenaciously stuck things out as you did. It moves me to tears to think of all you did, and the knowledge of you with me was so sure, I was never afraid. Please know that I'm with you, and love you, and it can't be any other way again.

Tara

~

[34]Serla Grewal of the Indian Administrative Service, in charge of family planning. She later became Rajiv Gandhi's principal PS, and was also Governor of Karnataka.

Wazarat Road, Jammu
January 24, 1965

You ask several questions. You also make some suggestions which express your misery. Are you 'corrupt'? Am I 'corrupt'? Is there morality in the so-called 'higher morality'? Is it mad? Should you be stoned in the marketplace?

Of these I can answer one straightaway. You *have* been stoned in the marketplace. The methods of stoning differ through the ages. If you accept that, you have already been stoned, *and* in the marketplace, as relevant people round you have known what, or somewhat, of what happened. You have carried your cross, and carry it. I have been stoned with you, (and been utterly helpless and useless to prevent it). I have seen what happened before my very eyes, and in my every feeling, to you. But this is not comparable to yours.

I have no doubt it is not you, but I who am 'corrupt' and 'mad'. You are comparatively a newcomer to this 'higher morality', this madness, a newcomer in practice, though I suspect it was in your instincts and bones. I have no such excuse. I have tried it and failed, and it is quite criminal that I should involve, after that failure, anyone in a repetition of what I know has happened. I cannot claim innocence. And yet I do not, even after this failure, look at these things merely in terms of practicality. It is immoral in my opinion, to hurt others. But it is equally immoral for another to hurt you. And it is in the clash of moralities that fine judgment is involved. Obviously, in the terms you mention, you do the social order great damage to depart from its norms; you create precedents and examples of bravado for further erosion. Yet no social order can survive to serve humanity unless it changes to meet new horizons and new conceptions. Particularly in the matter of women's freedom this has been so throughout the world, even the parts of it considered most advanced today. Again, it is a matter of fine judgment as to where and when, and for what cause, it is justified to defy, or attempt to change, the social order. It must be respected, and it must be changed. And in the process many have been, and will be, stoned in one way or another. Generalities do not help. The individual problem must meet the individual and specific conscience.

I am, unfortunately, in a position where I can hardly advise you. I am committed to my immorality and madness. I thought I had learned, but you came along, and accepted and gave 'wholes'. I do not have the resilience apparently, with this new and whole affirmation, to withdraw from my faith, and I am willing to be destroyed again. But you can benefit from what has happened to me. And whatever way you go, I will understand, and you will not be alone. It is fairly clear that Gautam will accept no association between us, no real freedom for you in coming and going. It is clear you believe it a duty to do the right thing, and not break with him. There are also the children. So you have your ultimate objective clear. It is also clear that reducing *us* to the correct proportions, compatible with this situation, is not an easy matter, even today, though we have known each other well only a few months. For I'm afraid you and I have fallen into a fatal combine, fatal in its stength, and that is love plus friendship. Love may be powerful and overwhelming—'electric' as you call it—but when years pass you may well find electricity is useful at night, but not needed by day. It is when you get the softer daily food of friendship combined with love that there is difficulty of escape, for it satisfies both nourishment and aspiration, and you may see the stars even on a walk through the fields, or a chat in the drawing room. It's where values and beliefs are always confirmed that there can be friendship, and if you love also, it becomes a difficult thing to break. And I think this has happened to us, and I mention it here to underline that you face a difficult problem. Part of facing it is to recognize it as difficult.

So perhaps my *objective* advice would be to act now—
you have experienced the potentialities in this situation
dramatically and terribly in these last few days—to reduce our
relationship to a friendship. No strain, no longing, not fought
about or heart broken for. Even to achieve that, with Gautam's
acceptance, will be difficult. So accept the discipline involved,
and I shall honour it too. I shall value it as what saves you (and
consequently me also) from a hell of uncertainty and torment.
I will be wholly with you for I love you. Do that now. Write
to me and behave with me as you would with a friend, but
only that. For more, it would be a matter of luck and sheer
chance. Otherwise, it may well be that after five years or so
of suffering, sweating and fighting, and having scenes and
violence to achieve something bigger and closer and more
exclusive, you may find that with Gautam you just cannot.
And in the process you may have made it too difficult, for
reasons internal to us, to retract to a friendship. So I'd suggest
we act now, and act together. I am with you and will honour
what we decide.

For reasons I have already stated, this cannot be my
subjective advice. I have gone too far in the process of
'corruption'. It is part of the air I breathe. My subjective urge
is that once I have seen the stars, and am certain of their truth,
let it rip. Then the only practicality is what arises out of a
particular issue or situation. That may indeed be tremendous
and may reduce one's affirmation to almost nil at times, but
the point is always clear, that given time and opportunity, I
will take this with both my hands. So, beloved Tara, I expect
you to draw the line. I can see all the facts and dangers in this
situation; you have seen them too. The best I can do is indicate
the ingredients.

I want to make you aware that there is a third factor,
perhaps the most important. And that is yourself. For in the
circumstances and elemental pressures that surround you, you

are in a class by yourself in this, and should realize it. You have to find a solution that gives you a reasonable chance of living at peace in your surroundings, and also enables you to write, an occupation which is obviously a love with you. Included in this is your safety and physical security, which must not be put in jeopardy. I repeat we must achieve this together.

While I am conscious I have brought you face to face with crisis again, and in a terrible form, I have not been able to regret it, except in particular incident or detail—not at all in principle. This is mostly because of 'the house we have built'. But also because this will be, perhaps, an experience worth having, for a person who writes.

I have longed for you and felt we needed to be together, if even for a while, to soothe some of the turmoil of December-January.

Much love
Bunchi

~

White House, Gamadia Road, Bombay
January 25, 1965

I seem continually to be faced with a new crisis before I have understood the last. Last night I was given a kind of ultimatum, to move to my mother's flat or go and live in Delhi. Gautam said I had let him down grievously and he didn't want me under the same roof. During the night I decided nothing precipitate would be wise. No change can be made till Noni finishes school at the end of the year. It would be damaging to her studies apart from anything else. I cannot simply move to my mother's with the children because I cannot be a liability to her, or anyone else. I would have to find work to support myself, and flats here are exorbitant and nearly impossible to

get. I need time to find work and plan for my future. Gautam
is an impatient person, and unreasonable when it comes to
accommodating anyone else, but if he agrees, I would remain
here till the end of '66, and then leave. But this again depends
on his change of mood and approach.

On getting back to Bombay I found a letter from Tariq[35]
asking me to be on the Tourist Advisory Committee. He will
hold a meeting of the Committee sometime in March. I will
wait for further information.

For myself this is another shake-up, more terrible than
any other, because it seems to have dried me up. I hear myself
expressing a view categorically when it might be more discreet
for the sake of peace to keep silent. I cannot shed a tear. I cannot
make an appeal. I feel a slice of life and feeling have come
to an end. Through all the shake-ups in my marriage I have
become a little less unhinged by each succeeding one. When I
was just married, I used to nearly die of unhappiness, long to
do anything, anything, that would set things right. And from
that stage of extreme vulnerability—which was also a state of
complete emotional innocence in these matters—I have come
far. If in the beginning I had been more firmly myself, I would
have been fairer to Gautam. I know this now, but I didn't then.
One doesn't realize these things when one is very young, and a
woman's whole upbringing, aside from her every instinct, is to
keep a thing healthy and working, protect it from falling apart.
I tried to do this, but badly, ineptly, bunglingly. I was curiously
innocent despite all my travels etc., curiously protected all
my childhood by loving, understanding adults. It was no
preparation for marriage, not in my case. So whatever way I
have behaved in this crisis was the result of having 'grown up'
the hard way, of having 'evolved' an outlook. I realized in '59
how far I had come compared with previous years, and now

---

[35]Minister of State for Tourism, Government of J&K.

I have come further still—but doesn't that mean, also, further from tenderness, from joy and belief and optimism? I have feelings for Gautam still, but they are what I would feel for anybody who suffers. Instead of affection, there is compassion, instead of willing cooperation, a devotion to duty. And I feel hounded by his threats of heart attacks and breakdowns.

Champa's calling me a tart—Gautam has called me worse than that. Perhaps there is an element of that in me, in every woman, a gypsy element, irresponsible, free, that simply because it is female does attract the male. She is right that I am aware of men and they of me. I like it that way, always have. Have never considered it wrong to feel this way, and I think any woman would be a hypocrite who said she did not enjoy male attention. I can see that it might be very trying for other women to watch this happen.

I am late already. Must be at Morarji Bhai's[36] at 12 for lunch with all the Swiss.

With much love
Tara

~

January 26 – Last night I was told the 2-year period of waiting would not suit and I must leave as soon as possible, end of February at the latest. If this turns out to be final—and I never know—I have decided it would be best for the children to stay on in this flat where their routine is established, and move myself to my mother's which is piled high with her luggage, but will otherwise be available as she will spend most of her time in Delhi. I would then be able to see the children every day.

Gautam has so much to him that is worthwhile and good. I feel horribly depressed at what I have done to him, dragging

---

[36]Morarji Desai, Chief Minister of Maharashtra at the time.

him into corners where he doesn't want to go, tearing off covers he wanted left undisturbed. Yet I know that every bit of progress we have made—and in a strange way we have actually made some—has been because of this journey into areas he would rather have left alone. But that is no reason for wounding a human being as I have wounded him. How wrong we have been for each other.

New Year for me always begins on February 1st because we are on holiday till nearly the end of January, and then it takes time to settle down again, transfer to a new diary, fit into the children's requirements at school and so on. So by the 1st I hope to be organized enough to start thinking connectedly about another book. Physically settled is another matter, and emotional permance is not something I expect, but even in an uncertain life there are areas of silence and serenity one creates, all the more indestructible because one creates them of necessity and desire, and in these areas life and work go on .

January 29—Your essay on 'Secretariat-Field Relations' has just come—something to go on with for a little while. The last few days have been very tied up with Ciba. The cumulative effect of the Basel crowd has been to relegate our personal troubles to the background.

It has been interesting to watch Dr Keppeli's reaction to Gautam. They are rather similar men and Dr K. says he knows, and approves of the fact, that Gautam is a positive, highly emotional man, also ruthless in his pursuit of objectives, and that such men are needed to get a job done. Dr K. has complete confidence in him. I have found the endless business conversations rather exhausting. Business, and its technical and other problems is not a subject of general interest, as is almost any other profession. The Swiss are wholly dedicated to hard work and they work like ants, with high organization and unremitting industry, and never another interest to deflect them. Their wives are, or have to be, just as dedicated, and none that I have met has any real preoccupation outside the home. There is hardly anyone less fascinating than a Swiss housewife. I think an Indian woman with education and opportunity is a far more rewarding and fascinating human being than her European counterpart. We are having a farewell lunch for Dr K. at the Ritz, for which I have to order the menu in a little while.

Much love
Tara

~

Wazarat Road, Jammu
February 1, 1965

My darling

First of all a happy New Year, since yours starts on February 1st. You need a New Year and a happy one. Second, I am impatient to contact you. I am distressed at the blank wall ultimatum Gautam seems bent on administering to you and himself. It is too unreasonable and violent to be believed. I am not only anxious that you are driven to the wall like this, but to know exactly how you can manage. The knowledge of your mother's flat in the same area and not too far away from the children, is some comfort. Whatever you may write, and however you may put it with all your resources of courage, you must be feeling terrible. I am certain, however, you will land on your feet. I am less certain for the children as such events are bound to bewilder them and be beyond their comprehension, and there may be some scarring of their being and confidence. But I am also quite certain that your repeated assertion about not giving in on the principle of this, is correct. And should there be the smallest way I can help, you must not hesitate to ask. I have a certain amount of ready money I could make available at fairly short notice.

I think what you say is very true—'Courage needs a witness'—that if what you do is understood and shared, it makes a difference to strength and capacity. That I would ever come anywhere near giving the sophisticated, disciplined and self-contained Tara anything of this kind seems quite unbelievable, and has made me feel very loving, as if you were really my child, my beloved child, and I could wrap you up in tenderness and take all the sore and bruise from your being. I am unable to keep my thoughts from when I will see you again, and though I banish them, too, as an impossibility, they appear as too nearly possible, as necessary, as even around the corner. And I have been continually aware in all these letters of Ranjit going off, and wondered if it was mother or son who was missing the other more before the event.

Thanks for the extracts from Gandhi's *Doctrine of the Sword*, which I enjoyed, and I don't believe I have come across it before.

Champa said the other day that some women were very practical where their interests were concerned, adding 'though I should not say this, as you are so fond of her, Tara would always be about Gautam.'

I said, 'I think she quite enjoys the way they can afford to live, but that is about all.'

Yes, you had the wrong type of upbringing for this difficult marriage. In many ways, though different in detail, I had the same kind of upbringing, at least complete adult trust and sympathy, and much about my milder marriage shocked me to the core when I got into it.

And these last few weeks I have often wished for the impossible, that you were not yourself, but in fact Champa or Kikook or Kaval, all of whom have much more reasonable husbands, who would not have raised this impossibly high wall around you. I could at least write to you when and how I wished. Please write and tell me all about yourself and continue to love me.

Much love
Bunchi

~

White House, Gamadia Road, Bombay
February 2, 1965

Dr Keppeli and Dr Rohner have left for Pakistan and Basel, and Gautam has returned to the attack and told me I must leave this flat by the end of the month. He has also given Dr K. the impression that something is wrong with his personal life and continues to spread the news far and wide, and, incredibly, to blame me for anyone knowing. I have not even spoken to my mother yet, and feel too weary to have any rational thoughts. I have told Gautam I do not seek a break but I will submit to being thrown out if that's what he wants. I've also told him I won't accept chaperonage, i.e., the rule that Champa, or preferably he himself, must be present when I meet you. He must realize I am not at his mercy and I will not toe any line. He sees this as a prestige struggle and feels he cannot lose face by compromise.

February 5 – I had a talk with my mother and she says there can be no drifting off to another flat to suit Gautam's whim. If he wants a separation he must (a) make up his mind, and (b) make it legal, and the children and I must leave this place together .

February 8 – I must tell you I can't reduce us to friendship. The 'fatal combine' is here to stay. So are the strain and longing. I haven't told Gautam of my acceptance of the Tourist

Advisory Committee as we have a drink party for 40 on the 19th and a dinner for 14 on the 22nd and I simply cannot face a cancellation of these if there is a blow up. I feel I am dealing with an invalid. His is no longer an unhappiness that can be put right or catered to because it has too long and complex a history.

I *could* cut you off, but is it a good thing to cut off a whole live area and carry on with a stump?

It's strange your asking if 'normal life' continued 'fast and furious' at Chandigarh. Curiously it did, with desperation, as if each time were the last. There was a kind of menace surrounding the house, as you know, so I couldn't sleep very well at night. I used to be afraid of Gautam's footsteps—they echoed loudly on the miles of uncarpeted floor and up and down the ramp—afraid of his voice in the darkness, and to see him when I opened my eyes at night standing and staring at me fixedly and intently, more often than not, drunk, or sitting up in bed and staring at me. I would have to stifle a scream and tell him in a very normal tone of voice to go to sleep as I was tired and it was late. For how in heaven's name could I even just acquiesce (which is what you say is all a woman does!) in that set-up? Every nerve in me screamed. In the morning there was at least the reassuring morning light, and not the unknown dark, and the drunkenness of the night before partly worn off, though it never quite did during those dreadful days. And that was how it went on.

Bought some bedspreads this morning though this flat is temporary, as we are to move to a new one in a year or so. And it strikes me as quite amusing sometimes, not knowing whether I'll be moving into it or not. As does your gentlemanly assumption that whether one walks out or is asked to leave, it is proper that a wife should be provided for by the husband. You obviously don't live in an emotional jungle, and I assure you such things cannot be taken for granted at all.

I am reminded, in this marital situation, of Milton's lines:

> And that one talent which is death to hide.
> Lodged with me useless…

My talent, yours, Gautam's, Champa's too perhaps (though I don't know her well enough to say) lodged with us useless, prevented from growth. I look back over the years and think all I've done for Gautam is haul him over red hot coals. Strange that he clings to me as he does, says 'I'll never allow you the kind of freedom you want.' Allow! I have always 'allowed' him his. You say I should give in practice, so long as I maintain the principle. But what's the use of an armchair principle? Sooner or later it has to be practised. So I am with you, every bit of the way, in your 'corruption' and 'madness'.

With love
Tara

~

Wazarat Road, Jammu
February 7, 1965

I got a call last night from SS and Serla,[37] at Chandigarh, about Kairon[38] being killed on the Grand Trunk Road along with Baldev Kapur, an officer I knew well and was trying to get to Kashmir. The news shook me and I was half inclined to leave immediately for Chandigarh, for I'd known and worked with

---

[37]Serla Grewal and her husband, Sukh Chain Singh Grewal, both of the IAS.
[38]Pratap Singh Kairon, Chief Minister of Punjab, who was killed along with Baldev Singh Kapur, on the Grand Trunk Road, while travelling in 1964.

this man for so many and difficult years in the Punjab, but I realized I could do nothing for a dead man, and had never come to know his wife and children at all well, and could offer them no effective succour or assistance. In the gush of reaction I scribbled a letter to the press which, however, possibly transgresses the limits of a civil servant's right of public expression, and so will not in fact be sent. It was done in a hurry, and on some whisky, nevertheless here it is.[39]

I spent a lazy morning today after weeks, and amongst other things read Odysseus in the *Eastern Economist* on your book *(From Fear Set Free)* and non-violence. My personal belief is we could have applied non-violence to the Chinese invasion of 1962, with results no different, though from the point of view of morale, much and significantly greater, than what actually happened. If we had defended our frontiers non-violently, with our 'bodies', we would have made an impact on world morality, and a tremendous impact on the confidence of the Indian people. The number of people required to face the Chinese with non-violence would perhaps have been no larger than the armies we deployed. And what is important, the Indian people would have understood what they were doing, felt they participated, as indeed they itched to do, and the whole campaign would have been one of organized unity, building confidence, which is what ultimately makes a people. We did not capitalize on, and make real, the enthusiasm of our people. It was dissipated eventually in cynicism, and lack of faith in our capacities, not congealed to a new experience of strength and inner resources, which I think it could have been.

Love
Bunchi

~

---

[39]See Appendix.

White House, Gamadia Road, Bombay
February 11, 1965

As I expected, Gautam says he will cancel the drink party of the 19th. I had sat hours on the telephone getting forty acceptances. The dinner he will shift to the flat of one of the men from the office—my dinner, my chosen guests—and that I can be present or not as I wished. A lunch at the Willingdon Club for the same visitor from Basel—but the guests were to come here for a drink first—he says I can be present at or not. And I must leave the flat immediately. He said he would pay for the children's food and their school bills, and didn't grudge me an allowance. How much should it be? I said I knew nothing about these matters and must get advice.

It does seem a pitiful world, from the horror of Kairon's murder, so close to Delhi, in broad daylight, to the way a marriage can be broken. I have failed to reach Gautam as a human being, to be to him the wife he wanted, failed him utterly. What excuse can there be for that? What have I done to an honourable man—a hard and harsh man but one who acts with integrity in his black-and-white world? But what else could I do? And I am doing nothing to halt the tide. What kind of woman am I? I see the enormity of what I am doing, yet when I see Gautam's persistent, continuing reaction, I feel he is a man gone beserk, and who from time to time since I met him has gone beserk at every crisis. Normalcy is always so temporary, so unreliable. This makes me doubt if there is a future with him, even supposing normalcy is restored once again. I am constantly the criminal in the dock, constantly on trial. I can live in this situation, and will if he wants me to. I can write in it too. But I'm not prepared to give up my relationship with you. The more I think about it—in the context of my set-up—it would be like asking mankind to give up mathematics and revert to counting notches on a stick. In all conscience I cannot do that.

Today is Speech Day and Gitu is getting a prize as she does every year. I don't know if Gautam is even aware of the fact. I am painfully aware of the gap in the children's existence. Aware, too, in flashes, of a kind of void ahead, of the immense effort I shall now have to make to put together some sort of life for myself that will be a constructive one. For I don't want to feel sorry for myself, or have anyone feeling sorry for me. Well *that's* a challenge ahead, a fourth dimension awaiting investigation, an *experience,* you will say, for a writer! So it will be worthwhile.

Yes, you have involved me in a repetition of what has already failed for you once before. Only there will be no failure between you and me, Bunchi. I am in this of my own free will. They can draw and quarter me for it, or continue to stone me, as you say they have. I do not blame them, for they must protect their institutions. Someone must.

I must ask you again not to worry about me. You and I have been expecting this development. Your life must go on exactly as before. All these goings-on at my end are interior to you and me, and have nothing to do with your marriage, your work, your outward daily life.

~

Wazarat Road, Jammu
February 1, 1965

And again you are perhaps asking yourself why I should write all this. I have done so, I think primarily, because I love you, and feel I must tell you all that I feel, and you must be patient with me, and also truthful, and tell me when I am an infliction, however small. I also do so because I want the whole of you, and am aware as to how I do. I don't want you physically behind a bush, or in sudden release of desire when there is an opportunity, a 'quick one' when the lights are out as it were. I do when the whole of you is with me, when I can give you the whole of my body and being, and take you gently always, as far as the spirit and being go, fully and wholly and almost as if it had to happen as a continuation of our togetherness—in conversation, and in warmth, and even in laughter—an affirmation of a full expression. I put it badly, but you know in your bones, I think, what I mean, and that it is possible, and has, in a sense, happened between us.

But let me talk about what you wrote about yourself during this crisis. You wrote singularly powerfully and vividly and beautifully—not one extra word, and not one false note—and I thought Gollancz need have no fears of your portraying passion. It's all there, clear as crystal. And I can see how you felt—almost exactly—and can hear the 'footsteps' on the long 'uncarpeted floors and the ramp coming upstairs'. I can understand, and even cling to you as I do, your 'blotting' me out 'deliberately' and 'welcoming' me back when you are again 'alone'. And your preference, queer though it may be, for the 'morning' with the beginnings of light, and not in darkness.

~

White House, Gamadia Road, Bombay
February 16, 1965

My mother arrived yesterday from Delhi on her way to America. She told Gautam she hoped I would have ten more men in my life, every one of them important to me, and that he must try and understand me as a person. He said his mind was made up. So she said in that case there was nothing more to be said, and the remainder of the evening passed pleasantly!

And now I have to think of the immediate future, with these parties, and then the dismantling of a home, and it will

take time before all the energies and hopes and efforts I have
centred on my marriage will be fit for any other task. I feel quite
ill when I think of telling the children, of packing, of moving. I
am acutely conscious of wanting to stand on my own feet. As
for our relationship, it has within a very brief period brought
me to a strange pass. I did not know on August 7, 1964 that
a landslide had begun that would end in an avalanche with
me at the bottom of it, buried under the debris. One thing is
clear, that truth is strong medicine. It should be prescribed
with great care, sometimes not at all, and in this regard I have
shown neither caution nor restraint. So in terms of common
sense I undoubtedly, rank as the biggest bloody fool of the
decade. I sometimes wonder where *is* this famous practical
side to me which people like Champa and Kikook, and no
doubt others, claim I possess? And by which I protect my
interests so zealously? For I am the biggest blunderer I know,
and that I haven't ended in disaster till now is surely the hand
of God upon me. Religious or not, I have faith in the hand of
God, which I prefer to call abiding goodness.

I don't know of any influence stronger in my life than
Gandhiji's non-violence, as a way of resisting wrong. But I
took no interest in it as an actual approach to living until 1959
when in my devastation I floundered for something that would
sustain me. And this did. I studied it carefully, proceeded to
apply it to my life, and the difference it has made is simply
that I'm not afraid.

~

Wazarat Road, Jammu
February 19, 1965

I have not added anything to this letter since Tuesday partly
because I have been rushed with work, preparing drafts of the

Sadr-i-Riyasat's speech to the legislature, which has to be done against time, and has to please many masters—the Cabinet and the Sadr-i-Riyasat—so that in the end it becomes a rather cautious, dull and sterile document, with the imprint of no single person or dominant idea. But partly I have not written because I have seen no clarity in your dreadful predicament. And this when I thought we were sailing into smoother waters, and I can see how hopeless and helpless this pistol-point decision of Gautam's makes you feel. The disproportion between what was happening to you and anything I could give you has been great, the fact that you are up against the loss and destruction of a whole life, thrust aside from what you helped to build and consolidate. I wish I had been able to visit you in Bombay and had some idea of how you live. Will I ever see you again, see you to have some time with you to myself, without the atmosphere of doom and disaster? Will I?

I have read and reread your passionate affirmation about non-violence, what it has meant to you personally. At the moment, however, placed as you are, life is driving you to either-or, giving you no chance in between. It seems a particularly difficult and absolute testing ground for faith, one that permits no choice of gentleness or non-violence, only a choice of one exclusiveness or another.

I am glad your mother has a house on Akbar Road, which is one of my favourites at Delhi. It has lovely trees and I often used to deliberately drive down it when I had a choice of routes, to enjoy the trees.

With much love
Bunchi

White House, Gamadia Road, Bombay
February 23, 1965

I could plot a graph now for Operation Crisis. Gautam has decided I must not leave, that he realizes I must, to an extent, live my life. This is a tremendous concession from him, though he has assured me he will kill me if I let him down, and kill you too.

I think he needs to come to terms with his own adventure in 1959. He should at least concede it existed, that he needed friendship and reassurance, if not (he insists) love. But to admit he had had *any* kind of satisfying relationship with another woman would (in his view) give me the liberty to do likewise, and he wants me in purdah. He is not insensitive; he doesn't allow his sensitivity to function. He is afraid it might be construed as weakness.

With all this mess here I haven't even started my new book. And now I have gone slack, loitering around the house in my dressing gown, not concentrating on anything in particular. It must be a reaction to tension, and having to hold together for a long spell without relief.

Your 'pedantic intellectualism' I would have liked even at the age of twenty. It's the sort of thing I never had enough of. The paradox was people assumed I was hungry for other things altogether, perhaps with some justice, since there was that side to me too. You are right about the 'life force' and its powerful urges despite one's better judgment. With Nicky there were other factors too, but he was European, and one thing I was definite about was that I must marry an Indian, live in India, and die in India, Basically, I am married to India in some peculiar, passionate and unalterable way, and nothing can change that.

The first of January is a good day for us to have got married. You are the only person I have ever known with whom I have wanted to identify myself almost completely—almost, because I know you so little after all. I'd put my life in your hands and my soul in your keeping, the soul you write of in your poetic scribbles. No one has ever cared about my soul before. Perhaps the fault was mine.

Sometimes I feel I've undertaken a fast unto death, and death of the spirit is all it can lead to. There is no way out. I am caught between two powerful opposing currents and drained of vitality between them, by the presence of one and the inadequacy of the other. The first time I was in Chandigarh, winter of '59-'60, all the people I met, including you and Champa, looked like characters in Sartre's play *No Way Out*, struggling futilely in a predicament that could not, in its very nature, improve. Now I'm there too.

I spent the morning with the girls telling them about the period between the two World Wars and the rise of Hitler, also Churchill's career, and they listened spellbound. Mummie brought back two pictorial souvenirs of Churchill's life and we have gone over these. And I enjoy nothing more than this kind of morning with the children.

~

White House, Gamadia Road, Bombay
March 8, 1965

I spent a long time on Saturday night thinking about everything all over again. When I encountered you (in January '64) I understood at once the encounter was full of danger for my peace at home. I argued with myself about it and decided I had a right to let you in, talk, share. So I walked into a very dangerous situation with my eyes open, knowing full well from all my past experience with Gautam, that this would never work. But I felt justified, for hadn't I worked for years to produce something worthwhile between Gautam and me?

I had submerged myself so that *he* wouldn't be hurt, so that whatever I had unwittingly done (through my past) to hurt him would be healed. But I never felt I had any return. That ten-year battering with its accompaniment of long morose silences, alternating with anger, took a great deal out of me. I was starved for companionship—not for sex or secrecy—just adult give and take. Then came this crisis.

I have never come across reactions like Gautam's. To this day he repeats with an incredible ferocity that he will kill any man who lays a finger on me. Now he says he has nothing to live for and his health is a dreadful new element in the picture. Having brought himself to this pass he is using his condition to convince me of my wrong-doing. Both he and I seem to be wandering in a no man's land where neither of us can discover a familiar landmark or a warming sight.

Darling, what makes you think I'd miss all the conveniences of modern living on a trek? If you knew the way I grew up, the way we travelled, third class in the dust and heat of summer, living in Congress camps, hardly knowing what it was to sit in a car—the two cars my parents owned at different times were confiscated during two different non-cooperation movements—and we used cycles and tongas throughout childhood. We lived in a big house, it's true, but within it life was simple by choice, and one's philosophy of life was in any case simple, in preference to one that accumulated possessions. The first inkling I had of what possessions meant was after my engagement to Gautam. I was leaving for Moscow (to join my mother) and his mother asked me to leave a sample blouse with her so that she could get blouses made and have them ready for the wedding. She told me she was giving me 99 saris. I hope I didn't look as dazed as I felt.

This crisis has loomed so large it has blotted out everything else for both of us and there has been no chance to talk of our interests. I seem to have occupied the whole scene and I hate that kind of limelight, even between us. Just as it was not in your 'tradition' to love in this way and with this speed, it was not in mine to let myself go in this fashion. And I wonder at the depth of this involvement, a kind of pledge made in sobriety, and with the full and perilous knowledge of all that hangs in the balance—one does not make a pledge in a trance.

~

Wazarat Road, Jammu
March 8, 1965

My dearest love

I complete a year here tomorrow, and can still feel myself travelling up in the car from Pathankot that morning, rather apprehensive and speculative about what I could do here, and how I'd fare as a 'stranger in a strange land'. And though I am at home here now, I am still apprehensive about the future as Kashmir does not seem to turn any very definite corners, and there is basically almost as big a question mark as there was. A whole set of arrests, about 160, was put through Saturday night, of which you may have read in the papers, as a start in the showdown against Abdullahites,[40] which seemed inevitable. It is a highly controversial decision and will invite a good bit of criticism, as we obviously cannot get into the vicious circle again of detaining these people over a long period. We want to convince them that beyond a point they cannot rake up communal feelings and hatred in the boycott campaign and the like that had started. It is hoped this skirmish will bring restraint and moderation. But it may have the opposite

---

[40]Supporters of Sheikh Abdullah, hopeful of creating a situation, through intrigue and disorder, of returning him to power.

effect and then where does it end? For there is no giving up Kashmir, and cannot be. At the same time one cannot, must not, hold these people sheerly by force. One must hope to win them over. The vast middle group of Muslims have to be won over, who are not really rabid, though they may have an inclination towards 'the book and the prophet', ostensibly more represented by Pakistan than by India.

March 9 – I enjoyed your letters of 1941-1943 very much. I think I was very different in my teens—did not have the variety of interests, nor the capacity of enjoyment and relish you seem to have had. And though you will argue that this is absurd, I saw the 'quality' of which I spoke, in these letters. It is all potential there, above all in the nuances. I felt you were much easier with it then than you are today, when too many people see only the facade, and you have learned to control the effervescence within.

You seem to anticipate or think almost simultaneously of what I wanted to write about. You wonder 'if a choice arose, what would you do?' It is not a question of 'if a choice arose'. I have made my choice. I have no urge whatever to keep the home intact. In fact all my urge is the other way. The only doubts I have on this angle of the business are in regard to you. There is much that could lie ahead for you. You have not only built on an inherited foundation, but one to which you have added your own sweat and labour. You have crossed the threshold and there is, I think, a harvest for you which, if it materializes, will take you to more variety of activity, of interest, of opportunity. It could be rich and various, particularly if it had the security, the happiness, and the background of a warm, understanding home to return to, and on which you could always rely. That home must not become a drag on your flowering. I am in the season of sitting back and gathering up. And yet, for myself, that does not hold me back, and I want and need you so much that I'd commit the selfishness of taking you, even if it worked only for a period. I'd have to be careful and watch that I did not come in your way, and be man enough if I did (I hope) to face it with you, and depart if necessary. I think I'm right in concluding that, today at least, your choice and urge are as clear as mine, and have become stronger over this crisis. We must talk about it when we meet and discover what we should do about it.

About Gautam's health—I'd thought this particular thing at least you would never have to experience. With Champa I was for years in the extreme plight of what your letter shows the first glimmerings. You never know whether this is a form of instinctive blackmail, and therefore, to be resisted, or whether it is real illness brought on in the other person by what you live by and believe in. It is tantalizing and excruciating, and I have often cursed myself for the sanity of my body and mind which would not in turn show signs of breaking and illness. Even today I am not certain what the truth is. You feel the responsibility of Gautam the same way, though with differences of detail.

I want to quarrel with you a bit, or with my obvious inadequacy—somewhere. *Do* you feel alone? Since you were with me in October—those lovely days which now appear an unruffled haven of nurture and delight—you have never been away from me. There has not been a day, nor even half a day, not even an hour that I have not been aware of the daily miracle of you in some way or another, as part of the scheme of things and the significance of living. It has never occurred to me I was alone. This palpable bond between us since October has not allowed me to feel alone, even if there is great and endless longing and a vacuum of unfulfilment, and all this may continue. If it does, we must face that together also, and not be submerged in despair or in a daily indifference to life around us. And now, all my love

Bunchi

Wazarat Road, Jammu
March 15, 1965

Over the weekend I have fallen in love with you again. I do not know why. Because it was wholly unnecessary. At the play I saw you sat beside me. And I was aware simultaneously of an intense longing for you, and an intense awareness of your presence. And I thought, 'She must be feeling similarly. Poor child'—and was somehow certain of it. For that also is how I have thought and felt about you, that like a child, in complete and simple faith, you have brought me all your problems and all your toys—'told you unabashedly about myself'—mostly problems, knotty, unrelenting problems. And I'm afraid you have become my child, and I have often felt like that about you, a complete equality in innocence which is only possible between generations. Yet I am much afraid to tell you this, for I have committed, and still commit incest then, and want you, my lovely child and also my woman, arrived to me in the abudance of innocence and yet fruition.

~

White House, Gamadia Road, Bombay
March 22, 1965

We got back from Delhi last night. There were crackling brown leaves all over Mummie's lawn and I wanted to tread on all of them, only there wasn't time.

I was quite used to *not* having a relationship like this. Sometimes I almost don't want it. I cannot bear the luxury of it for myself alone. It doesn't seem fair or right (in this 'socialist pattern of society'!) that I should have so much. Why can't Gautam have this too? Why can't Champa, or my sisters, or so many people I know? What have I done to deserve this? There's no rhyme or reason to it.

Are you right when you put so much emphasis on the 'Muslim' aspect of Kashmir? I think in time Pakistan might quite willingly part with its Bengal bit and be glad to be rid of a burden, but will never give up the Kashmir issue because it is an emotional involvement.

~

Wazarat Road, Jammu
March 20, 1965

You said you 'feel a little ashamed of having indulged myself so much in writing to you'—and somehow this hit me very hard. The letter famine, which we had agreed on, for the protection and growth of our love, our child, you are making an occasion to protect your soul from pollution and softening by too much association with mine. The more you reveal yourself, the more you confirm and discover yourself. Between two individuals this process may go beyond either of them to a new entity that has the richness of them both. You grow from roots that you plant in another, and from a renewed strength different and beyond your own, yet within you also. Surely this cannot conform to any preconceived notions of how far one can reveal oneself in decency or self-respect. The only limitations would be internal to the relationship, or the needs and responsibilities of practical life. Your putting a stop on it because of some idea of inviolability, to protect the core of yourself etc., seems to me to misunderstand (and to sin against) the meaning of love, which must, if we value it, surrender the core. For in fact you never surrender it, you merely strengthen and confirm it.

You may call this possessiveness, of which you have had a surfeit. It may well be a kind of possessiveness on my part, that I want and crave nakedness between us, the whole of what you can give, and I want to unload the whole of what I can give. Is that possession? Perhaps it is. But I can only love you in this way, that whatever you do, of importance, or even of unimportance, you accept my hand in yours. So I find it hard to accept a position that you should put limits on what you say to me. All my instincts go the other way, to tell you all there is. I do not think we are in any danger of an orgy of unrestraint. I also like a quotation that preceded Laski's *Grammar of Politics*—a great rage when I was a student of history—which went something like this: 'For liberty is like love; it has to be won afresh daily.' And I wish you were here with me so that I could love you daily afresh, give and renew and strengthen my being, take and receive and cherish yours.

March 25 – Thinking it over, queerly enough, (and in this case unwittingly) the person whom I have perhaps 'taken in' is Champa. Queer, because with her there was never any chance, or period, during which I exercised a relationship in terms of whole being. She was full of life and vitality and was one of the few women who could go about alone and do what she wished. She had many English friends who abounded in wartime Lahore and one of them was Morris-Jones, whom I got to know very well and like very well, who later became quite an expert on the Indian Constitution and has written a much quoted tome on the Indian parliamentary system. Marriage came swift and sudden, I still do not quite understand why, in a matter of a few days in 1944. After we were married I tried to be whole, as I wanted it, and also thought it necessary that she should really know me. So far, because of her talking about it, factually I knew much more about her; we had hardly talked about me at all. She was not interested in what I had done in the past, how brought up, what experienced, how felt, and so on. So I very soon withdrew, and she has, in fact, not even seen some of the things I wrote before 1944 (e.g. about Madonna, or the manuscript about myself) which you have.

So we lived on the day-to-day plane, and whereas I always tried to be truthful about anything important that came my way, in fact insisted on being so, there was never any coming to grips with each other as human beings. Over the years, of course, she has got to know a lot about me, but that is the accumulation and accretion of two decades of marriage, not of any voyage of discovery that we made as individuals. *Today* she is much more interested in me as a person than she was, but all this has come later. Now, *I* find myself cooperative, but not fully engaged or responsive. Nor do I feel she will take me as I am. So while her interest in me has developed over the years, it is still an interest on her terms, within her values, not necessarily mine. She is irritated (but seldom says so) by my ideas on freedom, on love, on frankness; she thinks I am too occupied with themes of the self, that I waste my time (and talent, for I think she believes I have talent) on them.

I have presented to her over the years the picture of a man whose values she has never been able to accept, yet she has been impressed by the fact that I have worked them, have been a success in my job, a tolerable success with many people, a great success with a few, that I am trusted, that even her mother, and brother's family, have more confidence in me than in their own relations. She has had to face a dilemma, for while she cannot appreciate my values, she admires and admits that I have worked things out in human, even gentle, terms. When we argue about freedom, for example, she concedes the principle, but cannot accept it. All her instincts rise up against it. I often feel my type of character has done her a lot of damage. For she has blurred her own intensities, and has not accepted mine. I may have been a peculiar kind of Waterloo—not unreasonable enough to reject, not weak enough to succumb to or compromise, and yet essentially not palatable to her system.

In the early years of marriage she had strong emotional interests outside, but they were not sustained and did not last. I sometimes feel that the very fact that I encouraged her whenever she showed any interest, whether human or otherwise, has far from helping her to an independent life within our marriage, convinced her that it was not worthwhile. And today she may resent the very real freedom that has always been available to her.

Possibly if I have taken in Champa in this way, you have done much the same with Gautam. For whatever he may say about your so-called immorality, it seems fairly obvious that in many ways he has accepted your cultural and aesthetic values in the home. He seems to think them good and worthwhile, and yet is unable to see they must be based on a degree of independent thinking, living and experience. Am I wrong in this assessment?

The only other experience I have of a type of 'taking in' is in the sphere of my work. For several years in the Punjab (and I say it only to you and for you) I had a kind of influence, almost power, over the organization I controlled.[41] It was a large one, eventually perhaps 2-3 thousand men, running food and supplies. The test came in 1947 when transport, and all normal living, was completely disrupted. I could only communicate with the field by wireless which was tremendously overworked and inadequate. In spite of thousands of people on the march, or locked into particular areas of towns (as, for example, 2 lakhs Muslims concentrated in Islamabad, an area of Amritsar, protected because of the concentration), I don't think anyone starved for lack of wheat getting to them. Even in Islamabad, a rationing officer named Mathur had enough personal influence and prestige to face the formidable opposition of non-Muslims in getting supplies to the area, and then the real danger of non-Muslims entering

[41]As Director-General of Food and Supplies, and simultaneously Secretary to Government for that department.

a Muslim area where a huge population was beleaguered in daily fear of their lives, and of attack.

These men worked often without instruction and often against all rules. And I think it was done largely because of confidence throughout the organization, and the fact that each man knew his objective and his responsibility. There was a kind of marriage of affection and responsibility between me and those workers. They had been 'taken in' by me perhaps. There are now too many chaotic influences that play on both workers and public, and make the creation of that kind of bond difficult or impossible.

You talk of barbed wire, and I am very aware of it, and that I am outside it, and even to approach it seems fraught with difficulties. But in a sense we are in that together also, for I am painfully and constantly aware of your barbed wire as not only a limitation on you, but on me, on us. I don't even know when you will get this letter, maybe only when you come here in April. You seem far away, my darling, and it is long since I heard from you. You say I talk too much. I do. I write too much, too, to you, and hardly want to do anything else but my work, and get back to you. You'd be bored with me if you lived here for I simply do not venture out when I have what I love. I only venture in, to more and more of them. You are lucky, for the barbed wire, as far as I go, enables you to escape.

You say you have grown in this experience, and in contact with me. That's how I've felt too. It has been a whole new experience for me. I have grown in the confidence that it is right to want, and fight for, freedom and individuality, that these are ultimates, and cannot be given up, even though they present themselves—not invariably in big national causes like the Congress had—but in comparatively smaller personal matters. In an independent and, one hopes, increasingly affluent society, they will more and more present

themselves in such matters. And I have grown in feeling not
only for you as a person, but also in the terrible rightness of
our association. It has never dimmed, this feeling that it was
right. I have also, queerly enough, been with you in your
instinct to preserve your home and life with Gautam, and
achieve a relationship, and sustain it, with me. That may be
asking for the moon, but I have asked for the moon with you,
and perhaps if we are steadfast enough, we shall achieve it.
And most joyful of all, I have grown in the warmth of finding
another person, in 'discovery' you will say, and I would
say 'in love', which may also be discovery. But I want a lot
more of that, lots and lots more, and wonder, will there be
the opportunity? Will she continue to want it too? My only
anxiety is the continual, unending absence of you. When will
I see you, how, for how long—and when will I see you next?
They all seem to merge into a horrible vacuum, stretching
out endlessly. People should not have to live like this. I
know so little of you, yet I feel I have known you for years,
that you and I are no strangers. Perhaps we were married,
or something like that, in another existence. For you are no
stranger to me, and I have known you—for long.

March 28 – I have had an unsuccessful argument with
the Sadr-i-Riyasat, and have failed where I badly wanted to
succeed. They were to appoint two Pro-Vice Chancellors for the
university here, following the Ganguli Commission Report that
Jammu and Srinagar should function as two semi-autonomous
divisions of the same university. I urged strongly that one of
them must be a woman (Kashmir has no woman in any real
top position) and it should be Mahmuda, who is easily the
most competent, and as it happens, the senior person among
the women in the academic line. Karan Singh has selected a
man named Mukhtar who has passed retirement so that he
has no claims, of right, to the appointment. Karan Singh said
Mahmuda was eligible but tended to be rigid about certain

matters. I said a university should give that kind of person rope, instead of filling it up with old and possibly discredited wood. I made much of the woman issue, that I'd like to import at least two women deputy commissioners and so on, that it provoked and stimulated a traditional society which has to get out of its ruts. And so it went on. He said bazaar rumour had it that Mahmuda was the Chief Minister's friend, and *Blitz* and other papers would headline it all over the show. I said even if they did, if the woman was competent and deserving, we'd be able to face any mud-slinging, and in any case people were saying about Mukhtar that he was the Sadr-i-Riyasat's man, and was to be retained. Mukhtar won, and I lost.

April 2 – Last Saturday, along with some Legislature papers, I got your letter about the possibility of having to call off your trip to Jammu to meet the danger of Gautam's mood and health. And I have dreaded the arrival of another letter telling me the axe has fallen on our relationship and it has to be given up. I have dreaded it these many months, but now that it has come upon me afresh I have wondered how I'll be able to accept it. It has seemed like an entirely new and devastating monster, now certain to take me in its jaws. And some of all this must have got into my subconscious also as Champa tells me I cried out in sleep, which is a thing I have not done before. I felt on the 30th, my birthday, that if another letter came in the afternoon telling me of the axe, it would be a stange birthday gift. So that the best thing that happened on my birthday was your telegram. It arrived at 7:30 when I had gone downstairs to lay out the drinks for Sadiq and Co. who were expected at 8, and was alone when the telegram was delivered, and I grasped the word 'Love' as if it was you yourself who had come to me.

~

White House, Gamadia Road, Bombay
March 28, 1965

I had forgotten how prolonged these deathly silences could be, how long they could last. I have no idea about Gautam's plans for going abroad except what I overhear him telling other people. He refuses to talk to me. Thank God for the children with whom there is talk and fun and laughter. But I am at sea otherwise, about day-to-day plans, appointments, summer holidays. I go out alone now everywhere and each time I must make an excuse for Gautam. Last Saturday to J.R.D. Tata's,[42] on the 3rd I'm dining at Rafiq Zakaria's,[43] on the 8th at Jehangir Sabavala's,[44] and excuse-making becomes awkward after a while. It is so unnerving, I've thought of letting Gautam have his way and calling my trip to Jammu off. I can, this very day, stop being everything but Gautam's wife, trim myself to suit his needs, and perhaps save him to some extent thereby. And I am prepared to do it with all my heart if it will help. Will it help? Tell me. Doesn't it seem a bizarre choice, either he lives or I? We can't both apparently. Tell me if I'm justified in coming to see you or should give it up. Something holds me back each time I consider giving it up—not only my selfish desire to see you, but the thought that this is not the way to solve this problem. Am I being too academic? Does it matter how the problem is solved when it seems Gautam's balance is at stake? And this, I suppose, is what you meant when you wrote of your fears about Champa. I keep asking you to tell me this and that, knowing full well you can't even write any more.

Over the past fortnight I've developed a fantastic notion that you are going to solve all problems, because of how, you

---

[42]One of India's leading industrialists.
[43]A well-known public figure.
[44]A leading artist.

tackled the crisis in Chandigarh. I have never known such steadfastness before and the strength of it has stood by me all these months.

~

Wazarat Road, Jammu
April 4, 1965

I am more than glad you are coming and we must get down to things in detail when we meet. You cannot go on living the way you have done, with almost no break, since mid-December and even earlier. When I count the months I just do not believe it possible. What it must mean for you, and how you have stood it and survived it, and can still write sanely, with argument and discussion, I just don't know. This time when we meet we must find the answers, as it is obvious Gautam cannot. I am wretchedly sorry for him but there is little point in saying just that, for I see no way out except as you put it, that either he lives or you do, which is idiocy, but seems stark reality also. I know you are in a virtual prison, all the more so because of your ability to see Gautam's need and worry about it. It is thus doubly a prison, for yourself, and what you have taken on for Gautam.

You sound envious of the 'clear road ahead' for me. I indeed am not in a situation of the dynamic and absolute proportions you face. Yet I do not feel a clear road ahead. I think it was Hegel who said, 'A man who has work that suits him, and a wife whom he loves, has squared his account with life.' In a way I have had work that suits me, the privilege of competing successfully for the ICS (at that time considered a great test of brains), with minor extras, like standing No. 2, and getting higher marks than the English in English Essay; having men and colleagues who have been good almost without exception; chosen to be Chief Secretary, Punjab, perhaps the youngest so far; chosen for Kashmir, etc. And as part of my work I have walked in the hills and made many friends. (Do I sound boastful? You must allow me to speak to you as to myself, my darling, for you have let me love you like that—why did you do it? I love you intensely—forgive the diversion.) Yet the ICS was not my choice. I did not want government service. For I was also brought up in the era of nationalism and the Congress. But I saw no alternative, and employment in the thirties was particularly difficult. Anyway the ICS was no great victory; it was a defeat ideologically. I tried hard to get a teacher's job at my own college, St Stephen's, and was rejected because I was not a 'Christian'. It was a little ironic because the Bishop of Delhi came specially to see me in 1957 (I think) to ask me to become its Principal. I said I was no more a Christian now than I was then, and he said, ' Ideas have changed as to what a Christian is.' I said, 'I'm fond of the bottle,' and he said ideas had changed about that too. I was very tempted but decided I did not have the sense of vocation any longer. I could not live the 24-hour availability that the Principal of a missionary college should be willing to do. But to return to the ICS, though I started a career in frustration, I have to admit on Hegel's first test, that I have had work that suits me. In the second matter, 'a wife whom he loves', I have never had that, and you have all the details. But here again, I have worked hard, made something of it, and to the observer it's a marriage that works. So all told, I do not feel the way so clear. It is as difficult as your way, for your way has become mine. Rereading your last letters so many things seem to climax and come up like a hundred snake heads whirling around me. It is all, my beloved, my darling, so dreadfully complicated, and so dreadfully worthwhile. Every hour and every day I am glad I love you, so glad that I could hold you against the taunts and strictures and 'better judgment' of the entire world.

You say 'God willing' and 'grateful for God's goodness' and God comes from our mouth and from our pen as if he—existed. *You* write of him almost without thought. So let us in future believe there may be a God who silences and understands anguish, who transcends dissension, and heals disrepair.

April 8 – I am unhappy. I don't want this from you ever, this holding back. While I will accept all your bloody limitations (I have no option) I will hate them for I cannot believe in them. I do want every thought it has occurred to you to express and you do wrong to mould these to 'balance', to the niceties of diplomacy, or of good behaviour. For we have gone long past that and accepted comradeship. I look at this as a personal faith, the one, and only one, place where there are no barriers. You are wrong that what you have written has no intrinsic value. It has, and we will never write exactiy like this again. When you are here, put all your letters in a locker, in your name, and keep the key. But don't destroy them. Also, you must not do this to me, this 'balance'. Let's be whole with each other. Do not tarnish it with limitations of any kind. In surrender and abandon there is much truth and much strength. Rubbish, you may say, but my darling, my beloved Tara, how do you explain 'us'—you and me—and what has happened to us in so short a time ?

April 15 – I enjoyed your essay on the briefcase, the crockery, and the geese. And the most interesting part of it was the admission that you had not packed crockery yourself, but neverthless knew all about it. Well, I have packed it, and know nothing about it. I did so before I was married, when I had very little, and the most difficult part of travel was arranging for my horse Asghari—who was terrified of being put into the horse compartment of a train, would go wild, and not even I who knew her well could assuage her feelings, so I had to leave her to the relentless process of travel, hoping that time's sordid gifts would bring her comfort as the train went onwards, and it did, for at the end of the journey she'd be quiet—a sort of dazed acceptance of the inevitable, and not normal again for many hours afterwards, in spite of gifts of carrots and gur. Where was I? Yes, I also packed all the crockery shifting from Amritsar to Ambala in the grim days of '47, and there were no breakages, but from Srinagar in October, I deliberately did not bother about the crockery. Till a week before I left for Jammu I had a very attractive visitor staying with me, who took some of my time and most of my thought, and who never even smiled when I got home, so that I never knew if she liked me as much as her work. So it was a deliberate choice of priorities. As for the briefcase, I don't agree to a leather one as a gift. From you I want something much more difficult—I want you—the most precious gift. And now the geese. You did not like my calling you 'upper crust' some months ago, but what is all this about flying geese to Chandigarh? There is also a daily bus and I could have got them there, but why take so much bother with geese—dead geese? What are they for, except to eat, and I ate them.

I'm afraid some people will think you are a 'scarlet woman' and I flinch from the idea as much as you do. I cannot give you any consolation that they won't, except this, that in time they won't. A cloudy morning, though many days in advance, makes me wonder if your plane will arrive. But the weather must hold, and you must be here with me. I wanted you to read this 25,000 word letter before you see me, but that seems difficult now. I have to remind myself you have never been here, never seen this room, the back veranda, the terrace. I have been assuming I have lived with you in all these places.

I have never written as long a letter to anybody, but these weeks it has been difficult to keep away from you, and I have come back again and again to you in this way. For people like you and I, who are not believers, this love is in the nature of a religious experience, the feeling that you are merged in something that compels and clutches you, that you cannot give it up, that you must follow, whatever the odds. In moods and moments it transcends your thinking, your planning, your good and considered sense—and yet without any feeling of shame, failure or frustration. Indeed the contrary, a feeling of belonging, of inevitability, of rightness. And God seems natural to talk about, almost a household word. There is so much I could only express with you near me, yet you are here with me, in some mysterious, unsatisfactory, but very definite way. I am terribly grateful God gave you to me for you are a gift, not an earning.

~

Anokha, 32/Sector 5-A, Chandigarh
April 12, 1965

We dined at the Grewals' and the talk turned to various Chandigarh people, dissecting them quite casually. And then SS said, 'And now let's talk about Mr Mangat Rai.' There was a sudden silence. Then SS said he found you a most interesting and complicated character, with something strange (or was it missing?) in your makeup. I said I wondered if it was happiness. SS said no, you always seemed perfectly happy, and it was others who attributed unhappiness to you (which I think is correct) and we didn't get much further than that.

Things have not been easy here, but I have committed myself to the Jammu trip and will take it—more stones in the marketplace.

April 13 – A hot day has suddenly turned to cool darkness, with a three-quarter moon hurrying through massed clouds. There are flashes of lightning and a rumble of thunder and I feel uneasy in this long wait to see you, and hope I will, and that nothing will interfere with it at your end either. Will you really be there?

With love, so much of it
Tara

~

Wazarat Road, Jammu
April 16, 1965

And now I am afraid of a letter from you, lest it tell me you are not to be here. When I got back from my walk a few minutes ago, four documents, two from Champa, one from Mrs Singha, and your letter FACED me. And I said, 'Keep cool', and deliberately changed first. Took off sweaty shoes, put on a long-sleeved sweatshirt, went round the corner, washed hands, in that order. And then made a telephone call to a man called Khaliq who had left some whisky for me, and a bottle of champagne for you—wanted to know what I had to pay, but he is not at home. And I don't know how I should cool the champagne and all that, or even open it for that matter. You will tell me. And then I could put off your letter no longer. And opened it, and loved it. The lightning, your longing, the three-quarter moon, which I also saw, and was sad it would go before you were here. And your words 'the ache of your absence' And I said, Why does she say that? Does she know I feel like that, and feel all her fears these days? Will she come? Will I see her? Will the weather behave? Will somebody interfere at her end? At mine? These churn through me, imagined, unreal, and yet so real. But I cannot quite say it like she has. Does she know I am her comrade in every word she has said? And I also thought this little note is like a deep sigh mingling past and future, the yearning of a whole life and experience. There is love in it, full and ripe with its longing and its fears.

I cannot destroy these letters. How can I? I know I will do what you want. But don't want this. Surely you cannot.

In many ways that seem so clear now, my previous existence and experience seem a preparation for you, a probation for love. Let me love you. And please love me.

Bunchi

~

This morning, Bunchi, you wanted to know about last night, and I was slow about giving you an answer, and finally didn't give one of any kind, and was aware that you must have thought something was missing for me. I felt a little hesitant with you. We were new to each other and I was seeing a side of you I hadn't seen, your 'relentless pursuit' carried into the physical realm. And I don't know why you should have any reservations about yourself. I have none about you, a lover aware of your beloved's needs. I did feel you are designed for a woman who not only wants pleasure, but for one who longs to please. And I would give much for the time to lavish myself on you, spend time in discovering you in this way, building a new intimacy between us. As for your 'ravenous hunger' to give me as much as you get, I do understand it. But in our circumstances, meeting as we do, so very seldom, should we worry about it? There might well be that need on an everyday basis, but just now I feel (dreadful confession) anti-equality, and happy, and to be able to give is a great joy for me. So let me.

~

Wazarat Road, Jammu
April 27, 1965

My new beloved and my darling

While you were still here I was looking out of the window in
my office, across the low scraggy hills and the layer of scrub
toward the plains, across the meandering sandy bed of the
Tawi, to the haze of the distant horizon, looking at it as if there
must be answers to all human contradictions, perhaps even
in the landscape, thinking of what I'd like to say to you, and
realized there was very little to say. There was a completion
and a fullness between us that had its own eloquence, that
required no questions and sought no answers. It just was. You
were rediscovered, reborn in rapture with me in another aspect
of what you call sharing, another aspect of us. And I almost
laughed at the thought that there was nothing to talk about
with Tara, that we were there now for us to use. We seem so
placed that our lives might be full of near despair, and if not
this, inevitably separation. Yet I knew, whatever happened,
we would love and believe. And this did not bring the breath
faster to the body, or the blood faster in the veins. It was quiet
confident, certain, and for always. Between you and me there
is nothing for the future, except fruition, no hills to cross, only
the valley to enjoy and cultivate.

But this is not what I wanted to say in this letter. I wanted
to say that for the first time in my experience (and you say I
am terribly experienced!) I have given and accepted without
bruise; it has not been a 'thing' between us, but a homecoming,
to the warmth and familiarity and pervading affection and
atmosphere of friendship and comradeship; to the excitement
of bliss; to the joy of ecstasy and poetry. All these I have felt
and had with you, all these as if they were in the natural order
of things, and belonged, and as if I developed to them but

did not have to, even for a moment, look at any of them as separate from myself, as something to achieve and win. There has been, for me, no beginning, and no climax, and no end. There may have been these in fact, and yet, even now with the miles between us, I feel enveloped with you, have you in my arms, know that this between us is a process of being, and not an arrival and a departure, nor a beginning, an act, and an end. And words like 'darling' and 'beloved' escaped from me as they have *never* done before in such a situation and at such a time. And I almost felt like crying out to God to take this frame from me, that it was too full a gift and ecstasy to carry. What could I do with it, whom give it to, and how share it? It could not be for myself alone; it was too much for me. And you were there then, an immediate reminder, unbelievably with me, and I could share what I had in my fullness, and you were then my 'new beloved' (with which I have started this letter), rediscovered and reborn. And you have been so gentle with me that I have hardly known you were there. You have had so much for me, so much without question, that I have been aware of armfuls of you, and more armfuls waiting for me. Does that sound contradictory? It is contradictory, yet there was no contradiction. Was it unnatural then that I was afraid that I had had so much and given so little? I was only somewhat sure when I looked at your face in the half-light we had, and saw on it clearly portrayed a kind of angel-like quiet animation, and rest, and contentment. Had I imagined it there? For myself—to use your words—I experienced and discovered 'areas of reassurance known only to the body'. I say experienced and discovered because I have not known such areas before. I have expressed the body and even found physical relief in such expression, but I have never been reassured by it; in fact, the contrary; it has raised questions in my mind and feelings, creases within the depths of my being, of which I was always aware and even wanted to run away from. Reassurance, strength, joy and baptism (if I may use the word) I have not had before. And all this has to do with your chastity, for there is something chaste about wholeness, and I have had it with you in our whole relationship. It has deprived me of debate, of thought, or even words about it. It has been a whole world we held aloft between us, and with and through us, like the sun in May on new leaf and lawn in Srinagar, and I have said I am glad I live, and was born, and reborn. With you I have been where I was never before.

And yet it was home, as if all was known, the passion of the intellect inspiring the flesh, and the earth of the flesh mellowing the intellect, so that I belonged to both. I was the prophet honoured in his own land, the traveller come home.

I am tired today—no walk—the crisis with Pakistan deepens, and I had long consultations with the army—got home a few minutes ago. I have bought my ticket to Delhi, but if things go as the signs are, I will not be able to make it, and will have to stay in J&K during the week's break. This strikes me with horror, as I must see you, if even for a very short period. So I hope and pray that I can. This morning I dispensed your tips to the sweeper, farrash and mali. I was lonely for you and dried myself with your towel. Please forgive the liberty. I washed out my somewhat marked clothes, not too successfully. I have thought of you intensely and repeatedly over a long day.

And, to continue from where I left off, for the future I appeal for your help. In future it must be something we do together, and help each other with, for which we must be able to talk, at the time, at least to the extent necessary for understanding and cooperation, in need and expression. Your letter is complimentary, and I accept it, but I also know you are prejudiced in my favour. Your writing you 'felt a little hesitant' with me was a revelation to me because your desirability is a) so manifest to anyone; and b) particularly to me, who so obviously loves you. So again, I would request your help, so that I (we) can understand how we want this between us. After I met you in October in Srinagar I was sure of your priceless value to me, and knew there was much to discover, not only in this, but about a variety of matters. I was willing to wait, and to sweat to achieve understanding between us. But the sweat has never even resolved to drops on my forehead. For you have been like the tranquil breeze from the endless and enduring mountains, and the sweat withdrew from my forehead even before it settled.

And queerly enough I agree with Kaka that you are a simple person. And in simplicity there is great strength, great beauty, great truth, and of these I partake with you, and the only credit that goes to me is that I recognize them and can worship them.

And you, my darling, also make me live three lives—the life that takes most of my time and energy: work, domesticity, duty; my life with you, for I 'live and move and have my being' with you, and whatever there is between you and me, however small, a letter, a telephone call, the possibility of a visit, are lit up with significance and concentration; and I also live your life with Gautam, its dark intense passions, its cults and superstitions. These are real to me. It seems strange, three lives to a man who longs to lead one, and one only. But I'd rather live six lives than give that one up.

Much love
Bunchi

~

13 Akbar Road, New Delhi
April 26, 1965

Something in me urges that, however difficult, we should continue to struggle to the next milestone, looking no further than that each time. For in that process some hope may emerge, or at least the next span of struggle be less of a strain, though I have no reason to believe it will ever be easier. We must count anxiety as part of the road ahead and learn to live with it. My journey was hot and unreal. I tried to sleep through most of it for I could not concentrate enough even to read the newspaper, my thoughts were on us. We were so much together, in love, in anxiety, in all our discussions of our problems. How easily and ruthlessly these things are decided in America through divorce. Why do we linger and ponder and discuss endlessly all the possibilities of hurt to all the people concerned? What could be simpler than that I should come to you, wherever you are, and we should make a clean break and start afresh. Only how nearly impossible that would be. Meanwhile, I want to thank you for everything, my darling, and send you all my love.

Tara

~

Wazarat Road, Jammu
April 30, 1965

The only part of your letter I would like to remonstrate with is that your wanting me to keep my visit to Delhi quiet is not for reasons of cowardice. I know you are not a coward. I do not know where you get your courage from. People usually do from God (even irrational faith) or from love based on principle and nature, like mother and child, or from great hate. I have dreamt of a courage born of the mind, and its comprehension of what is good, true and beautiful, a courage as invincible as the others, and yet infinitely superior, for it understands. Do you, perhaps, have some of that kind?

Jammu is strangely quiet with many already left for Srinagar. Yet it is an uncomfortable quiet and there is apprehension in the air. Where do we go with Pakistan? When I walked yesterday, where we went the first day, I was asked to go away as the army were busy digging. And today I went towards the Bahu (across the river) where we went the second day, and the army were busy laying lines and defences. The clean village you mentioned had been evacuated and occupied by our army. Will things hold for another day? That is the kind of question one asks quite naturally. For this place is gunpowder, and anything may happen internally (leave alone externally) if the extremists get going. I have got all the sanctions organized, the powers given to executives and so on.

Your letter of the 29th. So you have turned the corner again to normalcy. Let us hope this time it will be more lasting. I was immensely relieved for the break in tension, though I should be used by now to the high devastation between you and Gautam.

And now I have done most of my packing, and left the crockery to Ganesh: And I count the hours to Tuesday morning.

E.N. Mangat Rai. Delhi, 1969.

Part Two

My darling Tara

I have woken up this morning, about an hour ago, with pain at the thought and realization of leaving you. What can I do about it? Philosophy, does not seem to help in spite of years of practice at it. I have felt you were all around, a pervasive part of my being, in the feel of my fingers, and the air drawn into my lungs. And I have hated the idea of getting back to the ordinary world where I must carry on—work, eat, sleep, talk—for arid hours, weeks, months, even years, without you, in a way losing the feel and savour of you in the daily demand for adapting oneself to what the daily task needs.

What shall I say in praise of you? I need to praise you, for myself, not for you, to fulfil myself, to say what I am continually and repeatedly and almost newly aware of every time I get to know you better. And I cannot do it adequately. It comes to me repeatedly in terms of the word 'whole', whether it is the expression on your face, the fullness of your breast in my hand, the ache gone from me when I come within you, the awareness of your hand touching me—whether it is these, and I seem to experience them anew every time; or whether it is the childhood you lived, bits and pieces of which make a pattern of thought and home for me; or the incidents and situations you have told me of—all these are the completion of a person. They have an entity that lives as of itself. And somehow I have to think of you as untouched, and unspoilt, with a kind of innocence and strength. There is a completion in you for each occasion, almost each piece of conversation, each time I meet you, or write to you, or hear from you.

And I have never treated you as a child. I never could; you are very much my grown-up and my equal, very much and more than my match. You do not dazzle me, for dazzle is somewhat of a distance, separate, has a glitter of its own which may come and go. You kindle the depths of me, light up forgotten corners, bring alive substance that was not used and almost forgotten. You flow out to me in a mutuality of sustenance for I can feel myself taking and being strengthened, feel myself wanting and able to give. It's the dazzle of many lights, not only within you, but put on in me, and I know it is of the permanence of things, of their essential texture, full of the lustre of the intertwined fabric where you cannot see the strands, but there is the inviolable whole. I have never treated you like a child, I could not; I have thought of you as a child often, of your stretching out your hands to what is beyond, in steadfastness and innocence, and a kind of relentless faith. I have seen you becoming, as you have gone through the years of which you have told me, and I have seen you arriving, at places and stages in that process.

May 8, 7:35 a.m. – Am packed and will leave in a few minutes. This is to wish you many happy years ahead on the 10th and every day thereafter. I know you have a long way to go, many successes to achieve and enjoy, also that you will use them with moderation and consideration. I am a little afraid for you, that you may challenge some aspect of life with almost too much integrity and head-on, and hope the gods will protect you, as they should.

Much love
Bunchi

Delhi-Srinagar Viscount
May 9, 1965

Tara

We have just taken off and now there is no hope of turning up
at your doorstep again. And it is indeed the end of this visit
to you. But you have sent me away with the lights burning,
and I am strangely filled, even when parting from you, even
facing a long and uncertain deprivation of you. As you say, our
marriage was consummated and for me it is the first time I have
married, and you are my only and my beloved wife, now and
for the future. Much love, and please keep it close to you for it
will always be yours to make of what we can.

Bunchi

~

13 Akbar Road, New Delhi
May 9, 1992

My darling

I wonder if your plane is taking off at this very moment. I look
ahead to my own departure on the 11th, with a sinking feeling
but your love is with me as we go our separate ways. You
and I are not perfect but we have produced something nearly
flawless between us and nothing can alter that, though the
future stretches ahead like an endless campaign in the Rann of
Kutch—dry desert, occasional mirages, and never a solution.
Yet how wonderful it has been this time with you and how
much I look forward to all our years ahead together.

~

13 Akbar Road, New Delhi
May 10, 1965

Yesterday this place was a madhouse with people coming and going in connection with the election to the Deputy Leadership of the party.[45]Mummie held on, said she had a right to stand as she has the support of the rank and file, though she is opposed by the Syndicate. No word from the PM. The powers that be seem so afraid of her that this one election has stirred a hornet's nest of activity. And finally, half an hour ago the PM has asked her to withdraw her candidature. He is, poor man, terrified of the Syndicate, and I am bitterly disappointed at the outcome of this. She would have emerged as a leader with a following of her own and this is what terrifies the Syndicate. Currently the PM's name is Lull Bahadur (the lull in Kutch).

I shall be sorry to leave Mummie's house. There is an atmosphere of freedom and acceptance without questions asked. Even the children feel it.

I don't belong anywhere any more. 'With you' might be the answer, but where is 'with you?' What corner of the world, what time of year? Or is it just a piece of paper on which the pen eats up the paper with longing, on and on to no destination? Neither you nor I have the answer to that. I can hardly believe that the Jammu-Delhi interlude is over.

~

---

[45]The reference is to the election to deputy leadership of the Congress Party in Parliament. Vijaylakshmi Pandit wanted to contest but was opposed by the Party bosses (known as the 'Syndicate'). Finally they prevailed upon the Prime Minister, Lal Bahadur Shastri, to get Mrs Pandit to withdraw.

White House, Gamadia Road, Bombay
May 13, 1965

Maybe there is only one way out, renunciation complete and utter, the only possible release from a tortured situation. It would be possible because I would know it would be a release into suffering. I would then condemn myself to anguish for as long as I lived, and only thus could I legitimately end this thing between us. Whenever I have said 'this is my lot' I have been able to take the beating, as during the letter famine, or the horrible secrecy enjoined on us. I am far from happy in this double life.

~

1 Church Road, Srinagar
May 18, 1965

My beloved

We can live the love between us openly and fully, and even extravagantly, or we can practise it within the limitations of our responsibilities and duties, knowing that some degree of renunciation will be involved daily. Renouncing in your sense would kill vision and capacity, just as truly as the thief punished with the loss of his hands. I can understand your urge for truth completely, I have it too. I think we should ask ourselves, are we afraid for ourselves in telling this truth, and if the answer is no, then are we afraid for another person's happiness and capacity to carry on and live? If the latter is the reason, then we must relate it again and again to the need we wish to serve. It seems some area of compromise is inevitable.

I want and enjoy all the enclosures you send me. They give me a different light on you sometimes, through somebody else's eyes, and I want and love to see you in as many ways as I can. I am dreadfully in love with you, Tara, and now it is like an avalanche that takes me with it. I simply must get more control of myself and used to doing without you, as this may become torture. Why have you allowed me to love you like this, and why did you not produce some womanly tricks and difficulties, which would have left me wondering and puzzled, and unable to hold you and be with you the way I am? There are no barriers at all for me to hold on to, and hence the avalanche.

Please don't be depressed. We have to find a way out to constructive work and happiness; otherwise we will be dreadfully ungrateful, for, my love, it is still a miracle to me that we have found each other and there seems no end to what I can and do discover in you as a person, and through you even in myself. I do love you.

Bunchi

~

White House, Gamadia Road, Bombay
May 13, 1965

I have already told Gautam I am willing to be discarded. I have defined my position as clearly as geometry. I am not prepared to back out though I am prepared to compromise. I feel exactly as I've always felt in my life with Gautam whenever anything has threatened his domestic peace—like a bone being gnawed by two dogs, or a piece of property, a thing being fought over by two men, exactly as *I* were not to be considered at all, my feelings in the matter not to be taken into account, that I was to sit and wait till the two had hammered it out and then be dragged home by the victor. It is an impossible, ridiculous, and degrading situation to say the least. This happened with

Kjeld. It happened with Nicky when Nicky passed through Bombay and Gautam locked me up in my room, and it has happened on innumerable lesser occasions. 'No, my wife doesn't wish to dance with you.' 'No, my wife can't come to the phone.' While the wife stood by like a log of wood, not even consulted. Well, I'm a little tired of this nonsense, because nonsense it is. I'm not *capable* any more of toeing the line just to oblige. Something in me has had enough of that regime and can't take any more. Now, I can yield within reason, if some understanding is shown, not just because I'm told to, or told that someone's jaw will be broken if I don't. I don't want anyone's jaw broken, least of all yours, my darling, but I cannot be blackmailed in this way. The fight for freedom, the brazenness to demand it at all, has cost me dear. I would be a lunatic now to let it go.

There was much during this past trip that almost twisted my heart, the fact that you sat in that hotel room and waited for me, then the question of my birthday. I have a very birthday-celebrating family, but no birthday was ever celebrated as you celebrated mine, in so many ways, and over several days, and your phone call from Srinagar and your letter headed 'Tara's birthday'. I used to feel a little awkward going through the hotel lobby and up in the lift or by the stairs, and then revive as soon as I turned to the right and went past what seemed scores of servants in the veranda. Then at last my knock on your door and I was safe and cut off from the world for a little perfect while

May 14 – midnight: I got back from the Tatas a few minutes ago. Jeh[46] was not back from Europe and it was a small party. Thelly[47] is like scores of women who build their lives around their husbands, and stand or fall emotionally

---

[46]J.R.D. Tata.
[47]Mrs Tata.

depending on their husband's treatment of them. I think Jeh is impatient of this, wanting her to be an individual. It has not been in her temperament to take advantage of the quite unique opportunities her position has afforded her, or even to consider them unique opportunities.

I have been wondering how things will be when Gautam gets back from Europe. Even when he's here I wonder constantly, how will he be when he comes home this evening, how will things be in the morning, and so on. I am rocked or calm in proportion to it, rather like Columbus having set sail, and once on the high seas, able to do nothing but take what comes, wind, weather, mutiny, etc. Am I heading for a New World or a shipwreck? It is interesting to speculate on such things at midnight.

From Monday I must start work—there are no perfect circumstances, and I feel guilty when I do nothing. I am trying to start something with a Chandigarh background, for which I may have to borrow my diary back from you.

~

1 Church Road, Srinagar
May 21, 1965

I am glad you have written to me about the children, and especially interested in Noni's liking poetry. Poetry is a great trainer and discoverer of emotions. It lights up and means much more if it is read aloud by somebody who has a feel for it. I was lucky in two teachers who read us quite a lot of poetry when I must have been 15-17.

I think you'd enjoy living alone and would get a lot out of it. I know I would love living alone. In fact these days it is an insistent *need* in me, almost cries out in me. But that is very much connected up with you, and the way I feel about you.

There is a whole world you make me think and feel, which I long to express, at least on paper to you, and it is not all just love talk. For example, on renunciation I think I could ferret out a whole lot from my mind and experience. I cannot exploit the world your love, our love, has created for me because I have work, and I am not alone. I am dreading visitors, who start soon now. My trouble is that I am moved not so much by ideas and the intellect, but the emotions acting on these. This moves mountains in me and my love for you has had that effect, moved mountains within me, and I would like to travel among these, tarry in them, discover them, put much that I felt into words. And I get no time, and it seems a waste. I have been lonely for you and this whole business of you-me has seemed a terrible problem with literally no way out of it. In moods and moments I have felt wildly that we should push decision and go ahead with each other as soon as we possibly can. This whole business between us is too complete, too valuable, too much alive and too beautiful to submit to the slow ravages and compromises of separation. But these thoughts do not lead anywhere and I am always left with the question of what is right for us to do.

~

Janpath Hotel, New Delhi
May 28, 1965

Darling

You asked me to sleep and it seemed, as you left, an excellent idea. But how can one sleep when one is rested as if from a long long sleep already, as if—and you deprive me of words—there was nothing more to say, having known both ecstacy and rest. I have only one ravenous hunger, the need to know that I have given somewhat also, and not only received.

May 29 – I see no reason in my parting from you, no spark of hope or theory. I will have to collect these as I travel, and remain, it seems endlessly, away from you. And I thought I will have to love her with my mind through the letters I write in answer to hers, love her fully and passionately with my mind, for that is the medium of communication on paper. And whatever I wrote about would exude the strength and aura, the pervasiveness of the love I have for her, just as whatever she has written has brought me her love.

~

1 Church Road, Srinagar
May 30, 1965

My F and B

Which means feast and beloved, and you are both, for always, I'm afraid. I also think of you as GM which means gold mine, for I can delve into your mind and feelings and always and invariably get something from them—an idea, a confirmation, a bit of beauty, a bit of experience, a bit of revelation, even sometimes a categorical denial. I have not experienced anything like this with anybody at any time, this extension of love to realms of rambling and of response. So I should not be dejected, and whatever part of you I can live with is worth all my effort. I have, strangely enough, a child and a beloved in you, and you have drawn from me the tenderness of two kinds of love. I thought of one of my favourite poems in connection with you—'And all the wild sweetness I waked was thine own'. And would I not have been a fool, Tara, if I had not pursued you 'relentlessly'? *You* will have to be relentless now if you want to get away from my arms.

Of course I want to know whom you meet and what you talk about. I want all of it that you have the time and inclination to give me.

~

White House, Gamadia Road, Bombay
June 7, 1965

Gautam arrived looking well but tired and said it was the best trip he had ever done, both from the business and personal point of view. Everyone he met, he says, was struck by how changed and unlike himself he looked and behaved, and though he said it was due to overwork, no one fully believed him. Dr Kappeli remarked that when a man marries well, either he ruins his wife or is ruined by her. Gautam asked, 'Isn't it possible for them to do each other good?' and Dr K. said, 'There's a one per cent chance of that.' Gautam asked him point blank if *I* seemed ruined to him, and Dr K. said 'No, your wife is a great success. She has charm and beauty and she has a career. No you have not ruined her.' I asked Gautam if Dr K. thought I had ruined *him,* and he said not at all, there was no insinuation of that kind, that Dr K. liked me very much. Dr K. has shown great affection for Gautam and said he considers him a son, which is a great deal for him to say. It was on the basis of a medical check up, which he ordered himself, that the Kashmir holiday is being arranged. For the first time since the crisis, all is calm and normal.

~

White House, Gamadia Road, Bombay
June 10, 1965

Gitu rests in my room, reads for a while and then falls asleep. Today I asked her what the most wonderful thing in life was, and gave her the answer, 'To be an individual, completely oneself and not like anybody else.' And she replied, 'Well in that case don't keep expecting me to like the white of egg just because everybody else does!'

June 13 – Today Gautam told Captain Mountain (our American friend who brings a cargo boat here every year) that he would be leaving for Delhi on the 15th and would probably take a holiday somewhere after that. I asked if the place was to be kept a secret and he said he hadn't made up his mind.

We dined last night at the Jayasinghes[48] and for some giddy reason I held forth on non-violence-to Ernie Mountain,[49] and someone asked the classic question about what a man should do if another man raped his wife. Whatever else he did, I didn't think murdering the rapist's second cousin would be a solution, which is what wars and vendettas try to establish as a solution. Nor is there any injunction in the non-violent credo that says you must stand by and watch your wife raped. Anyway, Gautam came up with, 'What do you do if someone rapes your wife's mind?' So I said, 'If she cooperates, and enjoys it, then it isn't rape.' And I wonder if he means you have raped my mind. I don't find the suggestion very flattering for surely I have a mind of my own and am not rapeable material, nor do I think you fancy this approach to body or mind. To think, in any case, that I'd submit to such a process!

With reference to your argument with Selig Harrison[50] over Kashmir, I thought the following extract from a letter letter written to my mother from Owen Lattimore, dated April 6, 1964, would interest you. He is an authority on Asian, especially China affairs, and was victimized during Senator McCarthy's witch hunt in America:

> The last time I was in India, about Christmas 1949, your brother did see me, and sent me up to Kashmir. Things were going well then (in spite of that silly imitation Col. Blimp, Loy Henderson), and there was hope and the possibilities were great.

---

[48]Peter (PS) Jaisinghe, the founder of Asia Publishing House.
[49]Spoken of as Captain Mountain, above.
[50]A well-known American journalist.

I feel bitterly that we Americans have been responsible for a good deal that has gone wrong since. The suspicion and misunderstanding of your brother have been fantastic. There was nothing that a man in my position could do, because having been put in a false position about China, anything I had to say about India was suspect. Two major things have been wrong about American policy. Under the guise of a non-partisan approach we have, in fact, been partisans of Pakistan on the Kashmir issue, and have urged settlement in a manner which has helped to prevent settlement.

Even more fundamental has been our suspicion of the socialized sector in India's economic programme, and our persistent upsetting of the balance by pushing for private enterprise, regardless of the merit of the particular investment. If Wall Street were half as Machiavellian as the Communists accuse it of being, it would have lobbied in Washington for a crash programme in aid of state enterprise in India, as the only way to create in time the economic stability, on the basis of which then, and only then, openings could have been made for private enterprise, with the benefits of competition and increased production which private enterprise can stimulate.

We have now, I fear, compounded our previous errors by throwing our weight about on the Tibetan frontier crisis in such a manner as (a) to exacerbate the Kashmir issue, and (b) to give aid and comfort to those who, under a smokescreen of super-patriotism, are out to break up your brother's life's work, carving footholds of power (and mutual rivalry) for themselves.

June 15 – The only thing Gautam has said to me is, 'I'll send you a telegram if I decide to go away somewhere on a holiday from Delhi, in which case I'll be away about a fortnight.'

The gulmohar won't last long now. Already the trees, especially the coconut palms, are looking drenched and bedraggled, like beggars in rags, and at night the road I look out on from the drawing room windows gleams black and wet. Huge waves toss heavy spray over the sea wall along Marine Drive. It is suddenly much cooler, but only stays that way if there is not too much of a gap between showers.

June 18 – Ernie Mountain rang up and said in his nasal drawl, 'Since your talk about non-violence the other night, I've become so non-violent, all I do is eat and fall flat on my bed and go to sleep. I've even stopped taking any exercise.' I had to laugh and he said, 'Well, I thought and thought, what can I say to make her laugh, and this has done it.' The children and I are lunching on his ship tomorrow.

June 21 – I must be looking a sorry sight for Mummie remarked on this on arrival and linked it up with the chronic Gautam-me business. She said, 'If Gautam and another man arrived on your doorstep, would you know which one was Gautam?' I said, 'Only just.' And she said, 'That's what I thought, since he's never here.' She then suggested I go to Japan with her for a week in August. I told her I'd like to but must wait and see how things were on Gautam's return, whenever that would be. For I have no news whatever.

Ernie Mountain rang up today and said, 'I've become so non-violent that last night my ship caught fire and I didn't even know it!' Apparently there was a big fire at the docks and it damaged part of his ship and he had to call the fire brigade.

~

1 Church Road, Srinagar
June 15, 1965

My L and B

('Some we loved, the loveliest and the best' —Omar Khayyam)
I wrote to you last on Saturday, the posting day we decided on,
and it is, therefore, 72 hours now, and I feel almost as if I had
been unfaithful, and have itched to get back to you. Yet you
have surrounded me over the weekend, a day trip on Sunday
to Gulmarg, sitting watching the rich green of its meadow,
emerged only a few weeks ago from the snow, the sound of
the stream by Nasir's hut, the gentle presence of Prem,[51] a
disorderly game of rounders on an uneven lawn, all through
these Tara kept appearing, was missed and longed for, made
me happy, made me restless, all mixed up.

June 17 – Have you been to a place called Prang, about
24 miles from here toward Sonemarg? We left the house at
1:30, sat over a packed lunch at Shalimar, and I walked on
the soft green and thought long long thoughts of you. Then
to Prang in the evening, on the river Sudh, with the valleys
going upward towards Zojila and surrounded by hills, and
the thought of endless unknown and unknowable valleys.
You walked there with me and looked at the skies and the
mountains and the water.

Since I returned from you at Delhi at the end of May I have
gone through a crisis of feeling, have not been able to bear the
idea of living without you, have not been able to think that *all*
concerned must be considered. The only consolation in this
wildness was that I must put this from me till August 7th,
when we met here, or January 1st, when I married you.

~

---

[51]Prem Kirpal, a friend.

1 Church Road, Srinagar
July 24, 1965

And Champa used a queer phrase for me this morning. Talking of somebody else she said, 'Unlike you, he is not a desert unto himself.' And I understood how she meant it, and that there was an element of truth in it. I live with you, have now done it for months, nothing else interests me, everything outside is a secondary reaction, even my work. It does not grip or become real. I live wrapped up with you, and that is a hidden, secret life with little practice in it—some letter writing, an occasional strained meeting. For those like Champa who do not know how intensely and fully I am living this way, it must appear 'a desert unto myself'. But it is so in fact also, for I cannot live with you, you are too difficult to get near, you are a prisoner with your own walls round you; I am a prisoner of sorts also. We rarely get to a common courtyard to stretch our legs and take the sun. And yet, within my walls, I am always in that courtyard with you. It is a desert within the walls, and where will such desert living take me? Should I abandon the pursuit of living love forever, and proceed to live alone, with myself, not a 'desert to myself' but an 'oasis to myself', weeding and nurturing what still may grow within the bounds of my prison? And yet it is not in me to do this kind of thing, for I suspect I would take (and even beg for) any crumbs that come my way, and I know how very hard the alternatives you face are, and that I am with you in them. But please consult with me when you have decided what to do before finally comitting yourself to it.

I am glad I have spoken to Gautam. Whether we have gained anything is doubtful. It may confirm him in his determination to rid himself of me. I am aware of the tremendous possibilities and impossibilities you face as you go from me today, and I am with you, every minute.

I do not think Gautam will ever disentangle the unsatisfactory phases and qualities of your marriage from my coming into your life, partly because it has not been unsatisfactory for him at all except on those occasions when you have stepped out on your own and independent of him. And you have done that very very rarely. I do not think he wants more from marriage, not because he is ungenerous or inconsiderate, but because real companionship and friendship and equality do not represent real values to him. I think also that he is tantalized by your values and character, the whole background of a softer, more human impact as something worthwhile among human beings, and yet he may regard it as weak, and unreal to the hard facts and compulsions of life. For I think life has presented itself to him, perhaps from childhood, in forms of contract, of competition and struggle. Not economic struggle, but emotional and security struggle. So you are particularly difficult for him, yet particularly attractive. You challenge his whole emotional attitude, and to an extent he recognizes the same thing in me, and that has made his problem harder.

~

1 Church Road, Srinagar
August 9, 1965

There is a crisis on. Armed persons from Pakistan have moved in as guerillas — we do not know the exact number — no doubt to create internal unrest and to go for bridges (there have already been some blow-ups) and sabotage on a large scale. We believe 2000 men have already come in. All this has meant work and conferencing with the army and the police and others. I have been at it, mostly with DP, till all hours, lunched at 4 pm yesterday, and dined after 11. We are working largely in the dark but I rather hope that from today things will be more routinized. I have thought of you a great deal during all this, and missed your help and presence, which somehow seem to belong here with me in this crisis. Be very near me. I need you always.

~

1 Church Road, Srinagar
August 10, 1965

My dearest

Yesterday and last night were dangerous but today the planes land and I think we will turn the corner. Now that the matter is public I enclose my original draft of the 8th written at a police office just below Shankaracharya, with the hill sheer above me, lovely even in distress. You were much with me when I wrote this and I felt like sending it to you rather than Delhi. And Delhi did act next morning.[52]

August 11 – Again only a few minutes and a few lines for you. Had hardly any sleep last night as there was a continuous state of alarm, and firing round the city, about four miles away. It is surprising how a nostalgia develops about normal things when there is tension and crisis. People walking in the streets seem calm, unconcerned. The sun on the lawn is almost like a deep breath drawn from the body.

The birds start their twitter in the trees at the first break of light. All these seem immediately valuable, as if enhanced in beauty and in texture.

I am sorry that my brother and family (American), and my sister (Pakistani) have been caught up in an uncertain holiday. They have, however decided to stay on.

---

[52]Draft at end of manuscript.

I think of you constantly and there is much assurance and certainty in the thought.

My love
Bunchi

~

1 Church Road, Srinagar
August 12, 1965

I thought from an earlier letter of yours that Gautam would bring the children into this to put pressure on you but I am stunned at the savage way he has done this, and have known how unbearable this must have been for you.

And in our situation here, you have been of constant relevance, for it has seemed to me that my only absolute faith and absolute need for a human being was through and with you. So somehow it has been more relevant to act, to spend oneself in whatever way one can to be effective. You are not only a 'tryst with destiny' but a tryst with faith and belief .

August 14 – You cannot endlessly go on living like this, and now that the children are in it, they must be particularly considered. I am concerned for the children not directly only, but because you are their mother and will bear a daily burden if they are not restored to security and cannot forget the horror of what has been thrust on them.

August 16 – Your letters bring life, and a change from the now constant awareness of the crisis we are in. They are my only recuperation and resource. There is no doubt that this is now a war, and the enemy is within us. Nobody can any longer claim in this area that they are not in danger, and the town will continue to be till we have exterminated this vermin. Sandbags have come up and trenches dug at the houses of ministers and the like, and there is a degree of fear in each man's heart, and sometimes in his eyes and demeanour.

Yes, I, too, have been worried about communications between us breaking down. This is such a long road and is definitely a major objective with them, and if anything happens, only priority material will go by air, and I will only be able to send the occasional telegram. If so, to what address?

~

White House, Gamadia Road, Bombay
August 14, 1965

From the 11th onward I was able at least partially to seal off my problem as you are sealing off the ceasefire line, pending some further development or possibly some solution—remote as either seems at the moment, with no news, at my end, of Gautam's programme or when he will return. I have no notion how to handle it properly, tactfully, for as you said, my very presence is jolting for him.

I am sorry your brother and sister have had this experience in Kashmir, yet glad in a way, because with one an American, and the other Pakistani, it is as well they should know what goes on .

August 16 – In these last few days I have come to a 'solution'. I have decided not to press for an 'orderly separation'. Gautam has a feeling he will be trapped by putting anything in writing. I don't want him to feel this way. The money belongs to him and he feels himself the wronged party. I want to make no claims on him. I will remove myself from here and shift to my mother's flat. If he has the children living with him (and I can see them every day) he will not lose face and his own life can go on as near normal as before. I know I am a peculiar kind of woman, unable to separate my womanhood from by motherhood, or separate any part of me from another. The whole of me will have to go on whole. And the test of this will be that my children will, I hope, be able to respect me for what I am, and will love me none the less. And I will somehow see this through. The era of safe protected childhood ended long ago. Protection now can only lie in love and confidence and I can give my children no other kind.

I am numb over the way the children were told, but perhaps this is the strong-right-arm image they expect from him. Noni probably believes now that this is manhood, this is how a 'man' behaves and reacts. The image, for her and for Ranjit, is formed, and what I say or feel is somewhere out on the fringes of it, not quite relevant to what a *man* should be. Now that the first shock for them and me is over, we have been very close and talked a lot and slept in the same room .

August 24 – Gautam asked me yesterday if I would like to go to Europe with him, which is now impossible at such short notice as Gitu would be alone during her midterm break. He then asked if I would go to Moscow with him in October. How all this relates to a separation I don't know.

~

1 Church Road, Srinagar
August 24, 1965

I thought hard of an adequate way to address you this morning, and wanted to say 'beloved wife', but that seemed so near what you mean to me, and so far what it can be in practice, that I contemplated the gap in consternation, and did not use it. But you seem to have come even closer to me these last few days, if that was possible.

We now have much more information than we did, and have even labelled the gangs[53] A, B and so on, but in a terrain like this everything is vulnerable—a bridge (and there are hundreds of them), an army depot with ammunition and oil (there have been repeated attempts on these) and so on. Pakistan is also attacking now on the CFL[54] with regular army, and no doubt hopes to release another horde of infiltrators. Bad news keeps coming in at one place or another, as it must till we are rid of these murderers. Completely innocent people are held in terror in the countryside when these men come into the village for shelter, food or medical help.

And in all this process you are continually with me. Today I am so caught up with Kashmir, and what goes on around and within her, that it is almost an obsession, and but for you would be an exclusive obsession. You are my only link with another world, the only person, feeling, fact, that grips me along with this concentration. I have not sought or defined this. It has happened and is true once again in this turmoil and anxiety. And I take you with me everywhere and always.

August 26 – Now that we have crossed the CFL, Pakistan has to decide whether she means the whole desperate business or will find means to withdraw. But I doubt if the Ayub regime will be able to extricate itself from this and things may well become worse in the next few days.

I will meet you on the 4th, or send the car to the airport, as Amar Singh says the Tourist Committee will meet, and you must stay with us as there is a curfew every day at 8:30.

We are now irrevocably at war, and the whole genius of this country is alien to war. We do not think or feel in those terms.

---

[53]Refers to Pakistani infiltrators who were said to have come in gangs. This infiltration began in August 1965 and eventually led to the Indo-Pakistan war.
[54]The Cease Fire Line.

We do not thrive or revel in it. There is much more realism in people like Sadiq, Mahmuda, Sajjida,[55] who have no doubts that this must be seen through. Sadiq was saying last evening, 'The only solution to Kashmir is now in our hands. Let us not hesitate. Let us win or let us lose, but nothing midway.' And Sajjida, who occasionally gets very tense, 'People in the plains must not be allowed to stop this process. If they do, they will not have any regard for the Kashmiri, and do not understand what we have been submitted to for 18 years. This must be final and we must recover Kashmir.' But even our generals do not feel like that. We are deeply pacifist (though you do not like the word) and it is a tragedy that this genius does not find organizational forms. Yet we are fighting well.

I was glad of the brief description you gave of the ovalish garden and the house around you. It is soothing to read about other things which one tends to forget in crisis and tension. Sadiq was saying yesterday how terribly aware he became of the beauty of Kashmir when there is a crisis.

~

1 Church Road, Srinagar
September 13, 1965

My darling

I imagine you arriving at Bombay very shortly and have hoped it will be a peaceful homecoming and thereafter. Or is it, in view of our past experience, over-optimistic to think of peace? I think of it constantly these days, for you at home (and therefore for me), and for so many thousands in the country. I have wondered

---

[55]Teacher at Government College for Women, Srinagar, and married to Mahmuda's brother.

if it was quite right to wish and pray for peace with a war on our hands. But I think India has this will, whether it is army officers, policemen or civilians I have come across in the last few days. I wonder whether it also exists in Pakistan; surely it must, or are they really inspired by a hate which prevents its appearance? What is better for morale when you are fighting a war—a will to peace, or its absence?

I was very aware that this was not a happy visit for you, and at times positively unhappy because of the atmosphere here at home and the doubt about how and when you would get back. It could not, therefore, be a happy one for me either, for I was also aware of the atmosphere. And yet I am glad you came. I felt confirmed in the rightness of our love, that it belongs, and will remain.

Once you took off, though I was glad of your decision, I was afraid of every telephone call, that it may have bad news. I rang up Group Captain Sharma at 12:30 and he told me you'd left Udhampur safely and the flight thereafter was out of his beat, but no news was good news. And at 2 pm General Umrao Singh,[56] (whom I like more and more) rang up to say all was well and gave me some details of very low flying—300 ft.

September 16 – We have entered a difficult phase with the infiltrators in the area south of the Pir Panjal, round Rajauri, where so far, owing to preoccupations elsewhere, we have rather neglected them. They are there in considerable strength. Jammu is without electricity owing to some bomb damage to the transmission lines, the extent of which we do not yet know. I have spent the afternoon endeavouring to organize some deisel sets at Kalahote, for Jammu. Kalahote itself was attacked by raiders on the 14th.

---

[56]In-charge of a special command created for the defence and security of Srinagar city and its environs.

September 18 – In the morning came the alarming news of what seems a Chinese ultimatum.[57] I was summoned by Sadiq—missing my Control Room meeting—and found him in a temper about Jan Sanghi[58] attitudes and administrative postures in Jammu. He said no Muslim could be happy or live in self-respect in the circumstances, and wanted to remove some very senior men. I had to spend two hours with him, and later some of his Jammu ministers to sort things out. The fact is that Jammu is under great strain and pressure, with about 90,000 or more refugees, some areas where infiltrators are in command, and where there are great strains on the mixed population, and inevitably suspicions of each other. I have been instrumental in getting Tarlochan Dutt[59] appointed a minister and he is to be sworn in today. I think this should help present a united and determined administrative front. Sadiq thawed a bit at midday and said, 'I'm afraid I lost my temper.' And I said, 'In your position you must remain cool or we will lose the game.' He said, 'But I only do that in front of you'. And goodwill was restored.

I am sorry I have made this letter so impersonal, but it all seems so mixed up now, you and me, and the fact that I love you dearly, and all this anxiety in this dreadful war.

~

---

[57]China had, in early September, declared its support for the 'freedom fighters', who were, according to them, struggling to 'liberate Kashmir from the tyrannical Indian domination,' alleging that Indian troops had violated the Sikkim-Tibet border and intruded into Chinese territory, which India denied. On September 16, China sent a three-day ultimatum to India to dismantle these posts, failing which grave consequences would follow. The ultimatum was followed by reports of Chinese troop mobilization on the Sino-Indian border.

[58]The Bhartiya Jan Sangh, founded in 1931 and later known as the Bhartiya Janata Party (BJP).

[59]A Member of the J&K Legislative Assembly (MLA) from the Jammu area.

1 Church Road, Srinagar
September 7, 1965

Darling Bunchi

I don't like the thought of leaving you in these uncertain circumstances, not knowing from day-to-day what might happen. I can only hope Srinagar will not be bombarded, or further terrorized, and above all, not cut off. That is what I dread most, and can only bear it if I know you will keep in touch in whatever way possible. I have not been able to settle down here this time except on our walks when we were really alone. At your house the ceasefire line has definitely been crossed. But I want to thank you, my darling, for this visit and tell you how terribly glad I am I came to this beautiful, endangered place that has become so precious to us both, for I want to be in it, and with you, in every conceivable circumstance. You said (when we thought all air traffic had stopped) that I was now 'torn' from my 'vitals', and asked me how I reacted to that. But it did not seem like that to me. I was where I wanted to be and would have chosen to be. Once I had arranged for the children, and satisfied myself on that score, I had not the remotest wish to be anywhere else. All my love will be with you.

Tara

~

Delhi
September 12, 1965

Bunchi

There was an unreality about landing at Palam yesterday at a quarter to one. It was hot and still and suddenly a different world from Srinagar. And I couldn't quite believe we had made it. In the split second before I got into the helicopter at Srinagar I had a slight misgiving about the journey, but in that split second I also knew I'd rather make the journey than go back to your house and face the atmosphere! I don't know if you'd call it courage or cowardice, but I decided I'd rather face the Pak fighters—of which there were two, I was told—with us, and that was why we flew so low, between 300 and 500 ft., and took a circuitous route, through the woods and then low over the hot and dusty Punjab plains. The helicopter was so noisy we couldn't talk, and Bannerji[60] took out a pad and I produced two pencils (and a sharpener—and it greatly amused DP that I should be concerned with sharpening the pencil points as we all used them). He suggested we preserve the scraps we wrote so that if we survived they might have some historic value! We wrote scribbles to each other which Bannerji kept. At Udhampur we went straight into the waiting IAF plane. The crew were young and confident. DP apparently gave instructions that we should not be told of danger and that he should be called into the crew compartment to be informed of any dangerous development—which he was several times, each time by a member of the crew coming into the compartment where we were and giving a cheerful thumbs-up signal for our benefit! During the flight DP took me into the crew cabin beside the pilot. The sides of this were open, it was cool and breezy, and we had a wonderful panoramic view of the land below us. DP said, 'I have never known my country to look so beautiful as it does today.' And it is true it looked lovely in danger, worth every ounce of our dedication.

DP had some whiskey with him and one glass which we all shared, and he was, as always, full of concern and affection,

---

[60]Susheetal Banerji, at the time Additional Chief Secretary, Government of Jammu and Kashmir.

and never by a hair's breadth dismayed by any possibility. I wish you'd been on that flight.

Delhi is pitch dark except for the moon. Tonight the station was a nightmare, not a light, and the crowds and heat and noise made progress difficult. It gave one a feeling of troops on the move. I hope Ranjit gets to school safely. He seemed confident and told me not to worry.

It has been an emotional day for me, as if all the crowded emotion of the past week had been packed into it and spilled over. At noon I went over to Frank's (Moraes)[61] and found him much affected by the war. (Catching up last night on the newspapers since September 7th I had read some of his very moving writeups.) He talked at some length of the war news, said it was unhappily true that tenderness was not understood, that only strength was, and he felt as we all do that this *had* to be now, that we were right in doing what we'd done, and must see it through, and end it at the earliest moment. And suddenly he said, 'I'd like to talk about you' and he did, first about my writing which he said he now knew would be all right. He said, 'Others will be forgotten because they are stylized and don't have much else to them, but you will be remembered because you will grow in your work.' And he also said, with a great deal of emotion, 'But there is too much tenderness in you. You must learn to be rough. You can present your civilized equation, but present it savagely. For you will not be understood otherwise.' Then he said, 'Don't think I don't know what you have been going through. I know you have had your confrontation.' (Wasn't that a strange and apt word to use?) I did speak to him with almost relief at being able to, and it is astonishing how well and quickly he understood what I had to say. In my stirred up state I cried a little. Frank also asked, 'Does this man really understand you?' He also

---

[61]Editor-in-Chief of the *Indian Express* at the time.

wanted to know the nature of the relationship, and this I explained to him.

It has been a day of explaining for when I went to Prem's this evening, he and I were alone, and he wanted to know all about you and me. And then he dropped me at Lekha's himself because of the blackout, which was kind of him.

I have still not sorted out my impressions of the Srinagar trip, but I am so glad I came, and so happy about the times we spent together, no matter what storms brewed around us in the house.

We have had a very bad press in England and America, though the feeling is that the US basically understands our position while England deliberately will not. And perhaps this is the psychological moment for us to leave the Commonwealth. Strange—this new Commonwealth of African and Asian nations is really of India's (Nehru's) creation, yet the time may have come for us to sever the bond.

Much love to you
Tara

~

White House, Gamadia Road, Bombay
September 13, 1965

My love

I am sitting in the children's room which is the only one besides my own which is heavily curtained and doesn't show the light from outside. The children are sharing my room and have gone to bed. There is a total blackout and no vehicles allowed out after 8 pm. Bombay in its characteristic efficiency seems briskly mobilized for come what may. There was an air raid warning as my plane landed about five o'clock but the enemy plane was driven away. On the news tonight I heard there have been three warnings over Srinagar. Office and school hours here have been changed. From the children's balcony where every night I can see a thick sprinkling of lights, and usually a party on in the house next door, there is now darkness and silence, a strange un-Bombay-like night. And I suppose the city's nightlife is at an end until this ghastly business is over.

There was a letter from Gautam awaiting me. He seems aware of the war and the Indian news, but I suppose the urgency and enormity of it have not been conveyed to him by the papers abroad and I am disappointed he has been away at such a time.

My stay at your house which started in a fairly ordinary manner and remained more or less as expected till the day of my scheduled departure (the 8th) suddenly turned another corner when I got held up, and seemed to enter another phase for us. Crossing the CFL I called it, and we cannot give up the gains any more than India can, and whatever we have achieved, albeit somewhat recklessly and indiscreetly, is now for us to keep. Your visits to me, whenever you could manage them, were more than crossing the CFL, more like opening the Lahore front, for we did rather take the battle into new territory, and quite blithely.

The newspapers these days read dramatically, indignant at the enormity of the conflict thrust on us, yet determined to see it through. I like the tone of the reporting, and of the government's pronouncements, and the whole atmosphere in the country. For as Frank wrote in one of his columns, we are at the end of our 'patient deep disdain'.

September 14th – After the news tonight I heard an interview with an American correspondent who is reporting for *Life* magazine and has just returned from the Chambh area and Jammu. I could hardly believe that an American, and one reporting for *Life*, had come out so clearly and emphatically for us, and plainly stated the evidence he had found. I wanted to jump up and hug him, or anyone else, but there wasn't a soul around.

Gitu was most disdainful of the way her class behaved today when the siren sounded. She said, 'They were supposed to keep calm and march out quietly, but they all rushed and pushed. So I waited till they'd rushed out and then I went calmly!' Noni is highly excitable and nowadays jumps when she hears a sound. Apparently her class dived under their desks when the signal came, and only later filed downstairs. Ranjit sent me a telegram of his safe arrival at school.

September 18th – The news tonight was interrupted by the announcement of an air raid, I suppose over Delhi, and with the bombing of Ambala this morning, and the Chinese ultimatum, it is hard not to be full of foreboding. To think there was a time when our worst problems were personal ones. What is going to happen? Gautam arrives on the 27th from a different world, of peace, affluence, and placidity. How will I establish contact with him?

September 21st – I cannot believe any people or nation has a will to war in this day and age. It was true of earlier times, of Sparta, for instance, a nation born, bred and conditioned to war—the only testing ground of courage and all the virtues of that society. And in modern times, Hitler's Germany. But in between we do have the whole bloodstained history of Europe when territorial aggrandisement was part of statesmanship, part of the day's work almost. I think the centuries to come will judge Europeans the really untameable barbarians of all time, for in spite of the unique cultural heritage they evolved, their great ideas and great achievements in art and literature, and their Christian faith, they continued casually to lop off heads and territories until the middle of the twentieth century. The Europeans believed realism was life lived in compartments— religion for Sundays, blood and thunder for weekdays, a kind of realism they still flaunt in their 'realpolitik' and their arrangements and re-arrangements of their much-loved Balance of Power (to our detriment). But today I can't believe any people want war. India, as you say, has most definitely a will for peace, and she will no longer be my beloved country the day she loses it.

You said 'the debate may get transferred abroad' and diplomatic initiative will now take over. It will be difficult when not one helping hand has been held out, not one indication that anyone recognizes what the issue is about (with the exception of John Grigg[62] in England). And *our* crisis too seems to have shifted from the military to the diplomatic front. More and more any third person's reaction seems quite irrelevant. We should not in principle give up what we have gained at such cost. It would be like giving up the Haji Pir Pass now. And trying to please everybody will begin to resemble the man, the boy and the donkey, and which arrangement suits whom, and we should not waste too much energy on this.

With much love
Tara

~

1 Church Road, Srinagar
September 20, 1965

My own darling

I feel dreadfully cut off from you, empty and uncomfortable, even nostalgic for our troubled week of the 5th to 11th, when I wanted to get home because you were there, and your presence, even in those circumstances of strain, invariably

---

[62]A well-known journalist.

meant some richness, some consolation and comfort. I have needed you with me and realized more than once the truth of what you have said, that there is a refreshment from the physical presence and nearness which no words, nor certainty of love (such as I have with you) can make good.

We were all depressed yesterday with the terms of the Security Council ceasefire. There is no mention of Pakistani infiltrators, who are still with us, particularly in the Rajauri area in Jammu and the north area of Tilel in Kashmir, though the date August 5th suggests the infiltration is recognized, as regular hostilities across the CFL started much later. And the mention that there should be a political settlement after ceasefire seem to concede Pakistan's point in principle, though not in the manner she wished. With the Chinese threat it also seems difficult to look at the Pakistan war only on its merits and perhaps it would be foolish to do so. It is an extremely difficult decision for Delhi to make, to accept the ceasefire or not. An acceptance may mean this whole effort has been wasted; a rejection seems to mean taking on China, and all the consequences.

Sadiq thinks we must reject this ceasefire as otherwise we will not be able to face the country, and especially the people of Kashmir, who will once again be in grave uncertainty, and at the mercy of a future build-up by Pakistan. It is indeed a difficult decision and I wish you were here so that I could see some light on it with you, even though you and I do not have to make the decision. I value you greatly and am continually grateful for you.

My love
Bunchi

~

1 Church Road, Srinagar
September 30, 1965

My beloved

I have felt grateful that you continued to write, as if you were my wife, in spite of communications being so uncertain, and arrival delayed and erratic. But there are indications of normal communications. The Viscount service[63] started on the 28th. It is almost certain the government will go down to Jammu on schedule. As Jammu has borne most of the hardship and suffering, politically it is essential to stick to the move.

When I am realistic (about our personal situation) I see that you and I take from our marriages what they regard as the coinage of human association—an untouched spouse, a spirit not roused to joy by another association. Everyone seems to want a virgin. And I wondered why *I* did not want a virgin, and then I realized that I did, in a basic way, and that I had my virgin in you. I could have confidence that the relation between us was absolute, and you gave yourself to me in completion, and in completion there is purity. Because of this bond, this dedication, we have built and survived in a hurricane. The walls have constantly been assaulted, and as I wrote once before, I cannot conceive of any other woman I know standing up to it. One of the chief sources of strength in my companionship with you is that I can rely on everything being made plain between us, and on joint decision.

~

---

[63]The Viscount service to Kashmir had been suspended during the war.

White House, Gamadia Road, Bombay
September 28, 1965

Gautam arrived this morning and reopened the subject as soon as I opened my eyes. I felt jerked back from a different world, and quite unreasonably angry that he had been away from India at this time, not returned, not felt the need to identify himself with this country, for he has not been engaged in business discussions all the month and could have got back if he had felt sufficientiy moved. I just wasn't prepared early in the morning to reopen a subject we have already discussed theadbare. I found it difficult to make the adjustment from national emmergency to personal problems. And the way this separation has been approached and rehashed is like an interminable war that drags on and on. Some of the idealism gets obscured, the reason why one fights is no longer reason enough for prolonged 'bloodshed', and a kind of demoralization sets in that would bargain for peace at any price. Above all, I feel a failure, with blood on my hands and a human being on my conscience. And I could go on this way. But it all sounds academic now that it appears to be drawing to a close.

I went to buy steak for Gautam's dinner and it was painful to realize that years and years of building a home and planning for it, were ending. I thought of the years ahead, of bringing up children, their education, their careers, their marriages, their future families, all of this yet to come, to be tackled alone, without the semblance of any conventional support. I also knew I had to do one thing to have it all back again this moment—the softness, the ease, the stability—'eliminate' you from my life. But I didn't do that. I am afraid for the future, but fear is a negative reason on which to base decision. I cannot keep this marriage only because I am afraid to be without its shelter. It may be that I am the most irresponsible woman in the world, and may pay dearly for it, but I will have to take what comes. Do I love you still, your letter asks. Sitting here, at a time like this, I cannot conjure up any of the joys of love. What I feel is allegiance to a cause, one from which there may be no personal gain, or favour, but one which nevertheless has to be served.

You said in Srinagar you were abstract, and that I had a way of transferring the abstract into practical reality. I am experiencing some of the terrors of this process today, and wondering if some things aren't, after all, intended to remain abstract, and never meant (except by idiots and fools) to be translated into one's daily endeavour. There is Plato's Idea—the idea of circularity, but no perfect circle. Yet one tries to draw a perfect circle, and there isn't much use in even attempting to draw one unless one aims at perfection.

~

1 Church Road, Srinagar
October 6, 1965

My MFD

I was impressed with the indictment you draw up against yourself. You make a good case. So is Pakistan's against India, if you accept its basis. The creation of Pakistan accepted nationality based on religion. It follows that any contiguous Muslim majority area is Pakistan's by right. In regard to non-continuous areas (like UP and Bihar) the principle would be the same, but geography would make it difficult. It is a simple and clear case, so simple the world has tended to accept it in preference to India's more complicated (yet more civilized and humane) claim. Pakistan throws a person like me, who by chance and circumstance is a Christian, completely on the dungheap.

It is a conflict of systems, and in such a conflict, the only possibility of peace is some pattern that will enable each to flourish within terms which will destroy neither. In your indictment of yourself you have missed the bus completely. You have built your evidence on the very system that is the debateable issue. In marriage, Gautam insists you shall have no other god but him, that a woman's fulfilment and flowering can only be on these terms. Does Gautam accept this creed himself? If he did there would at least be logic about it. But he exercises his right to individual variation of a high degree. Here is a modern man, living in a scientific world, working in a scientific climate, accepting the variety of choices that such a world and climate necessitate, and which are its very essence.

In this background I cannot accept what you accept all too readily, that you have broken contract and faith with him. The platform would be a traditional one in a wholly arranged marriage. Otherwise it would have a degree of emancipation and a high degree of individualism. And that is what he stands for ostensibly, or implied when you told him of your American affair, that he would not care if you had had fifty such affairs. Yet even on that he turned his back once you were with him and a plaything for his psychological tortures, inflicted on you, and no doubt on himself. It is surely clear beyond words that this is also a conflict of systems. He has to recognize this, otherwise he gives you two equally impossible alternatives—submission or defiance.

Given the assumption on which you married—a modern educated man making a marriage of choice with a modern educated woman—I could, point by point, make out as good a case against his having let you down as you make against yourself. Both would be equally wrong, for you have to realize that you stand for different systems, and a constructive solution of coexistence—not elimination of one or the other—has to, and can, be discovered. I cannot bear the case you make against yourself. Much better accept, if you must, the practical consequences of Gautam's impossible choices, as necessary for the man, but not an argument that is false for you, and never can be yours.

In your analysis a feeling of guilt, or failure, in terms of the old (Gautam's) system is almost too likely. Particularly as part of the old is embedded in us. There are bits and pieces of it we are fond of and we hark back to its security and certainty. To go back to the example of India and Pakistan, in the Kashmir problem we have a dual enemy—Pakistan, and the enemy within us which supports the Pakistan thesis. You must have seen manifestations of this, including the extreme view that India has no right in Kashmir whatsoever. It is some such guilt that you confess to, and I think you should firmly turn your back on it, for you are not guilty. Just as you see the humanity of Gautam, and feel his suffering, he should be aware of yours. For then only can there be the mutual urge to transcend systems.

And it is wrong of you to presume that you will be left entirely alone to face your problems for I do not propose to leave you alone. All my love

Bunchi

~

White House, Gamadia Road, Bombay
October 5, 1965

Sadiq said at Tariq's reception in Srinagar that we were going through the fire 'like Sita', and this analogy rather troubled me at the time. He seemed to think that, therefore, all would be well, whereas nothing was well for Sita even though she proved her chastity by coming out unscathed.

I have to tell you again how much your support has meant to me. The other thing I must tell you again is that you do not owe me anything. This is the time to remind you, oddly enough, not of your bonds with me (which will remain) but of your freedom with and towards me. You must never feel I expect anything of you, because I don't; never take any part of yourself or your life away from your own home and set-up that you yourself do not expressly feel you must. I have no claims on you, none whatever. What I have with you will always be there, and your arrangement of your personal life will in no way affect it.

I have been thinking how much I shall miss Chandigarh, miss having it as my home, as being mine. I loved its sky, and the walk around the lake, and the hills from my bedroom window, and the December roses in their extravagant beauty, and all of this combined with the laughter of children. Sum total: an emptiness within me, and a realization that this is no time for emptiness. Once the settlement is signed there will be plenty to do.

October 8 – Gautam asked me if I realized how I was being talked about. I said I did, and that I would have to face it, and try, in time, to establish my worth, and that those who respected me would help me. I think, if I had not been his wife, he would have admired this, but made as he is, he could not in me .

October 12 – I am very low in vitality this morning. Last night Gautam demanded I leave at once and when I refused until the papers are through, he became insane with anger. And I felt life is such a fragile thing after all, just bones and flesh and it would not take too much doing to snuff them out. But it has been a religion with me that a bully must not be catered to, not by the flicker of an eyelash, and that he must not have the satisfaction of seeing me afraid. And queerly enough, I was not afraid, and asked him, 'Are you going to kill me?' He said, 'I *could* kill you. I feel like killing you.' And for a few seconds I thought he would. Then he hurled me aside and went out of the room, and I, strangely, went to bed and to sleep, and woke up this morning as if it were any other morning. Gautam apologized, adding the warning that I should take care not to upset him in future. And I wonder how many more days I must pass in this atmosphere which he has convinced himself I am reluctant to leave. One of the difficulties is that he won't stay put long enough to finalize the details. He is off to Switzerland again on the 20th for ten or twelve days.

I have been sorting and putting books into packing cases—and the floor is littered with them—to keep Gautam calm, otherwise he threatens to throw me out immediately. This is how I receive visitors, and it's like living in the middle of a blitzkrieg day after day. Ernie Mountain was aghast when he came, and sat for hours while Gautam talked of 'I'll tear him limb from limb'. Kill, beat, maim are the words he keeps using. Ernie said, 'If you throw her out you will lose the best thing you have. Keep her with you and she will help you back to recovery.' I do not think separation will be the end of this mood. I doubt if I will be allowed to live in peace even when I leave him.

You must not even try to extricate yourself from Kashmir. These are critical times and you must remain at your job. Nothing can be more important than that, and I am with you in it. Other details will be settled in time when we can discuss them. I am not panicked, and we must stick to our jobs. My state of paralysis even stands me in good stead, keeps me armoured and in good working order, and forgive me if I sound that way. Yet it is a wonderful world, Bunchi, and even this huge, hot, crowded city looks beautiful in parts, and at times. I shall try to work on the Kashmir article.

~

White House, Gamadia Road, Bombay
October 16, 1965

What does MFD mean? I am no good at guessing your abbreviations. I live in limbo, and wonder if this is what Catholics mean by purgatory, a state of terrible and prolonged uncertainty, not knowing what will happen and when, and failing any longer even to imagine an outcome.

I am ready to concede what you say about systems, but in practice these things don't work out so patly. To accept marriage at all is to accept limitations, no matter how modern the couple, and no matter what they did or didn't do before. Marriage is the law and one only experiments with it on pain of dire results. Any rejection of what it lays down must apparently be done in secret. The facade and the proprieties must be observed. And above all the 'home' is sacrosanct.

Philosophically and intellectually there need be no guilt in me. I can see that. And perhaps guilt is not the correct word. I feel shattered when I see what has become of Gautam, no matter how the blame is apportioned. The historic circumstances of this have been wrong, mismatched, discordant. And the result is frightful to see. But I didn't know such a man existed, so wild, so uncontrolled, that jealousy could be so fiendish, such a disease, that the instinct to dominate and possess could be so violent and total. And who but you would side with me today, Bunchi? People would think me criminally insensible to a husband's very obvious and quite frantic devotion. So though I may come out well theoretically, there must be dozens who will judge me criminal. Perhaps I am not guilty, but I am a freak. I am different. And the only other freak I know is you. And that is why we recognize each other.

~

1 Church Road, Srinagar
October 14, 1965

My darling

I have been frantically worried about you. I have felt all this was happening to me. I have never felt so completely identified with any person in my life. There is no sense of separateness, of contract as between two people. And so, my darling, I do feel responsible for you, for us.

I can understand your saying you are a strange mixture of self-sufficiency and docility for I have seen this in you myself in this year. You have taken me whole and on trust. I have never been able to take from anyone like I can from you. I find it possible because you just give, as if you were unaware that you were giving. Perhaps that is an aspect of docility. I've also had your self-sufficiency. You will not take on any commitment with me regarding money, for example, though we know each other so well and accept each other so much. And I could give other examples.

MFD means my most fulfilling darling.

~

White House, Gamadia Road, Bombay
October 21, 1965

About the other night—I forget which night—Gautam told me I was not to sleep in the bedroom. If I didn't get out of the house I would have to sleep outside the bedroom. He strode into the bedroom, tore off the bedclothes and mattress and dragged them across the room, through the bathroom and into the dining-drawing room, and left them dumped there in a heap on the floor, with the servants coming and going. I went into the bathroom and locked the door so that I could undress in peace. I was also nervous and felt like keeping him locked out for the night but I knew that would infuriate him and he was capable of breaking down a door if the mood took him. The other entrance to the bedroom is through the veranda room, by a glass door which would be easy to break. So after undressing I unlocked the bathroom door and went to my bed which now had just bare wooden boards on it. I made up my mind to sleep there. I spread the bedspreads on the boards and took a cushion for a pillow and a shawl to cover with as the room is air-conditioned. I lay down with a book and started to read. I wasn't, of course, reading, but I had to make a pretence of normalcy and I hoped it would restore his good sense. It didn't. He was in a furious temper. But I had decided to non-cooperate, and whatever he did in his black unreasoning moods would have to be accomplished without my help. So I went on reading. He snatched the book from my hand and dragged me off the bed and across the floor and into the bathroom, just as he'd done with the bedding earlier, only the bedding was probably more trouble. In the bathroom there was a table in the way and it wasn't easy to get through so a most ludicrous struggle took place and he became quite incensed and rough and I thought he'd break my arms and wrists. He raised his arm to hit me across the face but the blow didn't land. Instead he shook me fiercely and flung me down on the floor with much name-calling and said I could sleep in the bedroom. So I dragged my bedding back to bed and went to sleep.

But a *man* is apparently one who does these things. Ernie Mountain was saying to me that though he fully realizes the sickness of Gautam's condition, had his *own* wife been involved with another man, he'd have killed the man. He said it nonchalantly, like telling me the time of day. And I thought there is extraordinary and perverted progress—yet certainly progress—in which nations can assemble as they never have before in a determination to keep the peace, while individuals go their snarling animal way, solving their individual problems with hatchets and cudgels, or bare fists, and are admired for it.

I have been alone such a lot this year, Bunchi, not a peaceful aloneness, and now the year is nearly ended. I shall light the house for Divali on the 24th night and do Lakshmi Puja and think of the new year. About you, it is enough that you are there, somewhere. It is extraordinary how little I want beyond that scraped-down-to-the-bone-fact. I have no hankering for marriage, no desire to upset any part of any scheme that claims you for any reason at all.

I've thought of saying to Gautam, 'I'm offering you more than a wife. I'm offering you an adventure in living and thinking. Open your arms to that and let us share it.'

There is much tragedy in all this, the tragedy of inevitability, of things moving inexorably toward their destination, almost from the start, from August last year. The river flowed along its course. What I failed to do was erect a dam. But one light emerges from all this, for you, that a woman kept faith with you and did not count the cost.

~

Janpath Hotel, New Delhi
November 7, 1965

My Tara

I am very aware that you go again on an uncertain and (though I hope not) hazardous journey tomorrow, aware of parting from you, and of the presence and pressure of this problem that involves your future. One thing perhaps I hold more strongly than you do, and that is a belief in the essential courage and strength and idealism of your character. It will stand up to the dictates of destiny, of that I am certain. There is that in you which will not only survive, but will triumph, and make an oasis from the desert.

There is no basis or fact for my belief, but I hope, without reason, that you do not give in, even though I know that if you must, I will understand the necessity, and you will have my full support and all the help I can give. But *do not*. Somewhere spirit must live, in spite of all the odds. Somewhere, we who have seen and had love, must be willing to be chained, gagged and quartered by it. Somewhere there must be no separation between those who suffer, like you, and those who see and hear it, like I. Somewhere we must forge a bond of unity, halving your pain in mine. Come away and let us be together. I must live with you, otherwise this fever will not end. Fever is the wrong word. It is an infection, pervasive, addictive. I imagine sometimes that its base may be a mutual desire for a common culture, rooted in this land which we both love, and I recognize that love unashamedly with you, asahmedly with others. And perhaps our merging has a cause, apart from your beauty and your character, the need for science *with* compassion, the need for a love big enough to be both kindly and ruthless.

Much love
Bunchi

~

Janpath Hotel, New Delhi
November 9, 1965

My BD

Which more than Beautiful Diversion means my Beloved
Darling, I felt almost frantically like going to the airport to
see you off, and was not at peace about it till I saw the clock
hands pass 9:30 in Committee Room D of Vigyan Bhavan. I
had hoped to write somewhat about our being together for a
week at Delhi, of what it meant to me, but now with divorce
hanging over you, it seems somehow irrelevant to do so. I
spoke to you of the practical difficulties that hedge me round,
but whatever it is worth—and personally I think the substance
of things is in the human equation—I am wholly yours. The
legalities will come later, if I can achieve them. We should be
able to get sustenance and real help from each other, till the
other thing is possible. I want to cherish and love you and you
must make it possible for me to do this. All my love, BD.

Bunchi.

~

Wazarat Road, Jammu
November 13, 1965

I have been frantically worried about you, thought of all means
of communicating, and I wonder what happens in your world
over 1000 miles away. I can't post this to you till the fateful
Saturday; it may cause murder. And anxiety gnaws at me like
a knife cutting cheese. If only I knew what you did, where you
are at this moment. I sorted out your letters in the morning, 250
in all, and I have thought that this correspondence has been
something so big between us, almost a life and certainly a bulk

of its own. And now even if she gives me up, even if she ceases to love me, I have had a richness with her which neither time, nor man, nor even she can take from me. For today I have been full of fears that you will have to give me up.

I do not know under what law and procedure Gautam seems hopeful of a quick divorce, or even a valid petition for one. The very minimum period for grant of a divorce by mutual consent is two years, and for remarriage, three years, after you have lived separately for a year. Gautam's ferocity to save a year in the process may mean he definitely contemplates remarriage.

You really should have somebody near you these next few weeks, some really reliable person. I wish it could be me, but my very presence in Bombay may excite and exasperate. And I feel I have been through, for the first time in my life, what a parent must feel about its child at the brink of some difficult experience, holding the breath for it almost every minute, yet unable to be of positive concrete assistance. For that is how I have felt, cut off from you in this most gruelling experience. You tend at times to be impulsive and quick of decision, but in this divorce matter you must be very careful, whatever the burden on you, and I can see that you have been driven beyond all reasonable expectation by Gautam's attitude and ferocity.

Dinner at DP's last night, and a visit from Victor Kiernan[64] of Edinburgh University—he used to be in Lahore. He was there again from August to October and told us of Pakistan's complete control of news, of the lies they told, eg., Sikh regiments are controlled by Hindus to ensure that they fight, and are sent to the most dangerous jobs while the Hindus keep back. He did not give much hope of peace and said West Pak is hysterical about Kashmir; Ayub cannot throw in his hand. He

---

[64]A well-known writer and professor at the University of Edinburgh.

said, however, that their economy is buoyant and its growth rate is better than India's; Ayub is still popular, and there is no alternative to him. He thought the US would still try to win back Pakistan, as they had no fear of India. They knew India would now survive with its democracy, they knew India could be squeezed on food more than Pakistan. Therefore Pakistan was still worth winning back. India needed no winning back, it was committed nationally to what the US wanted.

All my love—and I hate always ending a letter to you, as if I dragged myself away from a part of myself.

Bunchi

~

White House, Gamadia Road, Bombay
November 19, 1965

I asked Gautam if he was happy about his decision and he said of course not, far from it, but it was the only one open to him and there was no going back on it. I was struck as I always am by the wholeness of his approach. It is cast-iron and unrelenting, and intolerant perhaps, but it is whole, and has an integrity and completeness. My tragedy has been my inability to go along with him through it, so that at the end and forever he must feel rejected, and I must feel guilty. I hope I shall not be haunted by this, but I do not know how to lay these ghosts, and am never free of them—except and only for as long as I am with you. I leave you and I'm splintered into fragments once more and a hundred voices haunt and plague me and tell me I must carry my burden of sin as long as I live, and since I shall live often, for many lifetimes. In the last few weeks I have understood Frank's predicament only too well, have understood the ghosts that haunt him, the burden he carries. Gautam will not be haunted for he does not see things from this point of view, so his conscience is clear and his course of action is both obvious and justified. I know that once I have moved to the other flat and some kind of life is established there, this pall will lift. And Gautam will be going abroad a lot. It is as well I shall be moving. It is not a year I'd ever care to repeat, domestically, full of dread and misery.

~

White House, Gamadia Road, Bombay
December 3, 1965

I got to Shri Bhai's[65] office to discuss the paper to be signed, and he told me and Gautam that my mother had phoned this morning about a talk she had had with Manubhai Shah,[66] who had been told of this by Morarji Bhai,[67] and the whole affair had become a 'national issue' and was being discussed at 'Cabinet level'. It came over me that Gautam has flayed me alive in the marketplace—was this what 17 years had meant to him?—and I would not submit to this campaign and would face the Cabinet and the President and whoever else. And what exactly was this 'national issue'? What heinous crime had I committed for which I was being victimized? I should not have spoken like that but I was at the end of my rope. I came home spent and exhausted, to make a list of all the jewellery and other items Gautam's family had given to me, and made a statement renouncing and returning all of these, so that they will know I have walked away with nothing.

I came home feeling that no one understands any of this. Even my mother and sisters feel it is the height of folly and unwisdom to see this crusade through. And far from all this

---

[65]S.K. Handoo.
[66]A Member of Parliament at the time.
[67]Morarji Desai, Member of the Union Cabinet at the time.

muddling me I see the terrible clarity of what I am doing. I feel almost as if the elements are ranged against me and that their fury is upon me. And if they are all against me, what can I do? And if I'm in the marketplace, what can I do? Paradoxically, my motherhood gives me strength. Alone, I might not have thought all this worth fighting for to the last gasp. But there are children for whom values must be defended, who must have values to uphold, and later, when they are older, they may realize and attach some significance to the fact that their mother held fast to her values. And forgive me if this sounds stupid and emotional.

December 7 – To continue my dull diary, Gautam informed me this morning we are to sign the papers at Shri Bhai's tomorrow, and the application for divorce the day after. He said, 'I hope you realize you are responsible for wrecking this home.'

Meghram[68] leaves for Chandigarh this evening, and the children and I on the 10th for our last time.

~

White House, Gamadia Road, Bombay
December 9, 1965

Today I went to the court and it didn't look like my idea of a court. It was a room off it, apparently, filled with typewriters and files and a great bustle of important matters proceeding. And a very sour-faced individual asked me if I had read and understood the document I had signed, and I said I had, and *he* signed it. And two things struck me as I entered the courtroom office. One was a large picture of Mamu on the wall, the one that appears on the stamp. The other was that today was December 9th, the day in 1947 when Gautam and

---

[68]The cook.

I first met, at a cocktail party in Delhi. And of course a copy of my marriage certificate was also attached to the document, with Mamu's signature as witness on it. And I took comfort from something he told me in '59: 'Don't be like Indu, leaving this issue unresolved for all time. She is neither married nor separated. Resolve it.' And though the resolve to end this marriage was not mine, I thought it is now ending, and I must think of the future, not the past. But though I felt, this is the last chapter, let me see it through with some dignity, I was feeling terribly shaky, on quicksand all over again. Where was I? When would I reach firm ground?

And now I must lock the suitcases and put them in the hall.

~

Anokha, 32/Sector 5-A, Chandigarh
December 18, 1965

I spent an hour with Kaka this morning as the children told me he had fever. He was lying in a long chair in the sun and made a great joke of my saying I wanted 'elbow room'. He said, 'What you want is a whole room, not elbow room.' He said he was anxious about Gautam, and though he was fond of me ('It must be your face because I don't know you at all') he felt I had overstepped 'the mark'. Where's the mark? And what's beyond it, fields, hills, lake, as on my walk today, or nothing much? I was in a cynical sort of mood on my walk, though I had the breathtaking beauty of the vast sky, the hazy hills, the thorn bushes, the ground sometimes hard and sometimes soft and thick with dust beneath my feet. The past six winters here (except last year) I've lived more with these than with people, stroking the hills, caressing the lake, putting my arms around all of it.

Kaka's cat came along and I had to get behind my chair. He said, 'You shouldn't be afraid of cats. You are so like a cat yourself. A cat cannot be commanded. It comes to one of its own free will. It makes good use of all the faculties God has given it.' I told him my cat-fear was 4000 years old, when I was buried alive in a tomb (in Egypt) with a cat. Then he said I was the healthiest person, mentally and physically, he had ever met, and I was *very* pleased. (Am I like a cat? I must show you the statues of me in the Egyptian section of the Metropolitan Museum in New York.)

In all my storm and stress I've hardly let you live your life, and not lived yours with you. I have drawn you down into my whirlpool and clung to you in a feverish way. I wish I'd shown more self-reliance. That would have provided more balance as between our lives, given yours a chance to show, and 'we' would have developed more evenly.

What kind of day is it in Jammu? Here it is now dull and grey.

~

Wazarat Road, Jammu
December 19, 1965

My lovely and beloved Nayantara

Even my real friends of the past, like Prem and Kaval, seem to find you lovely. I will have to try and find another word.

It is my last morning of freedom and in a few hours I shall be immersed in the arrival of the family, and in the auras and patterns created by two decades of domesticity and marriage. We human beings seem to weave cobwebs, like the spider does, of psychology and inhibition, I suppose also of paths in them of expression, affirmation, all mixed up—and then whom do we catch in them? The spider catches his food. What do we catch?

Only ourselves. I wonder if one could just walk through the cobwebs suddenly, or are they enmeshed in our very bodies, and would they draw blood? And is it possible—and as I read your letter this morning, I had a tremendous desire—to break free, and not compromise any more. No more cobwebs for the future. The straight and open road. The straight and open act. No subterfuge. So believe in me a little longer.

December 20 – DP and Sadiq came and spent a long evening over drinks. Much work ahead, preparing a draft for the Tashkent talks[69] with our government's points.

Much love
Bunchi

~

74/Sector 9-A, Chandigarh
December 31, 1965

My beloved

I do not know how many minutes I have before the household gets back. I am upstairs sitting out in the veranda near our bedroom, in the shade, with the sun shining almost still on the terrace, a few kites sailing, apparently without effort, in the sky, and the sound of a few birds whom my observation does not identify. And I have a great deal to say to you, and yet so little. And the little is repetitive. I came away from you yesterday again full of you, and full of happiness, and also missing you, and the journey to 4:30 pm today seemed a longer time than it is. Happiness and you were the same thing, and missing a part of it, as I miss you even when you walk away to

---

[69]Refers to the peace terms between India and Pakistan hammered out at Taskhent.

bolt the banging door as we sit on the lawn, though I know you are there and are returning; I miss you when we are together and you are not there, but with your railway bookings; even when I am enjoying your presence as when you looked over the poetry book in my hands. So possibly, happiness, you, I and missing are all the same thing. I will never get used to you for you are an endless and new joy each time I am with you. I have never loved, and admired, like this, without blemish and without reserve. I never could again.

I have said the little I had to say. The great deal today would be a meandering of the pen, and I could wander on and on, but I think with a pattern nevertheless, the pattern of a man who is home, who loves and is loved. Many blessings, much love and luck to us both in 1966.

Bunchi

~

Anokha, 32/Sector 5-A, Chandigarh
December 31, 1965

Darling

I suppose I should, on this last day of the year, wish you a Happy New Year. But I want to wish us both everlasting love.

Much of it from
Tara

~

Part Three

E.N. Mangat Rai at the Ministry
of Petroleum, 1970.

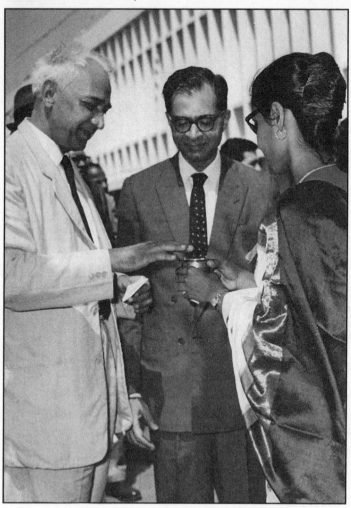

74/Sector 9-A, Chandigarh
January 3, 1966

My darling Tara

I have been impatient to get back to you ever since we parted
on the night of the 1st. I came home to find the party still going
on, during which they had played charades and other games,
and seemed in a mellow mood with little immediate desire
to go home. And I entered the room somewhat gingerly with
the feel of you still all over me, but was almost immediately
normal, and able to cope as I sat down, though with no desire
whatever to talk. I had a quiet warm inner glow of awareness
of you and of a profound satisfaction of completion, and the
only wish I had was either that I was alone, or with you. And
so eventually to bed, and to deep slumber.

No, I do not think you or I could tire of freedom. You will
recall you mentioned this subject as we got to your house on
the 1st evening. That will not happen to you or to me; mainly
for two reasons, the first, that both of us have developed over
the years strong resources to feed on in the way of reading
and writing. There would in a sense never be enough time,
nor lack of direction in dealing with this need and interest.
And for human warmth and aura we have an abiding interest
in each other. When away from each other we could, I think,
feel the need that Tagore describes:

> When the weariness of the road is upon me and the
> thirst of the sultry day, when the ghostly hours of dusk
> throw their shadow across my life, then I cry not for
> your voice only, my friend, but your touch.

There is anguish in my heart for the burden of its riches not given to you.

Put out your hand through the night, let me hold it, and fill it and keep it; let me feel its touch along the lengthening stretch of my loneliness.

I recalled the time when I was really free, between the ages of 24 and 29, when I had started work and was not married. ('The earth and every common sight/ To me did seem/apparelled in celestial light.') My only problem of chance desires was that of women, of the possibility of marriage, even though I was more convinced then that marriage was not a form of association that could make me flourish, and if I had been able to convince any worthwhile person that an association together, with loyalty and devotion, was more worthwhile than marriage, I am certain I would have worked for this and faced its consequences.

And as a parting idea, I think that for me even today many things are still 'apparelled in celestial light'. There is much I would like to say of these days with you but there never seems to be the time. I was myself as I have seldom been before, and was always and every day grateful for you, and above all for what has become us.

My love
Bunchi

~

13 Akbar Road, New Delhi
January 7, 1966

Frank asked me to have a drink with him and we had a long talk, with me doing most of the talking, and a lot of it about you, which I couldn't help, and it's always such a relief to talk about you. Frank said, 'Hearing you talk I've realized something, about you I didn't before. I think you are a rare woman because you feel with your mind. Most people think with their minds and feel with their bodies. I have done this myself and tried for years to establish relationships through the medium of the body. And I believe now that the only lasting relationships are those based on the involvement of the mind.'

~

White House, Gamadia Road, Bombay
January 13, 1966

My darling

I entered this flat last night with a sense of deep discouragement. It looked so dismantled and was a reminder of last year's hurricane. I felt very low in morale, especially when I read a letter of Gautam's to the children which said he would be away another month because this means I am stuck here till then. He also said he is now a director of the Jayanti Shipping Corporation and would have to go often to Europe and Japan, and apparently it does not concern or worry him that the children and I must live in this untidy fashion with the future uncertain and no peace of mind while he goes on his prolonged travels. (The letter is from St Mauritz.) I find it hard not to feel bitter toward him, a thing I have tried to avoid.

Thank you for being with me in Delhi, and so much with me. I find people's comments and discussions about us quite irrelevant. We are so different from what any other two people are or have, so remote from anything I have seen or anything in my own experience, that I cannot see any other factor as being relevant to it. And I love you very much.

Tara

~

White House, Gamadia Road, Bombay
January 15, 1966

My love

I listened to the news which indicates a preference of the Chief Ministers (including Sadiq) for my cousin Indi as PM. It has given me an idea for my article for the *Sunday Standard* which I might write along the lines that the PM is an institution, and perhaps we have arrived at the stage where it does not matter who is PM, that anyone in that capacity can be expected to fill the role with reasonable adequacy. This is not an age of heroes — we've had all that and it will be a long time coming again. I think it is not a matter to stir up much passion and controversy who becomes the next PM. Even the rigid Morarji will be limited by the task in hand, the brute necessities of food and other perpetually threatening problems. Even Morarji (whom I'd be afraid of as PM) has one saving grace. *He's* afraid of no one, and this country would maintain its integrity and no nonsense about it. But I'm afraid of Indi too, and of anyone like her who is so far from having solved even a fraction of her personal problems or evolved any kind of constructive philosophy of life, as leader. Of the present lot I think I'd rather have someone a bit more anonymous than these two.

I wanted to correct your impression about our child, the one you say I 'passionately don't want'. I have never had a father for my children, and I have longed for one. It took me years not to feel wretchedly lonely in this matter. It would mean much to me to have a child whose every moment of pre-life, and life, I could share. And history is full of illegitimate children.

I suggested to Sri Bhai that the problem of my moving from this flat to Mafatlal Park without Gautam's signature might be overcome by my just packing a suitcase for the children and myself and leaving the rest of our personal effects here. I cannot go on like this and he seems supremely unconcerned about anything except going on his travels. He is less and less concerned with the children and doesn't seem to realize there are many matters concerning them that need his attention. I am disturbed by my undefined position and this whole situation gives me no relief or release—but perhaps that is what Gautam intends.

~

White House, Gamadia Road, Bombay
January 19, 1966

Bunchi

I heard the news of Indi's election at 3:10 pm as I had kept the radio on all afternoon especially for the announcement. And I wondered what reaction you have had to the news, and if by any chance you thought, 'What in heaven's name am I mixed up with?' I wish we could have been together now, because I would have told you I sympathize with such a reaction, that families—the best of them—are formidable things, often closed corporations that admit no outsider. And I would have told you that as far as I'm concerned *you* are my family. I have no other passionate attachment except my country and that embraces us both. I love my children dearly but I recognize I am a trustee for them, that they are, and must be separate from me, and will form their own allegiances and attachments.

In the matter of you-me, the question of family, or Indi being PM, or any other consideration, hasn't worried me at all. I could face a horde on this issue. This, between us, is a simple fact. It has, however, been of concern to me to carry my family with me on this issue, to convince them of what it means to me, to go with their blessing so to speak. I have had nothing but affection and trust from them and I would always like to return that.

~

Wazarat Road, Jammu
February 11, 1966

I am sick and tired and depressed with being away from you, and your absence clings to me in a dull, and sometimes sharp, and always constant awareness the whole conscious day. And I wish I was 'infatuated' with you, 'led by the nose', 'under your spell' as the conversation at Khushwant's reported to me seems to imply. But I do not have any of that kind of feeling. This is slow and pervasive, not separate from me. This is 98.4, the warmth of the normal body, which remains that way. And I am fed up with this correspondence; it is wholly inadequate. Yet it is the only link we have.

We must talk about our plans, and there are difficulties we must face together. I depend on you. You and I will walk the earth *together*, and if it is rough we will hold hands and take each other with us. Those are the only terms I can understand with you. I can only offer you a comradeship of the trenches, where the only certainty is your objective, that you will win through. All else, much else, is always uncertain, method, procedure, what the next hour will bring. Also there will be fears and doubts. I shared yours, and was with you in your trenches. Will you not share mine? Remember you were afraid and clouded with uncertainty when you went through your fire. I have mine ahead of me. I walked with you in yours, though I was far from you and could not be available and at hand. Will you not walk with me?

Yes, as you say about the Delhi talk about us, there may be situations in the marketplace 'in which gold looks like counterfeit and a million dollars passes for two cents'. We have to pass through the misunderstandings of people around us. I would have preferred that such talk did not take place, but it has, and there is some value in knowing of it.

~

E-8 Mafatlal Park, Bombay
January 31, 1966

I moved here to Mummie's flat last evening. It may be the change of residence, but I feel I've travelled miles and left everybody behind somewhere, way back. I've had an experience, and no one else has had it. I'm changed, and no one else is. Life seems to be going on just the same way for everyone else.

I have been going out a lot, and have had expressions of genuine concern and regret about the separation, and offers of help, quite unlike the Delhi atmosphere relayed to you, by Kikook, of scandal and gossip. Delhi terrifies me. How does one feel safe in a jungle? What way is there to keep oneself intact and enclosed? I don't want to live like that, shared out in the marketplace by all the vendors. Tommorrow I'm lunching and dining out, but my 'tread' isn't what it should be. I'm just going along somehow. The day's saying in the *Times of India* yesterday said something about having to make a choice between 'truth and repose'. Apparently one can't have both. The thought of being plunged into turmoil again on Gautam's return is very disheartening. I really don't know what he wants.

Two nights ago Sharuk Sabavala[70] was saying that Lal Bahadur's uncertainty over the Tashkent decision[71] was

---

[70]At the time representing the *Christian Science Monitor,* later associated with Tatas.

[71]The decisions arrived at in Tashkent.

very real and plagued him, and he was afraid about its acceptance in India. It is incredible how quietly it has gone over in the press, though this coming Parliament session may throw up a clearer picture.

~

E-8 Mafatlal Park, Bombay
February 10, 1966

It is difficult to describe my state of mind since Gautam's return. I feel wrung out and squeezed dry. We covered all the same ground even to his saying he would kill you. I had the feeling I would never be free, and that if I was, he would still not allow me to marry again, and that my freedom would in some way involve dire consequences.

I asked him to drinks yesterday and he refused but asked what I was serving, and when I said Black Knight, he said, 'My wife cannot serve Black Knight' and sent four bottles of Scotch and a carton of Kent cigarettes. And he continues to say 'my wife' though he has said I cannot use the car and he has no further responsibility for anything, including the overhaul of the frig, which is a necessity in this climate, and with children in the house.

I have been terribly shaken by his condition. He's lost in space somewhere and it's horrifying. I also know he will rule the children out of his life once the divorce goes through.

~

Wazarat Road, Jammu
February 14, 1966

It has rained, my love, at last. On Saturday afternoon the heavens poured down for over an hour, and then a steady rain most of the night and part of Sunday. It cleared up last evening and the snow was visible, for the first time this year, on the hills from our terrace, and even on Vaishno Devi. The river which had shrunk to a small stream of transparent water, was last evening a swollen, fast moving, reddish brown, almost solid with the churned up mud from many hills. And as I watched the rain lashing the earth from my office window on Saturday, I was somewhat humbled, as men who do not believe in God (or gods) are apt to be on such occasions.

And whatever your personal circumstances, I am going to come to Bombay in March, for I am a free citizen of India and can visit Bombay if I wish. Even if your circumstances do not allow you to see me, I will be there, and will ring you up every morning at 10:30, whether you like it or not!

I have worked practically round the clock on the draft to be prepared for our Delhi discussions.[72] The ground we had to cover was large, the time limited, and it has been a rush job which Bannerji[73] and I have tackled together, producing a small booklet, nearly 10,000 words between us, in about 36 hours of drafting, discussions with Ministers, and recasting. And I have wanted to send it to you at once, but I can't at the moment, as it is somewhat secret. Will show it to you whenever I can.

~

---

[72]Discussions held in Delhi at which the Kashmir government presented its point of view to the Centre. E.N. Mangat Rai had prepared a draft meant to serve as a background note for the discussion.

[73]See Note 60.

Wazarat Road, Jammu
February 16, 1966

My darling

Not since knowing you have I felt so completely lost, as if the
earth had opened at my feet and was crushing me of breath.
I thought to myself—it was hardly thinking—that we are
involved in two 'rights', each of which involves senseless
death—the agony of Gautam, and the agony for us if we throw
each other away. And I wanted to cover you over with love
and to tell you that, in these circumstances, these truly awful
alternatives, whatever you did would be done by us, and not
by you alone. I even felt I should take the responsibility of
deciding for you, that I should take us to the sacrifice. But I
could not bear the idea. Over a long evening at home I was
much calmer though somewhat depressed. And I thought in
less extreme terms. I felt you should endeavour to achieve a
breathing space, and persuade him that things having gone
so far, you and he must give living separately a trial. Both
of you, and he particularly, must have a chance to view this
whole matter in some degree of calm. Now that he has signed
the papers, he and you should relax, get a feel of it, and see
where you both want to go.

I would be inhuman and unimaginative if I blamed you
in any way for this turn in our plans and decisions, for I have
grown to love you in a way where everything important that
happens to you happens to me. I am in a very real sense you,
if such a thing is possible. Because I understand what has
happened and why and how, I do not feel anything but a
party to it. I only want to make my need clear—that from you
I will value and love even the thimbleful. So in any decision
you make that should be a consideration as far as my position
goes.

But I think you should also consider the effects of this for *yourself.* Suppose I did not exist in your life, or suppose I was your brother (which I would not like to be) or your father (which is a feeling I do sometimes have for you) I would certainly advise you, having gone so far, and faced so much, not to make a decision in a hurry. You can reasonably ask for time. My point is, my darling, you must give *yourself* a chance, and not be bludgeoned into a life back with Gautam because of his suffering. You have hardly been eighteen days at Mafatlal Park. Is it not premature to make a decision that will involve you for decades when you have been through absolute hell getting to this position?

February 24 – I am glad I wrote as I did, and that we have cleared this so completely between us, and it has been almost like a re-baptism, a reaffirmation of our love. And I also agree with you, many times over, that our life together has already started, and that we do live together. I love and trust you enough to assure you freedom of action; and while this crisis stage is on you must not feel inhibited at any time, or uncertain of my love and confidence, and must take them for granted. And you need not consult me in advance when it is difficult. So my darling beloved, you are my wife and my comrade, and I know that with you whatever happens, I am always, and forever, safe.

~

Wazarat Road, Jammu
March 5, 1966

Even if I had deliberated and calculated, I would, if I had the opportunity, have chosen you. For you are the woman I had wanted in my twenties, my idea of a woman. I had always imagined that if I married, it would have to be a) a woman with the tenderness of a woman, b) a person interested in ideas, willing to appreciate them and talk of them — call it if you like, though the word irritates me, somewhat of an 'intellectual' and c) a person with a sense of humour. So I have chosen you and everything that has happened since that choice has confirmed it as right and apt and happy. My 'loveliest' and my 'best', you must not go back to any prison again. You have fought through a compaign; let us not have a premature Tashkent. Give it time, my love, and let me plead with you that should you consider returning to your marriage, it should only be on terms that do not enslave you to a rigid lack of freedom. And now, my darling, much love, and do not on any account run away.

March 8 – I am much more certain now that you should not give in. I have been forced to the conclusion that there is in Gautam's makeup a driving mania to possess, to express himself only, and without compromise in terms of his own need. And the issue with Ranjit conclusively proves this. It can only be explained in terms of his needing to hurt you through Ranjit, a child far from you, and because the child was yours. It is the act or the instinct of supreme ego and vanity.

You will say 'he is a sick man', but what do you do with a sick man? Whatever the answer may be, it is certainly not that you give in to the disease. A Gautam who has you return his slave, may well break out later in the same form regarding the children. I do not think you have any certainty that you are 'saving' the children by giving in. And then yourself. Yourself, as a person, would have to be abandoned. Therefore, today, I think it is right that you should resist, give Gautam a chance to discover himself. It is possible that holding out will not cure Gautam of his malaise and that he will drive himself to breaking point. But at this stage try it out fully, give it time.

~

Wazarat Road, Jammu
March 9, 1966

Incidentally, I could add to your list of 'strong-minded women' in your family, and my name is Nayantara Sahgal, for I think you have survived an invidualism under remarkable conditions, and one day when we have time and leisure, and the sky overhead, we must lie down on a lawn beneath the trees, and talk of how it happened. For you, to take one example only, had not loved (or never believed you had) a man till 37, and yet you knew all about it, better and less tarnished than I did who had loved for years. By 'knew about it' I mean the nuances and strength and aspirations it created; you arrived there with these almost ready-made, as if they were already there, on the shelf of a well-ordered store, merely to be brought down and used. And yet one could see that they had not been used, and that was a part of their inarguable strength and lustre.

I do not know what I would do without you. The other night as I wrote DP's article on Law and Order, I thought I just could not do this if Tara was not here; it would just be meaningless; I would not even try. And that's how I could not do without you. I'd carry on; I'd not be sick or grow thin or waste away. But there'd be no meaning, no tread, no savour to all the processes of doing and thinking and feeling; they would suddenly be without light. I crave (really crave) time and quiet with you. It's a kind of thirst, and I am always thirsty. And now please do not let anything come in the way of our meeting, for which I count the days.

~

E-8 Mafatlal Park, Bombay
March 13, 1966

As to keeping my morale up, I need my signs and symbols around me just now, all the familiar hallmarks of living, to cover my bouts of panic. It isn't exactly panic either. It is the feeling that one is walking along and one suddenly steps off into nothing, a fear of falling into nothing that envelops me from time to time, quite often when I've just woken up in the morning. And I feel amazed at my predicament, and say to myself, 'What has happened, and how, and why?' And during these fits of panic I've had a nostalgia for my marriage, for the safety I once knew, the protection, the predictable future I was going toward with the children safe and their lives assured in it, an easy, steadily more luxurious life, with everything under the sun one is supposed to want, merely for the asking. It must have been another lifetime. I started leaving it behind when I wrote to you in 1964 that I was already too far from anywhere. And there may be a touch of madness in all this, the 'voices' I cannot do anything about, turn my back on.

I have no firm or vigorous hold on life. I don't love life for itself. I have a sense of responsibility about it, to give back a little of what I've received from it. I feel about life a bit as you do toward your marriage.

~

Wazarat Road, Jammu
March 13, 1966

I have read *From Fear Set Free* very slowly. I think your descriptions of the life around you in Bombay are good, and without being dramatic, are effective in portraying a great and helpless kind of sorrow all around us in this country, with which we are only able to live by ignoring it most of the time, as far as consciousness goes.

I'm afraid my record correspondence (collection) is with you, my sweetheart, and you are very much a party and contributor to it. As Sampson says (in *Equality and Power)* of Elizabeth Barret Browning: '...The struggle was one of great mental anguish. We are fortunate that she who suffered it was also possessed of rare literary gifts. The correspondence began in January 1845, and concluded with the elopement in September 1846. In the 1913 edition the letters extend to over 1100 pages.' I was trying to calculate the damage we have done in the nearly twenty months since August 1964, and I rather think we would beat the Brownings. I'm afraid I may continue to write the occasional letter to you even if you were there right with me.

~

Wazarat Road, Jammu
March 18, 1966

A gruelling day with a Cabinet meeting lasting till 9 pm. And a queer talk with DP yesterday. He rang me up at 1 pm and said he was at my house, so I came home from office and he had 3-4 gins till 3 pm (when I had to leave for a meeting). As we talked he said, 'Do you mind if I tread into your affairs and say just one brief thing?' I said, 'No, not at all as I know your intentions about me can never be anything but genuine.' 'You are going to Bombay. Do not go beyond a friendship with Tara. Leave it where it is. Do not begin thinking of marriage and the like.' He said it hesitantly, apologetically, and repeated it two or three times during the course of the ensuing conversation. I got a bit categorical and said, 'If you said this for Tara's sake, or her children's, or Champa's, or mine, I'd understand. But I get the impression you say it because it's not done. The conventional facade must be kept.' He did not admit or deny that, merely repeated what he had said. I said, 'Well, that does not appeal to me. You see, I do not belong anywhere. I am in Kashmir today as Mangat Rai, that's all, a civil servant whom you thought you needed. And that's been my way of life since I was 21; I am where I am on my own. It's too late to expect me to conform to patterns. You'll have to put it to me in terms of human value.' And we did not get any further.

March 19 – In fifteen minutes I will step out on the first lap of my journey to you and I cannot believe I will see you in 24 hours and pretend to (and succeed) to look quite normal with no indication of the birdsong, now an overwhelming exultation that can hardly be kept within me. This waiting has seemed a long, trying travail.

~

J&K Govt Guest House, Bombay
March 26, 1966

My beloved Tara

I should not be writing. Perhaps I have nothing constructive to say. Yet I do write for I want to be in touch with you the moment I leave; I want never to be away from you; I love you, whatever that unsatisfactory word is worth. The only questions are of practical difficulty, and what can be done. The rest is suffused and confirmed with rightness. And that is how it has been between us; how I hope it will be; and that is how it is *not* now; and the loss seems unbearable and I am wretchedly alone and lost and floundering. But I shall love you, and shall never leave you, till these processes are worked out, and then I shall, I hope, see and abide by their answer, whatever it is, and however difficult. Meanwhile I shall continue to cling to the only answer I have now known for many months. My love, try and forget where I have been unkind. Look after yourself for you are very precious.

I enjoyed getting to know your children a bit more than I have. I felt that a barrier of complete ignorance had been removed. I am also pleased I know your surroundings and your daily way of living. I will not feel so lost about guessing what you do, where, how. Your way of living has very much the stamp of you on it, so that to an extent it was even familiar. I can understand your 'obsession' for the 'home for the children' I have it too, an obsession for a home for *your* children. And I think we could make it together. Am I asking you something against nature or against heredity? Is there something unnatural about love? I do not think so. Why couldn't we take your children with us? If you only believed, I feel certain we could, my love.

I will remain very much with you these next few days when I am surrounded by people and festivities, which I would much rather have shared with you than with anyone else in the world. In a matter of a few hours I will again be miles away from you and very aware of the growing distance.

~

E-8 Mafatlal Park, Bombay
March 27, 1966

My darling

I waited at the airport till your plane left, all the time aware of your sadness, that I was for the first time since I've known you sending you away not full and confident. And I knew it stemmed from my state of mind and that it was in me to fill you with power and purpose on the one hand, and despondency on the other.

What I am suffering from is some kind of inertia that has taken hold, which we have discussed and tried to understand, and though it is your way to probe and analyse and try to discover reasons at such a time, and my way to retreat into myself, yet we must, I think, be a little patient at this kind of backfiring. It is a fault with me that I retreat at such a time. It is how I'm made. An intense isolation grips me, sends me adrift. I am convinced of your love and your nearness and your belief, I have all that, and yet it all seems to wait on the shore for my return. You pointed out my individuality even in small matters—matters I hadn't even noticed. I am like that. I've always made my own decisions. And yet I've lived with you intensely and closely and in detail (in ways I did not know existed) for the past year, and been able to at least on paper, and whenever we have met.

I read your letter in the car coming home. You have not been inconsiderate. There was tension between us and I don't know what I would have done myself in similar circumstances. My love and affection are still there. What seems to be in abeyance is the ability to react. But I beg you not to be despondent.

We had no peace this time. Please let me know about the bruises (which still look severe) and the bloodshot eye. I have felt helpless to say or do anything about this, appalled that it should have happened, and dreadfully unhappy about it. Perhaps it is I who should apologize for bringing this upon you.

I would give anything to be able to say this minute, 'The fog has lifted, the paralysis passed.' I am miserable in it myself and floundering myself. I have still not got the hotel scene with Gautam out of my mind. There have been times when this whole business seems to have had little to do with individuals. It has seemed a reflection of something much bigger, a microcosm of violent passions and abiding belief, of love and terror and joy and sadness all mixed up. I am very anxious to know about your eye and the bruises. Has there been any pain since you left? And I hope getting back into routine hasn't been too painful.

I was very conscious this time of you being possessed by urgency, and myself lacking it, and perhaps the relationship itself demanded a let-up, a slackening, a loosening. I can't think of any better way of describing it than Byron's lines:

> So we'll go no more a-roving
> So late into the night,
> Though the heart be still as loving
> And the moon be still as bright
> For the sword outwears its sheath
> And the soul wears out the breast
> And the heart must pause to breathe
> And love itself have rest.

I am filled with fears of Gautam's return and further encounters. Time is needed, you said, and he will get time, but I doubt if time alone will solve his dilemma. Time must have some direction, some meaning. In his case it seems to move shapeless and muddled and its passage resolves nothing. But since no other help is possible for him, you are right that it must be left to time. But I have been full of fear that this will not end except by blood-letting. That is the kind of absurd, extreme, and yet terribly real feeling I continue to have.

With much love
Tara

~

Wazarat Road, Jammu
March 28,1966

My beloved girl

I have been warmed by your telegram, and yet unwarmed, if such a combined feeling is possible, because I have felt that our love should now carry us further to its acceptance, to the vision and courage to establish itself, or the courage to be destroyed by our inability to do so. Having tried, we may fail, but let us at least try.

I have had to tell the story of bees biting me many times, and I've added many details in the process. DP who came for a drink at lunchtime said I should write a story on the subject, as it was so vivid and so clear what had happened. And Sadiq had his own story to tell about a man surrounded by bees at the Shalimar at Lahore, and putting his head below water, and lifting it up each time to find them settling on him. And queerly enough I am feeling very fit, except for this occasional sickening, drooping doubt as to whether you will believe, and we will see this through. This visit to you has been a rather terrific experience for me and I am much too near it and too full of it to write about it with any confidence. Everything became different, what you did to me, the way you were with me, and I was quite lost, Tara. And since I returned I have been quite lost. I know that you were good to me throughout, and kind to me, but I did not want goodness and kindness. I wanted you intensely, and your acceptance of me. I could not hold this experience. It drove me in a sort of desperateness for you; I could not be reasonable. I could see the facts, and that they required, and justified, patience, and yet I got driven in a kind of despairing need for you. And I wondered if somewhere deep in you this relationship with me, which is conscious and known and understood, came up against a passion more subtle, less known, even dark and compelling, and of driving force. Perhaps deep down in you Gautam held you in some way just like that.

And the only solution I could find again and again was that you and I should be more and more with each other in every way possible and on every occasion. I never lost faith in you as a person; you were strong and clear and, if I may say so, pure.

~

E-8 Mafatlal Park, Bombay
March 30,1966

Your birthday – What are you having for breakfast? And what are you feeling like? How is your eye, and the bruises? Did Prem believe your story about the bees?

Mummie told me Gautam had told her, 'This time I thrashed Bunchi (he said not a word about hitting me) and next time I will kill him. Then you will have a Nanavati case[74] on your hands.' I do not put it past him to do some insane thing. If a man makes public his intention to shoot another man, is one not entitled to police protection? And *should* this matter be kept quiet? I have felt, as with his threat of watching me, that it should be made public.

~

---

[74]A murder case involving a naval officer, Nanavati, who shot his wife's lover.

Wazarat Road, Jammu
April 1, 1966

My sweetheart

The eye, and the black marks are much better. The redness has almost gone. The only thing I feel is a slight crackle when I touch my nose. There is, however, no pain. You must not feel bad about the incident with Gautam and the thrashing he administered. It has passed over me though I have felt a kind of horror that there should be such things between people. But ever since January 1965, I have felt that it was not you but I who should suffer in this way with Gautam, and that it was wrong that you did. In that background I have almost felt restored to you in some strange equality and in some strange comradeship. So please do not feel bad about it.

Yes, economics is important for us. But if you examine the figures it does not seem an impossible task for us to face and solve. We need not be disheartened by it. On my part I am quite determined to start making the necessary enquiries now, and will do so as soon as the birthday visitors leave.

My love to you
Bunchi

~

Wazarat Road, Jammu
April 4, 1966

The whole reaction of these last two weeks has descended on me now that I am alone, and I am glad I am alone. Champa and I talked before she left. Her points were that I was deluded as far as judging women goes, 'You do not realize a woman will never tell the truth about herself to a man, at least not to a man she is keen on keeping. She will deceive you.' She was scathing about my 'worship' of you and said my activity was almost 'classical'. She implied that the 'new lease of life' you had given me should make me wary of its meaning. 'She is a young woman who has you at her feet and no woman like her will ever give that up, as long as it is new and you worship her as you do.' I spoke at some length, that I felt as if I had come home, that my whole life had been a probation for this, that there was no infatuation or tumult about this, only the tumult of external circumstances, and there have been many, borne down on Tara, and that we have been truthful, even blunt, with each other, and hidden nothing from each other. And so I have broken the ice, and made my position clear, and I am glad I did, for I hate living a lie with anyone.

Though I say it, your children are as important to me as they are to you. Perhaps 'the world' and 'the family' are not so important, and we will have to face them. I have thought and felt about little else than the problems and pains within you, and which are within me, and mine, also. But we are married, and let us recognize that marriage as a fact and trust, without blemish, between us. This, between us, our marriage, is certain.

It is time for you to see that you do not have to 'shoulder' any guilt. You have repeatedly given Gautam every possible chance for a reasonable settlement, again and again and again, and it has been rejected. There is no scope for guilt.

And what does all this come to? The issue of 'the world', 'the public', cannot be solved; it can only be faced, and lived. But I do not want you to try this experiment unless you are prepared, and want to do so, with open eyes and knowing what you are doing, and what risking. I think another thing you must get into your pretty head is the simple fact that there is a whole world available to you as an independent person. I know you value it very little. But I also know that the way you have reacted to an independent life even in this short and troubled time, is of significance. You have great and abundant resources for individual development and enjoyment. It is a worthwhile way of living. I do not suggest you accept it as final. I don't want you to, as I want you to live with me; but it is important that you should know yourself and not think of life in terms (necessarily) of a man about you. If I lived with you, and had any sense, I'd have to discover means by which you could exercise, and enjoy, yourself by yourself, and yet live with me. I say this because we too readily assume that there are only two alternatives for you, a life with Gautam, or with me. There is a third, very real alternative, yourself, and you could make much of it. That would not exclude me. You are by no means hung with a man; you could flourish on your own, and never underrate that possibility.

About 'blood-letting', I think both you and I must dismiss this as a consideration in our actions or thinking. If blood is to be drawn, we must face that. I am a little sustained by the fact that if it is drawn in any final sense, of killing, it is likely to be in my direction rather than yours. And while I do not welcome the possibility, I think one must just ignore it. We should, as we decided, meet at least once in three months. All my love, *and* always

Bunchi

~

Wazarat Road, Jammu
April 9, 1966

I have wondered, and bothered, whether I have influenced you wrongly in this whole matter, considering your comparatively innocent and sheltered life as far as breaking social convention goes. I wonder if I have been cold and objective enough, or too greedy and subjective, in analysing what I can give you in the way of happiness and satisfaction in this literal revolution in your life. I know you are very much a person who needs and fits into a home, and I think I am also that kind of person. I see you go lightly from one room to another, and I just watch, and do not say a word, but it is of tremendous comfort to know you are there, a continuous presence and influence in and around me. That is why my time with you in Srinagar in October 1964 was so abundant and happy, for we were in what became our home, also at Chandigarh this time, even though we were distracted by the situation, and even on this visit to Bombay when I enjoyed the making of breakfast and your presence around the kitchen. And that perhaps is a reason why my whole instinct revolts and rebels at any plan where I cannot get up and find you there with me in the morning, even if I do not say a word and allow you your longer sleep.

And that is why, again and again, we must be clear as to the nature of our relationship. We both rejected it as an affair only, which we could have carried on clandestinely, for it was clear that it was not just that, and could not be. We accepted it as love, and gave it our dedication. And I, who am a man who has had no use for marriage certificates, have longed these last two weeks for a symbol of our voluntary decision, like married people have marriage certificates. And by that I do not mean you should accept any commitment of finality. It is love in freedom; that is its very essence; and it is final only because we want it that way. And it need not take only one form of living between us. You must, for your own confidence, consider the third alternative—life on your own. For once you do you will understand that there is no compulsion in regard to me. It is a choice that is open to you to take when you want it, and in any way that is possible between us. So you should assess the possibilities of living on your own, looking after your children, pursuing your interests, and having your own friends—including me, I hope, as a very special one! We should regard this as a great adventure between us, in which we know we are together, wherever the road leads, even in periods of prolonged absence. I am terribly, irretrievably, and finally married to you, Tara, and there is no going back, not one inch, for me.

~

13 Akbar Road, New Delhi
April 27, 1966

Gogu had already been told of the hotel incident by Gautam. Gogu said Gautam felt remorseful about hitting me, but not about you, and when I repeated what he had said to Mummie, Gogu said it was not impossible. I asked if a man could go around creating terror in other people's lives this way, and he said he himself didn't believe in violence, but he really did not know how he would react in a similar situation, perhaps just like Gautam. Moreover, public sympathy was with Gautam. You had alienated my affections from him and for this the simple and direct remedy was a thrashing, it being a man's world and so on. I said I didn't put it past him to carry out his threat of killing, and Gogu said, 'Well then he'll pay the penalty, but I don't see how he can be prevented.'

I felt very depressed after this talk—the effect of their kindness generally, and they were both very kind and concerned about me—and the shock at Gogu's attitude that the attack on you was justified! Gogu thought I should let a year or two, or even ten, pass for things to mend, that Gautam is living in a 'champagne bubble', throwing wild parties, and getting drunk but had by no means given me up. I thought it an extraordinary outlook, when *he* has insisted on the divorce, to expect me to hold my life in suspension, remain his wife in spirit, waiting for the day when a return will be possible. And most people in this country would support that sentiment. Marriage is marriage. And I said it was hard to feel sorry for a man who throws champagne parties every day but cannot spare the car for his children.

I told Prem the story about the bees. He understood why you had had to hide the real story. I asked him if he had ever encountered such a situation, or such a man. He said, 'Only in books' and that we should leave the country. He said it was hard to believe such threats, but that he believed them.

Sonny,[75] who was at Gogu's, told me his 'respect and admiration' for me had gone up a hundredfold after seeing the agreement between Gautam and me. 'I don't know of any other woman who would have given up the claim to all that money and all that jewellery.'

~

1 Church Road, Srinagar
May 5, 1966

I have not been able to put an ounce of tranquility, or normality into anything. It is as if I still wait—tense—for something to break through. There seem ages and months of vacancy ahead. And yet, purely intellectually, I think we have been wise not to force the pace, and to hold our hand, and that is the cross we may have to carry for quite a few months. It has seemed infuriating and absurd that you should be so near me at Delhi, that I should have leave from the Government, and yet must be here—a tool in the hands of another person's will and movements, because he was married to you, and that is the law, and my doing otherwise may create

---

[75]J.K. Srivastava.

difficulities for you, me, or your children. This meaningless waiting has quite overpowered me. And I have wondered how you felt, whether with your human responsibilities—the children, your mother, your sisters—were not so submerged by the stranglehold of circumstances.

~

13 Akbar Road, New Delhi
May 7, 1966

I feel guilty that I did not let you come, but there was no alternative. Whichever way I argue it, this whole question of Gautam's condition burdens me with a sense of responsibility. I've wondered how to purge myself of the burden. Marriage is a merciless tie. I seem incapable of feeling positive. I do not with any clarity see a future for us. I see us together, but when I try to think in terms of *getting* there, I can't seem to do it at all. Even writing letters is not the free flow it once was. At times it all seems a tremendous, endless effort, not a blaze of glory or a crusade any more. I have got my way, got thrown out, been left to my devices to make what I can of my relationship with you. I also know the relationship is good. But the circumstances surrounding us continue to be difficult and exhausting. You say, 'I am a little afraid of this arid year or more, and what it may do to us.' That sums it up. And is it not frightening that with all that we possess, we should have these fears? Who is safe from such fears then? Anybody? And how does one feel secure?

~

Wazarat Road, Jammu
May 6, 1966

My darling Tara

This is perforce my birthday letter to you. Of course I should have been with you, but that cannot be. Anyway, whatever the limitations, this brings you all my love. It is rather pointless for me to send you good wishes or to consider you apart from myself. By which I do not mean that you are, in any way, an adjunct to me; but that I, and my life, and its hopes, and sighs, and wishes, its meat and drink, have become so inextricably and so deeply mixed with yours, that I cannot wish you separately from myself—which again is not meant as a commitment, or a halter for you, but for myself: a commitment, a halter, call it what anyone may, a beloved destination, an affirmation, a home, a resting place, fulfilment, from which I desire to go nowhere else, where I feel I belong. A 'prison' if you like, with which the gods have blessed me, and from which I will not move. Call it any name, it is always inadequate, it always misses the mark. I am glad I am involved, that life gave me you, that I want and need to move no further, whatever this may bring, even turmoil and anguish, disease and devastation. Thus am I twice blessed that you were born, for each blessing of yours shall be salt and savour to me and shall add meaning and texture to my existence.

I am sorry I have plagued you and that you have written to me at such length to explain yourself, and written as you have, reasonably and with affection. I could never ask you to give up any association, or any activity, even though you have offered to do so. I do not want that. I trust you completely. In fact, in many ways, I trust you more than I trust myself. I have never had that feeling with anybody. In all these months you have had the faculty, in almost uncanny degree, of making me feel what you have felt, of what the last few weeks of living in the same flat as Gautam meant, of the sheer weariness and doubts and difficulties of even packing your things, the heartbreak this brought, the daily strain of overwrought nerves, where even a sound may make you wary. I am also quite certain that I want to know and understand and love whatever you are. We have had some adjustments to make in point of view before, and gaps in understanding to fill up. There may be other gaps in future, for that is the process of living between us. So accept that, and believe that I trust you completely, more than myself.

Yes, I keep hoping that all this ugliness and violence and strain will abate, and pass, and be forgotten. Once this bloody year is over, I'm afraid I am going to force the pace a bit with you, and come out a long, long way in the open.

All my love
Bunchi

~

Wazarat Road, Jammu
May 10, 1966

Another marked manifestation of my feelings has been that I can no longer think in terms of 'no way out'. For it has become very clear to me that there is only one way out as far as I'm concerned, and that is the way to you, and I will not, cannot, give this up even if it produces ruin. Previously I rather prided myself on the fact that I could face being given up, or circumstances which made it necessary that we should for practical purposes. Now I don't think there is any reality whatever in giving this up, under any circumstances, however difficult or impossible.

I was in a somewhat rebellious mood yesterday and could not bear the idea that I seemed a kind of prisoner in my environment. I wanted freedom of action and movement in place of being tied to a domestic routine, tied also to a regime of official work and discipline which restricted me unduly. But my main rebellion was against my domestic strings, which involve the acceptance of a kind of human bondage, to which I am not loyal, which is not spontaneous, and yet which takes a daily toll of being and living. It seemed to me absurd that this should be so, and quite natural that I should go my own way, and refuse the bondage of years. I even felt I should, on my own, say that I regarded myself as free, but will have to wait even for that till the time is ripe.

I am not trying to cajole or bully you to change your mind. I am quite certain you must come to your own feelings as to the base between us for action. You are in many ways an unfolding flower and I have got involved with and associated with that unfolding. You must bloom on your own, and I must glory in that bloom and must nourish and love it. So I am quite certain this is not an attempt to blitzkreig you to my way of thinking and feeling. If possible we should both try and snap out of this malaise of depression and uncertainty. Let us, my darling, beloved Tara, look at this as a venture together, and face it together.

~

E-8 Mafatlal Park, Bombay
June 2, 1966

I don't know, Bunchi, any more than you do, what brought about the change in March, but I have found my encounters with Gautam very unnerving. There was within me the desire to blot out his misery somehow, anyhow, if only he permitted a chink, and some kind of compromise. It is in such situations that traditions and old-established patterns rise up to meet and engulf one. And as Sheila[76] wrote, 'The facts of relationship cannot be undone.' An act has endless and continuing repercussions, and each day might reveal a new, unseen, even undreamed of factor. If that is true with reference to externals—and I have faced so many 'externals'—then it is doubly and trebly true of 'internals'. I cannot be without qualms. I cannot put this marriage behind me. I live with the wreck of it because it goes so against my grain to have so many years of effort reduced to rubble—and more than just effort, a home built to endure, a loyalty given, a future for the children. But it *has* been reduced to rubble, and I have not been able to prevent it, because Gautam would have it no other way. I don't any longer (except perhaps technically) hold myself responsible for the rubble. He just wouldn't have it any other way. But the destruction is there just the same, and his suffering is there just the same, though he may have brought it on himself. And you are in so much the same position, you will understand exactly how I feel and what I mean. It robs one of something. One lives forever in a haunted house. You know that yourself.

Earlier I was at the peak of a sort of defiance. I had been driven into a corner and made to do as Gautam demanded. By that time, too, after the long siege, I was ready, even longing to have it all over with, the nightmare of scenes, the heartbreak of packing, all the bits and pieces of shrapnel lying around me. There was no other thought in my mind. And so our plans could be made. I didn't realize then that they could be badly shaken, and not from any new situation arising, but from the old one re-asserting itself. A long relationship like marriage has for years and years sent out too many shoots and tentacles.

---

[76] Sheila Lall, E.N. Mangat Rai's sister, former wife of Arthur Lall.

Its holds spread out and go deep down. You can cut off the part of the plant that shows, but the undergrowth persists. The pattern of marriage is ineradicable, if one has ever put anything of oneself into it—and then divorce is stupid and senseless, the solution of fools—which is what Gautam is. I don't think the extent of this struck me until I saw Gautam again, and thought, 'Here am I planning to live with another man when there is this unfinished business between *this* man and me.' And the dreadfulness of this divorce hit me, along with the thought that Champa would be similarly deprived; and I thrust all my misery on you, and you took it.

Yet I have been going through a strange experience since my separation. After being in solitary confinement for years it is like being out on an open prairie, with limitless space all around and a huge starry sky above me. It is something of a continuing psychological shock. I cannot get over it. I am face to face with the world, with people, with no screens between me and anything. It is an extraordinary sensation. I have got used to a very full social and working life of my own. It would be hard to go back to any curtailment of it.

~

1 Church Road, Srinagar
June 8, 1966

Don't you see that unhappiness is an indulgence when it springs from a decision that Gautam not only made, but remade again and again, and thrust you from him because he would consider only his decision and no other? It is an indulgence, and also a sword with which he seeks to bring you to your knees. Apart from that, and apart from me, do you set no value on yourself, what you stand for, what you have fought for, and achieved at such enormous and daily cost? Let us not reopen the whole arena of this battle. I do not think you have ever realized or understood how much I need you.

~

Janpath Hotel, New Delhi
June 28, 1966

A strong ingredient of my feeling for you is your utter validity for me. You stand out 'burning bright'—even when separate, you are there and you are valid for all that I stand for, and admire, and can respect and love. In that sense I have a commitment to destiny with you. So the difference of point of view makes no difference. It doesn't seem to count.

Prem said he was amused at Chandigarh reactions to you and me. The undertone was that Kaval was a godsend compared with you. She obviously did not take Bunchi seriously, and it was all just an extra, which had its tensions and its amusements also. *This* seemed serious business, an absolute, clear association with each other, openly done, in front of everybody, and with a complete strength and rhythm of its own. Prem says Kaka bewailed and bemoaned that fact that we did not appreciate the surreptitious, stealthy, secret amour, and was eloquent in its praise.

I had a busy day yesterday. The Indira Gandhi meeting took place at 4 pm. I notice she has the bad habit (I think primarily Indian) of looking at papers that come in, or scribbling instructions on files while conferencing. She did that so often that I can hardly believe each item was of such urgency that it could not wait. Sadiq practises this habit ad lib. (DP says, 'As far as time goes, his approach to it is feudal'.) Apart from this the meeting went well, and I think she has developed a distinctly more practical attitude to many matters which we have now been discussing over 2-3 meetings. As we sat there (my first visit to this room, where I gather your

Mamu used to sit), I could not help picturing you in Mrs G's chair, and the feeling came so often it was uncanny. And I even spoke (a sentence or two) once or twice, which I normally don't when Ministers are conferring.

~

Janpath Hotel, New Delhi
July 20, 1966

The Chief Ministers' meeting yesterday seemed a kind of exercise in paralysis as far as any firm attitudes to the economic crisis goes. Indi presided, but again looked at notes off and on throughout the meeting, which created a vacuum so far as the chair goes; in effect, Sachin Choudhry[77] held the chair. He was polite, patient, and gave the impression of an immense weariness at what faced us, and though there were streaks of determination, these did not make any sustained impact. The response from the CMs was not that of a leadership seeing a crisis, and adding their mite to face it. Altogether it was a dispiriting and distressing business, lacking in guts and vigour. I thought, if this is the character and calibre of our determination in financial crisis, we are going to have a revolution within 2-3 years. In the evening I mentioned this to Krishna Bhatia[78] who said, 'No, there will be no revolution, as the wherewithal does not exist. There may be violence here and there. What we are heading for is chaos. And perhaps from chaos something, a clique or the like, will emerge. In a way the quicker chaos comes, the better.'

I wondered, if there was a substantial change of regime and methods in India, how we, the more mobile classes, would

---

[77]Sachin Chowdhry, then Finance Minister.
[78]A well-known journalist.

react? Would you, for example, think of leaving the country if you could, and watching the storm abate from abroad? I'd be inclined to stay my ground, where I was.

~

E-8 Mafatlal Park, Bombay
July 22, 1966

I've wondered a lot about this last meeting of ours in Delhi. I knew that I was definitely frightened about a life under one roof, and suddenly every aspect and detail of it seemed to loom large and terrifying. It was just too much to cope with. So I sat silent most of the time, mute and seemingly deaf. I was with you in your disappointment with me, but we were for the first time on different levels. I did think we could live under two roofs without causing shock to those near us, and from there move on to the original decision. But I was afraid to say so because of what I have done to you in the past. We can talk about it in September when we meet.

And Bunchi, you do ask a strange question, would I leave this country if there was a substantial change of regime? I don't think I would leave this country if there were any way of staying alive in it. Unless speaking one's mind meant being shot I would not leave it. Even if it meant that, I am not sure I would leave it. I don't know if I am capable of leaving this country in any circumstances whatsoever. The emotional surgery might be so great as not to leave much of a person to enjoy life anywhere else. I would be afraid to cut myself off from India. And that may be foolish when one wonders what is India, and why should going away mean cutting off? Yet it would, from the soil, the smells, the sounds, the sights. I would be intensely lonely and exiled in spirit as well as actually, an exile like the Sahara desert, endless, arid, torturing. I would be afraid without India. Nothing has ever had the power to move me intellectually or emotionally as the image of India has done, and does, a vision that filled my being to bursting. Beloved was a word that applied only to my country. It leads one to wonder what country is and means. I'm not sure, only there is not a day when I am not aware of it in some form. I think I would stay my ground here whatever happened. I feel as if I were indispensable here, and something dreadful would happen to the controls if I went away! Years ago I made up my mind I wouldn't marry in the Foreign Service so that I need never be away from India for years at a time. This, needing to live here, is one of those love affairs that cannot be fully explained. It is primitive to some extent, necessary for security. It is far from being only that, of course. And I'm afraid I'm one of those fools who believes in India's great contribution yet to come.

The child? Yes, of course we'll talk about it: Him? Her?

Yes, I love your idea of a ring. Let's think it over.

Remaining in touch with Indi is not a personal thing. It is a family thing. I have a strong sense of immediate family, of doing the right thing by them. I pay a great deal of attention to my sisters and their problems. We are sentimental about our shared childhood, about having a common language that shuts other people out when we are together. There is a strong attachment between us, and a common hero, Mamu, who himself had a strong sense of family. And now there's no one to hold the larger family together. Indi does not have the interest or capacity.

About conformity, I react as I do today because quite simply it takes more courage than I possess to make this jump when I consider the children. Since having to make a life for myself I have been conscious I must provide them with a mother on whom they can depend, one who may have to bear financial burdens for their future, be able to create a life and opportunities for them. I know I give no appearance of being either shaken or unsettled, but apparently only of such total self-possession as to seem abnormal and cruel. Yet there's a howling torrent raging in me at times. What can I do but look unconcerned? It's either that or some untidy lapse.

Ernie Mountain was here. He said to Gita, 'You know if this had been 200 years ago, your mother would have been a royal princess and I'd have been executed for looking at her too long.' I said I had never heard of any such law, but Gita sagely said it was true, and she'd heard about it somewhere.

~

1 Church Road, Srinagar
July 26, 1966

Your briefcase (ours, I mean) is behaving a little badly, and reminds me more of you in consequence. For it is being a little difficult, and I do not quite know how to cope. The clasp used to spring quite smoothly into position; now it does not do so; it does, but with a little coaxing, sometimes quite easily, sometimes with harrying. So it began reminding me of you. But unlike you, I am able to take it to meetings, and it sits near my desk for long hours.

It is difficult to accept the possibility of a life that is not 'under the same roof'. And I do not agree about the baby. I resent somewhat your opposition. If you agreed perhaps I'd not be so keen! And you *do* have qualms about the second alternative, i.e., not living under the same roof. In our attitude to the future there is now a vacuum which previously was filled by our commitment to an act and a programme. You said I was generous and patient with you, but in fact I was almost speechless (which is a great achievement for me!) for even now I cannot accept any limitation. But I am certain we must go step by step *together*.

We went with DP and his wife to Commander Kaul's drink party. DP took me to the edge of the lawn and showed me bands of disappearing sunset at the horizon, and I looked longingly for you in the still silhouettes of the poplars and the moon travelling mid-cloud. I wish I could say to you with all my heart that I will never again try to persuade you forward a step more than you decide on your own, not make you cross any threshold of my pleading or desire or need. But I cannot. I will persuade you to accept more, and more. You will have to put up with that. It is a new experience for me, a hard and unusual realization for me, that I am dependent on you, as if two machines now had common essential parts and could only work together or be smashed asunder and one would hobble away with what remained, and have to try and make a new machine with whatever was left. And the only explanation I could discover for this feeling of dependence was that I have had with you the experience of loving, and of passion, with my mind quite apart from my emotions. I have not only had the softness and wealth of a woman's love from you, but a strength of soul and intellect, even though you are so much and so sweetly a woman, mine.

~

1 Church Road, Srinagar
July 30, 1966

I am sad at your saying you do not think much of yourself. You are, as a woman, beautiful. (I will not elaborate on that as I may get involved in too much detail!) You will say that is an act of God, but we do things with God's beauty, and in yourself you have added to it rather than left it as it was. Then, you've had three children, and have till now brought them up well. There is hope they will be good ships launched by you. You have a name in the writing world that few achieve. You have also got through a personal crisis of extreme dimensions (for Indian, or indeed any society) and in doing so you have retained the essential respect of your set-up, which includes children, family, society, I think even your husband. A few people here and there may attribute motives and immoralities, but even they do not consider our relationship immoral or insincere. I may add to this list that you have the complete devotion, and complete faith in your integrity, of what must be assessed as an experienced and practical man like me. So what is this assessment you make of yourself, Tara? You have much to be grateful for, and much to be proud of.

Unlike you, I was always aware of being a Christian. At home my people were conscious of their background, proud that they had accepted a revolution in their spiritual life, and I was aware of this pride. At school I was made to feel different, called 'karanta', albeit playfully, a contemptuous term for Christian. My reaction to this was not of dislike or suspicion or fear. I was arrogant, I suppose, for my reaction was that Christianity was not the final thing. There were other things, other human beings behaving differently. I reacted away from Christianity as an ultimate.

~

1 Church Road, Srinagar
August 10, 1966

Yes, the reactions to Gautam's thrashing are depressing. Kikook said the subject had been all over middle class Simla and Chandigarh, and she had been 'astounded' that almost without exception it was accepted as all right. Even her father and Jivat,[79] neither of whom could she imagine as using

---

[79]Jivat Thadani, husband of Kikook (Jaya Thadani).

violence, or advocating it, had felt it was understandable, or at least had not registered any protest. Nor did Kaka. The only person who had done so in her presence was Krishen Khanna.[80] Yet the reactions are not only, as you say, society assuming that a woman is her husband's possession. That, of course, is basic. But with people like Kaka and Co. there is a definite element of jealousy, with regard to you particularly. I think you had rather endeared yourself to Chandigarh, both as yourself and as part of a background — Gautam's wife and the country mansion and hospitality. Your deviation to a distinct individual, with a will and mind of your own, creates a sense of insecurity.

Please do not be difficult about the ring. Next time we meet let us choose one together, from me for us. I have a longing for a 'symbol' between us, so do not argue about it.

~

E-8 Mafatlal Park, Bombay
August 23, 1966

The Teja affair[81] gets more and more complicated with his apparent disappearance. Mummie has written to say it is rumoured Gautam is going to marry Ranjit Teja. I doubt it, unless she is a good deal more docile than I imagine her.

August 25 – Have just heard on the news that Parliament has passed the bill to take over the Jayanti Shipping Co. This morning's paper carried a comment on Teja in Parliament and I enclose brief bits from *The Times* and *Express* regarding

---

[80] A well-known painter.
[81] Dharam Vir Teja, an industrialist who founded the Jayanti Shipping Co. He was later discredited and sought refuge in Central America.

Gautam. So now the break between Gautam and me has been announced in the Lok Sabha.

I don't believe Gautam will marry Mrs Teja but there is no doubt, since he entered the international business arena in the past few years, his standards have greatly changed. He has been drifting away from the Indian scene, and his India is more and more first class air travel and huge air-conditioned suites in hotels. And I think he will marry.

~

1 Church Road, Srinagar
August 26, 1966

Darling, much loved, and much else

You do not value yourself as a person for a very simple major reason, and that is that you have had very little opportunity to live as a person. You got married very young and stepped into a 'system', with which you made your peace, and within which you developed a constructive, pattern of living. In writing, and in bringing up children, you had your own exclusive field but I daresay you did not connect it up with your development as a person. I am surprised you have survived the 'system' you entered so early in life. But you *have* survived. And I do think you should avoid involvement and entanglement until you are certain that is where you belong. Perhaps it is just as well we have had this long period of difficult, chancy contact, when we are separated most of the time, and yet living with each other. In a way we are still at the beginning, and have a long way to go together.

~

E-8 Mafatlal Park, Bombay
September 8, 1966

In many ways I have not yet assimilated what has happened
to me. It's like being told I've grown two heads all of a sudden.
In any case how disposable, discardable I am. First it was my
body that wouldn't do because it did not come to him virgin.
Then it was my mind which he claimed had been raped.
And yet men have loved and cherished women whom other
men have wanted, and had. Men have stood by unfaithful
wives, even dreadful wives. I have stood by him in all sorts
of situations, which were strange to me and I couldn't feel
one with them or agree with them. But I never tore him to
pieces on that account. And I don't know if I've taken my full
medicine or there's more to come.

~

1 Church Road, Srinagar
September 9, 1966

No, we need not start any controversy again about our child,
as we have both decided we want it but would not have it.
But darling, we do have a 'child' already, this thing between
us, which is of us both, yours and mine. It must have had a
date of birth; it has certainly grown before our very eyes and
in our very being. So let us love and nourish it between us,
make something of it for us both to be proud of, and in time
for the world to see and accept and respect.

~

1 Church Road, Srinagar
September 20, 1966

Beloved

I have nothing to write to you as I am full of you in every part of me as if there was no separateness. What am I to say? That I liked being overfed, at every meal, every day; that I liked looking at you; that I liked being in and out of your flat and felt very much that it was my own; that I fell in love with you many times, each time more quietly and pervasively than the time before. What indeed am I to say, my beloved? What am I to enumerate to thank you for? I do not want to thank you at all. It seems so inadequate. Should I scold you, for that would help to wake me up to a separateness, and prepare me again for the long probation we still have to go through without each other.

What kind of woman are you? For even though you were troubled and burdened in spirit when I was in Bombay, I felt you were a constant presence, a constant support, a constant friend and affection. There was a kind of balm about it. I thought yesterday that you were a woman who created a background of home, peace, good order. I felt carried, surrounded, caressed with love and understanding.

I had a long talk with Sadiq yesterday. He asked me if I had enjoyed my holiday. I said I had. He added, a little slyly, I thought, 'No bee stings this time?' And I said, 'None.'

~

E-8 Mafatlal Park, Bombay
October 5, 1966

Last night I thought there was really no logic to being unhappy about being thrown out of my home, the home I had made for so many years. What is a home? It is when you come into your own place, leaving the strangers outside. And that's home. But if you widen your place in life and the world, if you make more people your concern, then there need not be that sense of release and detachment from the world on entering your own particular four walls, for then even outside your four walls is your home. And I thought there was no other answer really to happiness except that 'home' should come to mean a bigger and bigger place. I thought rather vividly of Gandhiji going to Noakhali in 1946 during the communal frenzy there, walking unarmed and unafraid into the madness as if he was walking into his own home because it was his home and those were his people. He had made them his. If I walked into my flat and found Gita brandishing a knife, I would not abandon her or be afraid of her. I would calm her. And that is what he did, with never a feeling that he was where he should not be or didn't belong. So why should I worry about being thrown out of four walls and why should that be so hard to bear? The huge impersonal world has already become mine to some extent. I do not feel strange or flounder in it. The lions do not frighten me. I even feel I can walk among them unharmed, and in time they might even lick my hand.

~

Wazarat Road, Jammu
November 15, 1966

The next few months will be a difficult period for our relationship, and its working out, and we should be prepared for that. We have been through months of tension and crucial decision. Now we will have to go through a period when there are few highlights, and we have to stick much closer to the ground, even the arid ground at times. There will be little occasion for stimulus or drama or great thoughts. We may even feel a little flat and fatigued and irritated with sheer, small, multiple practicalities, and at frequent cross-purposes regarding details with each other. I think we should both be prepared for all this and stick firm to the objective, and be patient with detail. I have also to face Champa and her reactions, and practical details with her. I say all this so that we both try and understand what we are to face. It will be a lean period, with little brightness and spark. We should not mistake its dreariness and bother as indications of lack between us. We have to go through it somehow, and together.

I am glad you mentioned the jewellery and that you enjoyed wearing it for me this time in Delhi. It was odd that I had wanted you to bring jewellery, and that I had loved seeing the heavy necklace on you. It is odd because I have been hostile to jewellery. It has seemed altogether a symbol of subservience of the sex, and a misuse of national and personal resources.

~

Wazarat Road, Jammu
November 20, 1966

Yesterday evening was highlighted by a haircut. 'The Lucky Hair Cutter' is a little hatti a few yards down Residency Road (now Vir Marg). There's a smart looking barber in charge, fair, lithe, you'd find him quite handsome. I've always had him to the house but I decided to break middle class Jammu traditions and walked into his shop for a haircut, a tiny place about 7 by 12 feet, two chairs for customers and another two behind them for people who wait. He cut my hair and parted it, without any instruction from me, on the right. I paid him Rs.2. He said he charged only Re. I at the shop, but I left it with him as a gesture of goodwill. I am certain my colleagues would have been a little taken aback if any of them had seen me. This event, and the fact that I walked to and back from office three times yesterday through smelly streets, made me wonder again how cut off my type of person is from 'native' India. The streets, mostly narrow, except the main car roads, are endless in their ramifications in this old town. There must have been an improvement scheme at one time, as they are mostly brick-paved, with a drain on each side. The drains smell foul as they carry not only the refuse but, I believe, the excreta of the population. They flow grey-black with lumps of vegetation discarded by people. But they do flow, and Jammu is lucky to be on a gradient so that it continually (and with a little rain, fully) flushes itself out to the all-absorbing, all-suffering river Tawi, which takes the refuse through miles of Indian and then Pakistani countryside to the sea. And I felt a strong link with this real India, this dust and squalor and poverty. I felt a haunting sense of guilt that I did not belong, that I was cut off in the method and manner I lived. After all, this society, this poverty, this squalour has fed me, made me, and maintained me in my special way for fifty years. And I could almost see its skeleton fingers stuffing bread into my mouth.

~

E-8 Mafatlal Park, Bombay
November 29, 1966

I went to Jeh and Thelly's party for the BOAC chief. The talk among the Indians was bitterly, deadly anti-government, even to a point of farce and unreality. Duggie Sawhney[82] said, 'I say the Americans are fighting our battle in Vietnam and I don't care who knows it.' Bobby Kooka[83] said, 'Ayub's a damn good chap, a clean soldier. What we need is a soldier here, not these

---

[82]Lesile Sawhney who was married to J.R.D. Tata's sister, Dabe.
[83]An Air India executive at the time.

dirty politicians.' It was left to an Englishman to say mildly that he did not think a dictatorship here would be such a good idea. Mrs Hamilton[84] sat very close to me and I got lost and buried in her millions of wrinkles and her brilliant green eyeshadow. She was wearing a harem-pants outfit, a Hollywood version of what the Sultan's favourite would wear when she entertained him. What was I doing there?

~

Wazarat Road, Jammu
November 30, 1966

And last evening on the telephone you have raised another difficulty about the ring. Please don't go around the subject like that. It doesn't matter if it looks like a wedding ring; it should. So please don't be difficult.

I feel the circle of 'fatality and finality' has gone round full and I know we will face the rest, and the future, together.

~

1 Church Road, Srinagar
December 2, 1966

You mentioned daily letter-writing and I was taken back to the first I heard of this, from a man named C.B. Young who was Professor of English at St Stephens. This was not my subject but I had quite a lot to do with him as I was Secretary of the Dramatic Society for some years and he did a lot of ticket-selling with the barra sahibs of Delhi. They were mostly English then and we used to go round from house to house

---

[84]A visitor from Britain.

selling tickets. I was added, I think, as 'local colour'. On one of our excursions he told me he dropped a line every day to his wife when she was on leave in England. She was Principal of Lady Hardinge (Dr Ruth Young), earned three times his professorial missionary salary, and was said to 'wear the pants', mostly because she was less absentminded than he, more attentive to the world and its affairs. I said something like 'Surely there's not much to say every day.' He said, 'Of course there is not, but then I do write; it's become necessary.' It seemed quite crazy, till Kaval and I started writing, about 1954 or '55, about thrice a week, and in '62 it became almost a daily business. But she wrote briefly. I also wrote much more briefly, except on occasions when I'd describe something or propound a theory. And then came—you—and you are as much, and more, responsible for the habit between us than I am. I had to discipline myself very much from January '65 owing to your circumstances. We had a drill about it. And yet we did write. It seemed necessary, and has continued necessary.

And you wrote some days ago that you were 'very patient'. It does seem incredible to me that in these many years you did not get caught up in the sheer atmosphere around you of defining an attachment as love, of seeing it that way, though later you may discover it was not the genuine thing. At the time most people accept it as that. And I shall always wonder how this happened with you, for it is most unusual, and I do not know of a single person of our class or background who has had a similar experience. There must be something terribly restrained in you, and terribly true to an integrity, to have survived so many years in the kind of milieu you experienced. One day when there is time, we must talk of this.

We must consider how long we will wait for something to turn up at Delhi. Government affairs drag on for months. If there are signs of delay, which would mean that I just stay on here or at Chandigarh, then should we take the plunge when the divorce is through, of my putting in my papers, and roughing it out the best way we can regarding work for the future?

~

1 Church Road, Srinagar
December 5, 1966

I cannot imagine what Mrs Hamilton's 'harem pants' looked like or what the Sultan's favourite would wear when she entertained him—I should have thought very little. And it is embarrassing when Indians run down Indians, government included, in the presence of foreigners. It is a continual lack of confidence in our environment and its leaders. Does a 'good general' (like Bobby Kooka's Ayub) help? A dictatorship is rather like clapping a man onto the surgeon's table, where in the privacy of the hospital, and under special knowhow, he is deprived of messy material, patched up, and put on his feet. The question is whether healthy tissue will be cut away too, apart from the possibility that with a people you cannot just cut away material (like an appendix) as it reappears through the generations, unless it is changed by the process of education and experience.

I have to assess myself as a party, to an extent, to the Kooka creed of 'a good soldier, not a dirty politician'. I would understand this country accepting communism, and would not oppose it, or assist it. The only kind of government I'd oppose would be a communal-fascist type. And why was it 'left to an Englishman' to oppose dictatorship here. What did Tara think, and what did she say? Or did she merely listen? And if so, why?

I am glad you have looked at some rings. I now will leave it to you to do the needful and not take too long about it.

Over the weekend I decided I'd live till the age of 94. My grandmother died at that age and I don't see why I should not.

So I thought, my beloved, that I'd plague you for forty years and I was quite pleased with the idea of seeing you eighty or so yourself, and wondered what you'd look like. That's how I feel about living with you, and I've never had any such ambition before. Please agree with me, fully and immediately.

I was pleased on Saturday when Ghulam Ahmed Sheikh[85] said something which he meant as a compliment. We were discussing who should be Commissioner, Srinagar when Anwar Karim[86] goes on leave to Bihar. Sadiq has decided Nasir Ali[87] should act as Commissioner plus his present job. I told this to Sheikh, adding, 'I am doubtful if Nasir will like it. He'll have to stay in Srinagar at a very cold time.' Sheikh said, 'Nasir will take it in his stride. He is much more philosophic and mature now. You've had that effect on many of us. I, for instance. Even if a man swears at me I keep my head now and do not go off the rails as I used to.' I said it was a pity if I had thwarted his 'youthful exuberance' and he said exuberance was all right, but ego was another matter.

~

Wazarat Road, Jammu
December 11, 1966

Have been with you a lot today—before the station, getting there, in the train, and now, if it is running to schedule, you must be between Godhra and Dohad, perhaps dinner at the latter.

I started the social game in quite another world from yours, at quite another time. I was landed in a highly artificial,

---

[85]Secretary to the Government of Jammu and Kashmir, working directly under the Chief Secretary.

[86]Commissioner of Srinagar region.

[87]Agha Nasir Ali.

but highly developed, Anglo-Indian social order. I was entirely on my own, far from my background, both parents dead, literally no contacts in the Punjab. Society's tone was set by the English. The clubs were dominated by them. The Indian official served English food in his house. The non-official Indian kept aloof. There was much hunting and shooting and cards and the like. Where was I in all this? Rather bewildered. I naturally wanted to get on, do well. I was at the start of a career. As a human being I felt a little guilty that I was in such a set-up. I felt a little determined to show myself Indian. I felt ashamed that we copied so entirely a western form of social behaviour. So it was a mixed reaction. And I kept out of it except on my own terms. I was never a member of the famous Gymkhana at Lahore though I could have been. I called the occasional Englishman to my house and gave him Indian food and mixed company. I went to their homes sometimes but hardly ever to their social institutions. I missed out much of the organized entertainment. I was not 'one of the boys'. I was, in a way, always myself, and could not conform. Before I was shattered out of Lahore in the catastrophe of 1947, I had my place in the social set-up, though a small place, yet an effective and happy one, not a powerful one. In 1947-54 I was a club man, associated with all the social efforts at Simla and Chandigarh as a sort of duty to get the institutions going. But then I gave it up, and was again an individual, pursuing and touching society on my own terms, as myself, and not accepting what was done or expected.

I never endeavoured to establish contact of a social kind with the higher-ups in Delhi, political or civil service. I felt they neither had the time, nor I the inclination.

December 12 – If the train goes well, you must be getting near Mathura now, not so far from destiation. I hope you have written to me on the train. And now, my darling, beautiful, well beloved—I could say more but will save you a collection of adjectives, but I felt I should say some, as we are likely to start quarrelling soon after we meet this evening!

~

74/Sector 9-A, Chandigarh
January 1, 1967

My own darling

May it be a year of constructive action for you, and for us. There are difficult days ahead. I suppose an accumulated realization of all this seized me in a kind of frenzy last night. Please write and tell me we are together and strong. I want to be with you as I leave, and when I am away. I am devoted to you. My love for 1967 and always.

Bunchi

~

74/Sector 9-A, Chandigarh
January 6, 1967

We left Guddo's[88] at 11:10, and passed Noni and Gitu, on a single cycle, on the main road from the station. I would have stopped, but did not notice them till I had gone past, so waved frantically when I did. It seemed a last glimpse of you, and as I drove out of Chandigarh I thought that they came from your body, and I was filled with a new wonder and tenderness at an old and well-known fact. As I drove away from Chandigarh and you, and knew I could not drive back, I thought of the times we were together—12:15 when I would shout 'Tara' at

_____
[88]Mrs Navin Thakur, a friend.

the 'begum's balcony', hoping you would appear; 4:30 when we would walk across the road, with the feel of your hand, as if already in mine, as soon as the *cho* hid us from the imagined binoculars of the Boat Club, and the not so imagined eyes of the odd person cutting wood or grazing cattle near the *cho*. And was it only yesterday I was eagerly waiting for 8:05 when I would pick you up and bring you to drinks at our house?

~

Anokha, 32/Sector 5-A, Chandigarh
January 5, 1967

Your departure has depressed me very much and now there will be months without you. I've grown dependent on your daily presence, your voice calling up to me at noon—and at 4:30 there will be no one to walk with.

The children all collected while I was packing, and quite unpremeditated, I decided to talk to them, telling them I was upset with Gautam on the score of Noni's further education, which he was doing nothing about. From there I got onto the coming divorce. I do not generally get near the subject without feeling distressed and showing it, but managed not to get too emotional, and was very conscious of three young persons, torn in two, giving me their affection, yet wishing perhaps that they didn't have to listen. But I thought it best to go through with it, and did. I said that after the separation I had decided to live my life fully and not to mope, and that it was not my idea of life to sit around waiting to grow old and die—(this brought some weak laughs)—but that I intended to stay very busy, work hard, get lots of joy out of living and share that joy with them. Noni wept a bit surreptitiously as I talked. We even ended up rather cheerfully, and feeling rather close, which lasted all through lunch. After lunch Ranjit went off to Mark's, and the girls and I sat on the veranda talking of divorce and sex and family planning and politics. I did not think of going upstairs to rest, and they did not budge either, and it was a most sweet and full experience. I felt my love and friendship for them could soften their hurts, and my confidence continued all through the walk Gitu and I took together, stopping several times to 'drink in the view'—her phrase.

~

E-8 Mafatlal Park, Bombay
January 16, 1967

The whole day has been spent shifting my things to Noni's room, which I am now sharing with Gita, to give Noni a room of her own. Ranjit and his friend Jimmy Mody moved all the furniture, but I had piles of books and clothes to rearrange. It took hours. I don't know what I would have done without Ranjit. He has mended fuses, washed walls of stains, been to the PO for me, and shopped, and I have a list of things for him to attend to tomorrow. He does it all with such willingness and love. There is so much sweetness in this child. And as I got into bed I felt suddenly glad to be with Gitu and realized I'd been lonely in the other room, listening if I woke at night, to the eerie sound of the sea. Now I feel I have links and roots. It's odd, as I thought I'd mind sharing.

Now that the children have been removed from Gautam's horizon, a return to normalcy for him will mean forgetting about them. I am terribly afraid he will consider his duty done if he gives them lunch at the Intercontinental twice a year. S.S. Grewal said in Chandigarh, 'He never meant to hit you. That was just by the way.' So he will not 'mean' to deprive the children of all the opportunities that are their due, but he'll just do so, without a qualm.

No, you don't 'interfere' about the children. I don't know how I'd manage it all alone and I count on your help and advice. I feel miserable at the thought of Ranjit's departure at the end of the month. The flat will be very empty without him and I will have lost a handyman as well as a support.

~

Wazarat Road, Jammu
January 18, 1967

I think the really nice thing about my family was that it never quarrelled, nor had any strains within itself about money or property or goods. I used not to think this remarkable till I entered a world where this was a common phenomenon amongst families. There has been a full trust between us and never a murmur or a suspicion of any kind.

It is difficult to associate your efficiency with a glandular condition—which is what you call your depression, saying it makes you linger in the shades and shadows of death. Anyway, I thought, I love her glands, whatever they make her say or do.

~

Wazarat Road, Jammu
Republic Day 1967

Nayantara, I am cooking. This morning a present from the Transport Commissioner arrived, two birds, from Srinagar. I have put them on slow heat with salt, onion, garlic, tomato, ghee, etc. I'm told that works. Let's hope it does. It sizzles (slowly) at my side. Wish you were here, need you badly, not to cook, my beloved, but to be with me. I'd cook for you if you gave me a chance, which I'm sure you would not do, for the wrong reason, that a woman should cook. I never thought I'd fall in love with a woman who accepted her womanhood, but I have. I hardly believe it.

January 27 – DP and Co. stayed till 9:15 last night, then DP whisked my meat off to his house (next door now) and I dined there.

I'm glad you've put Noni on a special reading routine followed by discussion with you, and a review of the book later. That should cover at least some background reading these next few months. And the French may open up a new set of contacts, apart from the language itself. I have written to Noni about another curry I cooked, sitting here in my study, a stove at my side. What are you worried about, darling mine? I will help you with your children. There is much more that is going well than badly. If we bring up these children well, they will face the world, and do it well. You cannot guarantee everything in advance, and one should not be too fearful for the morrow.

With reference to jobs, my whole priority is yourself and us, and I keep that in the foreground. I am certainly not making a change except on the basis of a definite proposition. If nothing materializes, then at some stage we will have to cut the cackle and decide what is the best we can do. I am not willing to chase two moons. You are the moon, and the other moon will have to be dealt with practically, and not take me from you. We must discuss all this in March when we meet. Can we now close our ranks and face what comes with faith and confidence?

~

E-8 Mafatlal Park, Bombay
March 1, 1967

Perhaps I should begin by telling you the divorce was granted this morning. I felt a mounting fright over the court appearance and prayed for some sort of equilibrium to see me through. We each had to go into the witness box in turn to answer some routine questions. And then it was over. And we'd been divorced. In the courtyard Gautam put an arm around me and said he'd take me home and in the car I started to cry. He took out his dark glasses and put them on and looked about to cry himself. Then he started upbraiding me, saying I had brought it to this, and I quarrelled back. And the whole thing was incredible and childish considering we had just been divorced. The divorce decree did not seem to have made a scrap of difference to the crisis and its impact, all the long months of it, and the year of separation after it. We were quarrelling as if it was all still relevant.

I felt all evening I loved you in an enduring, absolute way, and if that is so, how can a marriage that was dissloved today still play upon my feelings and emotions and continue to haunt me? How in heaven's name do people marry and divorce so blithely and with such apparent ease in the West? The word sticks in my throat though I've said it several times to the children to prove that it doesn't stick. The predominant feeling is of having been axed, lopped off like a dead branch, instead of kept like the living branch one is. An act like this should have been impossible. Yet I should have grown used to the idea, since Gautam lost no time in ordering me out of his house in Chandigarh in December 1964. But the mind does not accept such a solution. I felt it should not happen to Champa. So what comfort can I give you for the 'mountain' you now face of your break with her?

~

E-8 Mafatlal Park, Bombay
March 13, 1967

When I write every thought and feeling (even if it lasts for a day or a few minutes) I never think of you or that its result might be devastating. You deserve better from me. And darling, nothing I wrote was intended as a re-thinking. Let us be absolutely out in the open. I have no inhibitions about that any more. You must know that I am beside you, in all that we have been through, and what is yet to come, in this dreadful, inevitable drama. We seem to have been so long on this exhausting journey. I somehow recoil from being cast in the role (in Champa's letter) of a woman who breaks up a home. Above all, I have a wild desire to get all this behind us, to emerge whole and together out of this maze once and for all.

~

Wazarat Road, Jammu
March 30, 1967

Faith and belief are extremely important to people like you and me. They have been crucial to you in this whole crisis and without them you would not have withstood the shock you had to take. Faith and belief (and confidence) are not what I created, but what we created between us. It would be difficult to unravel my contribution from yours; they were inextricably one. But one of us can unmake it or put it to great strain. My attitude has been quite constant; the changes have been within you, as your change to 'two roofs'. It drove you back into yourself, an independent and isolated individual, and not forward to a new nuance, or a new texture of joint comradeship. I do not suggest you should not be yourself, or should not change, but there has to be an awareness of a partnership you have created. After all, I am a partner; after all, I am a friend; after all, you love me; after all, we lived and practised an idea of ourselves, a pattern, between us. Am I to blame if I continue to want it? Does not some responsibility rest with you for definition, if you change it?

~

E-8 Mafatlal Park, Bombay
March 30, 1967

I began your birthday with a visit from A.J. Shah (who is Ashok's tax man and now also looks after my mother's affairs). He is quite appalled by the 'Consent Terms' and says the note you drew up is quite correct. He thought Shri Bhai, who has been advising me, was 'Mr Sahgal's man.' 'If he is not Mr Sahgal's man, does he have any idea what living costs are in Bombay? How can he have agreed to these terms? You are absolutely stripped. And Mr Sahgal has saved himself a large amount of taxation.' He was quite taken aback by the terms, kept saying, 'Where is the philanthropy in this? I heard there had been some.' What did the children get? I said the children and I together, for all expenses, got Rs.2,000 per month. It is incredible that the 'rate of tax' question did not strike Shri Bhai and he assured me again and again I would not be tax-burdened on account of Gautam's shares.

It is a bit incongruous that I should be breaking through to some joy over us just when you are deep in the heart of your separation problem, and this tax news has hit me. Perhaps you will even be amused by my new-found determination.

~

Wazarat Road, Jammu
April 4, 1967

I have been taken aback, even infuriated, at what you say about the tax situation. I cannot believe Gautam would do such a thing. It is a simple matter of justice, and that you allow and dispense even to a stranger, even to an enemy when war is over and there is truce. But it appears even worse than injustice, for it tilts the thing finally and fully against you, and your personal income has to take the *whole* burden of the higher rates. This change between the old terms (where he paid at 'average' rates of tax) and the final terms (where he pays as if you had no other income) seems diabolical, though the original, to which I had objected, was bad enough. You cannot and must not accept this enormity as it will maim your effort at independence. If necessary, you have to fight it. Gautam must create a trust, whatever the taxes involved, and you should be finally rid of this mix-up with him financially. You have been cheated and you must protect yourself.

I spoke with committed and strong feeling about you, and about myself, to DP. I think he was quite shaken at the conviction. I said I did not feel immoral at all. He said, 'You do not know yourself. Nobody has ever thought you immoral— nobody has ever uttered the word—nobody has thought Tara immoral. Both of you are *known*.' He also said, 'You are intellectually an iconoclast. You do not allow humbug. But emotionally you are humane and kind. The mind is saved by the feelings. Here, however, you have integrated both in headlong decision. And you are committing suicide.' He said he would say exactly the same of you.

~

13 Akbar Road
May 7, 1967

Rita's[89] information is that Shri Bhai arrived today on the evening plane, was met at the airport by Gautam, embraced by him, and both drove away in Gautam's car. It sounds arranged, and for a purpose. And the implications of this get-together chilled me.

~

Church Road, Srinagar
May 9, 1967

I cannot understand the deliberately untrue statements Gautam has made to Kikook. He talks of your 'control' over the money in your name, whereas you clearly have none at all. He says you will be a very rich woman whereas none of the money is yours. Above all his saying you will pay no taxes on it when you remarry is not borne out by the agreement. Perhaps he is bothered by what he has done and is making a special effort to undo the impression it may create. I think Shri Bhai has played a double game, since a man of his experience could not possibly have misunderstood the terms of the agreement.

My week with you has done me a great deal of good. I feel a strength and nearness of you as if you were still there. We must develop an attitude and policy towards the next phase. We are bound to hear talk of various kinds, that you are a loose woman, or I lecherous, and we should take it with equanimity. We have created a strong instrument between us, which is inviolable, and will stand by us. We must lean on it.

---

[89]Rita Dar, Nayantara Sahgal's sister.

I met Kuldip Nayar's[90] brother at the drink party at Nedou's and he mentioned 'many rumours' about me. I took the bull by the horns and said, 'You mean the scandal,' and explained that I intended ignoring that kind of thing. He said he thought the Kashmiri pandits were hostile to me as I had tried to carry out government's policy for representation of Muslims in the services, and the like. I said I had considerable sympathy for them, as a small minority with the fear and spectre of Pakistan making a long-term future for them rather difficult and uncertain. (Sadiq has told me Champa had talked a great deal whenever you visited Srinagar last year and implied she was responsible for much of the chit-chat. He also told me he had talked to her mother at a party, perhaps six weeks ago, and told her he understood that when Champa and I married, I had defined clearly that I was not certain of my feelings—I do not know how he got this information—and Mrs Singha admitted this was so.)

I am glad to hear you have been eating well in Chail though I do not quite believe it. Except for gulab jamuns and gelebies I don't think I've ever seen you get into your food with zest or gusto.

~

Chail
May 16, 1967

Darling, I can feel your 'constant dread' in this entirely new phase for us, with your side of the problem looming large. This, combined with the 'scandal' talk makes this a particularly harrowing period. It is rather sad, too, that 'scandal' is synonymous with 'divorce' when the two things are quite different. I suppose they aren't in the Indian

---

[90]A well-known journalist.

mind and a divorce is viewed as disgraceful. Yet it is many marriages that strike me as disgraceful and scandalous, but that's another story. You seem so surrounded by an aura of opposition, disapproval, and even hostility that I feel a little frantic, as if you were being thrown to the wolves and I were watching, helpless. Only we must not consider ourselves helpless. The helpless do not travel so far against so many odds.

This Chail countryside is curiously bland, ideal for soothing and quieting a ruffled mind. There is nothing in the way of emphasis. The air is clean and cool, but not enough to exhilarate. The woods are dense, but with a cultivatedness about them. Nothing runs wild. Even the sun sets without our noticing it almost. It just slips gently out of sight and there is the barest tingle of colour in the sky at the time. It was Gitu who pointed this out to me, saying she waited for the sky to get painted pink as it does in Bombay but the sun just disappeared without warning. And the silence, though deep, is soft and friendly, not the kind to harbour secrets and create mysteries.

~

1 Church Road, Srinagar
May 20, 1967

It is bad luck that all this should happen when a Nehru (of Indi's type) is in power. It is now clear I will never go right to the top of what the ICS can bring. And I do not grieve at all. I have never kept even half an eye on it, never lined up for the contacts and build-up for it. What struck me was another thought—that I was willing as a young MA, with a first class first in my pocket (and very proud of it) to join St. Stephens at 250 a month, with perhaps a rise to 700 in advanced years, with a chance of a professorship or a University job at a higher figure. Today I hesitate to retire on 1100 which I estimate I will have after meeting obligations to Champa, and the like. How times have changed. How *I* have changed perhaps? And I have wished ardently (like you so often have about your dependence on Gautam for the children) that I could throw it all up, quit the government. It would also be an immediate solution for us. But I seem as bound to this job as you are to Gautam and his finances for the children. I had all these, and other long thoughts this morning, that I would stand *my* ground, the ground they cannot touch. I'd be proud of my deviation, for it is wholly worthwhile and wholly lovely, with you. So do not, darling, tell me to go back from our plan. Just be with me, my friend and my wife. I am strengthened by the fact that you would join me in Kashmir if nothing else works out, and I want to hold you to that, for I am certain we should not continue separated much longer.

~

1 Church Road, Srinagar
May 24, 1967

We saw *My Fair Lady* at the Broadway cinema last evening. Bits and implications of the picture made me feel rather bolshy about us—the reference to middle class morals. I suddenly had a great desire that you and I should never, even as a principle, bother about marriage. It seemed so unnecessary, a blot to have a legal tie between two persons. We have been so beautifully and utterly loyal and devoted to each other these last years, and there has been a complete commitment between us which neither of us has ever doubted. Would not a legal tie weaken this rather than enhance it, make it something of the courts rather than the souls of us?

I also realized I was on the brink of a revolutionary action in my life regarding work, should Garware[91] make me an offer. If I accepted it, I would be turning my whole past upside down, and abandoning it forever. I would be 'casting my net upon the waters'—and the waters were Nayantara. It also seemed apt that I should do such a thing, put myself to test again—though I wondered if it was wise, and if there was something of the gambler in me—but it seemed inapt not to try. And I am glad, very glad, my sweetheart, that you would be with me even 'in some planless capacity (!), and we would still be together in whatever way we could possibly work out.' For we will have to face a long period of illegitimacy. This procedure will take a full five years for remarriage—three years after registration to apply for a divorce, plus one to wait for a decree, plus one to permit remarriage. Going down to Chandigarh in July for the registration has added to my problems, and you must remain with me, whatever the difficulties. In a way we expected all this.

Yesterday while Champa played badminton with Jagdip[92] I walked the loop where you and I have been so often. My thoughts were full of our predicament and the delays we face with this divorce law. But I also felt you were my rock, and would be there for me, and there was nothing basically to worry about, except that I was sick and sorry I could not give you marriage with me, whole, ordinary and everyday.

~

---

[91] An industrial house.
[92] A friend of Champa Mangat Rai's, and lecturer at the Government College for Women, Chandigarh.

1 Church Road, Srinagar
May 31, 1967

Sadiq sent for me and I told him I would stay on. And, darling, we will have to put our minds to how and when you can come.

~

E-8 Mafatlal Park, Bombay
June 3, 1967

It is strange and poignant what you say—that for the first time there is complete honesty between you and Champa. There was never that between Gautam and me, even now, neither on the personal nor on the financial level. I hope you're right that Champa 'has achieved freedom in this truth'. I understand too well what you are going through, conscience, the whole past, all that. It is all too close to the nerve for me, too. No words or arguments can make a break easier. This is certainly not true of some couples, and some nationalities, who seem to break without bleeding, take it in their stride. I wonder what there is about them, or their culture, that they can do it, and what is there about you and me that reduces us so miserably to pulp in our respective situations?

You talk of explaining us to the children. But, my dearest Nirmal, we haven't even been able to explain us to adult society; how are we going to carry the children with us?

I notice you never say 'my mother-in-law' but always 'the mother-in-law'. I'm glad you can call me 'my darling'!

~

23 Safdarjung Road, New Delhi
June 16, 1967

My beloved Nayantara

I hope this will be waiting for you on your arrival at Bombay, as I hate the idea of your getting there, or anywhere, without something of me with you. Now that we have had these few hours here together, and all the facts of the future seem clear, the time it will take to get a divorce, work for me at J & K, the income tax issue to be fought out and reckoned with, we should face it with affirmation. I wish most ardently, and daily, that we could marry. But it seems that all I can give you, beloved, is the thought that I have never wanted to marry anyone, at any time, the way I have wanted to marry you. I want it passionately. But that does not help.

~

1 Church Road, Srinagar
June 26, 1967

L.P. Singh[93] rang up midday that Ashoka Mehta, Minister for Petroleum and Chemicals, has agreed I should be appointed Special Secretary to his Ministry. My first reaction was one of shock rather than relief. But that seems settled and I am to be in Delhi presumably from August, and the implications of all this have been going through me—where would I stay, where should we look for accommodation for you, when would you shift, and so on. I've also been in a bit of a fever about your dismantling your home in Bombay, and have been nostalgic for its loveliness and order, as if one were destroying something.

---

[93]Home Secretary, Government of India.

Mahmuda has been saying for some time that she wanted to see me, and made an appointment to do so at office yesterday. She skirted round the personal, said I had not talked to her, and implied all the talk had been from Champa, and therefore one-way. She said she was glad I had taken a 'stand'. She said she had heard 'the lady' was insisting on this decision for a divorce. I said that was wholly untrue and there had been nothing of that kind. She said she thought so too, and had not believed what she'd heard, and added I was 'very lucky' and that 'a considerable sacrifice' was involved on your side, though she'd been told you were 'grabbing'. She did not believe you were.

I wish I could get away from all this to you, and some peace.

~

1 Church Road, Srinagar
June 29, 1967

Making love. I find you a continual wonder and sustenance. I can only give the analogy of nature, though that is not a good analogy, but each time I come to Srinagar the chinar takes my breath away, and so with the sight of water, of paddy fields swayed in the breeze, and much else. So it is with you, each time a new experience that takes my breath away, perpetually worthwhile, constantly lovely, constantly mine. And that I think is the crux of it, a constancy about you and your giving which is neither abandon nor restraint, but a quality of both, and sometimes one is stronger, and sometimes the other. But there is a feeling of complete giving, and I feel I am at home, in my very home. I am aware, yet gone, as if in something purer, chaster, more innocent and stronger than myself, as if your spirit ran in my veins and partook of the texture of my skin.

~

E-8 Mafatlal Park, Bombay
July 1, 1967

My darling Nirmal

I was glad to know the arrangements about your departure.
I will think of you on the 6th, and then at Jammu, which has
become ours, before you get to Chandigarh. And I'm so glad
Delhi is to be the new chapter. Perhaps it is good even for a
'provincial officer' who loves 'a smaller canvas' to shift to a
new stage. The shift has its challenges and this time we shall
face them together.

Your mother's handwriting is not easy, and her letters
don't give me very much in the way of what sort of person
she was. I think better of Arthur[94] after reading his old letters.
He seems to have gone headlong into his experience with
Champa and made no bones about it, even to the extent of
detailed arrangements. And your attitude was that she was
a free agent and must do as she wishes. Champa's attitude is
the riddle, for while you and Arthur were able to talk frankly,
even to the extent of practical details, she did not say a word.
Why? And in the end how did he leave without her? And
why did she say nothing when the affair between them was
known? It was no secret. I've also felt it is strange how people
when they judge a situation—like ours—tackle it in its present
framework, and never historically.

I wear the 'wedding ring' on my right hand, beneath my
other ring.

I have got used to you in Petroleum and Chemicals and
have been reading every item about fertilisers, etc. that I find
in the papers.

~

---

[94]Arthur Lall, a friend.

74/Sector 9-A, Chandigarh
July 27, 1967

Priobala[95] had another talk with me, more collected in tone but hardly in content. She asked if you were divorced, and when I said yes, 'Well Gautam is a normal man' and almost with regret, 'It's a wonder he did not get you thrashed.'

I'm so glad you have worn the ring. It has given me joy each time I have thought of it. Darling, you've written almost a page about our child, and I am not at all convinced. I think we should try and have it.

Yes, Arthur was very downright and straight about his attachment to Champa, in every way true with it. That's why he and I could respect each other in that whole affair. You are also right that I was not 'involved'. It almost happened outside me, even though my sister and my wife were involved. Also, I really believed in freedom, and experiments and mistakes were part of it. Champa's behaviour even today seems incredible. Arthur and Sheila and I were corresponding; Champa was, I know, corresponding with Arthur; all of us knew all the facts; and yet Champa never talked of them with me. Between us it was never mentioned until last year.

I was tested, and almost broken, by my idealism. I prescribed and worshipped personal freedom; to me it has been as crucial as political freedom, and once political freedom was gained, more crucial. And personal freedom, as you know, I have never conceived of except in terms of truth. It is not a matter of doing what you value; it is a matter of being what you value, and being is a daily business, not an occasional activity. Thus truth becomes the glory and the disaster, the condition and the stumbling block of personal freedom. In my marriage I think I met the biggest personal

---

[95]Priobala Mangat Rai, E.N. Mangat Rai's sister.

daily challenge to this conception. Champa had no use for this kind of truth. It seemed academic, theoretical, even cruel, certainly unnecessary. And I had to live my creed with her. What is your belief worth if it does not work? Freedom (specially when it is not understood) involves suffering, and part of the suffering has, on occasions, to be one's own. So in a way my marriage has been a challenge to my whole value system. Whether I have proved that system correct is doubtful, but I have certainly retained it as worthwhile for myself, worth trying for again.

~

E-8 Mafatlal Park, Bombay
July 29, 1967

Your tax note and the new complication we face went round and round in my brain last night. Then I woke up several times with a cyclonic wind howling round the house, a huge, heavy, persistent sound, and pelting rain with it, quite terrifying. I thought the building would go over. The wind got mixed up with taxes and both howled like fiends. In the morning I wrote a letter to Muhsin incorporating the two main points you mentioned. You have made suggestions of Gautam filling the gap if the share income falls below 2000 and this is a vital point. But I have noticed Gautam never wishes to be bothered with provisions outside a main proposal. He wants a package deal and an end to the matter. So it is no good asking him to fill in gaps. All this has to be safeguarded by a trust.

The novel is done.[96] I still have no title and I am dissatisfied about not having made enough of it. I greatly regret my mental pressures and strains of the past months. My problem has been

---

[96]*Storm in Chandigarh.*

a total inability to unwind, have eaten meals on a taut tight stomach, gone to sleep with a muddled mind. It amuses me to see myself as others see me—a person devoted to myself and my satisfactions, with a colossal bank account, and a vast appetite for pleasure and 'scalp' collection.

I have often done exactly what you advise: 'I am very much like you, and if ever you are at a loss to understand me about anything, put yourself in my place, and I do not think you will be far wrong.' And that works, almost infallibly, I think. I have got into tune with you, entered another rhythm, become conscious of different kinds of needs. You will say I have got back to myself in this, not something that has happened to me through you. That may be so. The fact is I am not where I was for years. I'm on another level.

~

74/Sector 9-A, Chandigarh
August 7, 1967

Champa signed the application for registration yesterday, thirty days residence having been completed. The signature was accompanied by a rather unhappy aura and I felt quite shattered by it. Priobala said, 'I suppose the ICS are like the maharajas who just put aside one woman and took another.' I left the room, infuriated that a matter so serious should be treated in such an utterly ridiculous way. In the evening over tea Champa said to Priobala, 'Shall we call Bunchi Hitler, or Caligula, or Al Capone?' It has been painful, and I have been very much aware of the break-up of a home and a past for Champa.

Jagdip has written urging reconsideration and that in any event I should legally settle the house and such money as I proposed on Champa. She says she understands I 'helped Tara at each stage of her settlement, to protect her interests'. Little does she know how futile any efforts I (we) made about your monstrous tax/financial settlement have proved. Mrs G.D. Khosla[97] has told Khushwant that your mother 'summoned' me and demanded I marry you. I am shocked at the lies people invent. My brother has written from America, 'From all we have heard Tara's marriage was in a precarious state for some time, and not because of Bunchi.' It angers me that people have the impression that Gautam was in any case in difficulties with you, and I am at a loss to understand how this has been accepted. Perhaps Champa has given Raj this idea.

~

23 Safdarjung Road, New Delhi
August 27, 1967

I wrote my first longish note yesterday on a file dealing with synthetic detergents and felt quite happy that I had got something off my chest. I went to the Ashoka last evening for the opening ceremony of Indane (an IOC product). Ashok Mehta presided. I was very much a stranger but thought I should show my face around a bit at official functions. Was glad to escape after an hour.

Ref. people's assessment about us which you find 'unbearable', you must not feel like that for it is not true. Given Gautam's temperament and to an extent, Champa's, neither of them has accepted *us* on merits. It is what they have said that has got around. You and I have been mostly quiet, except about taxes. We have tried to understand motivation. I could have told people Gautam has thrashed you in my presence. Yet I have not said it to a soul. And surely that is the right thing. That is us. And the talk will right itself. Now

---

[97]Wife of Justice G.D. Khosla.

that we enter a new phase of living together, we must have a definite policy—to make the truth between us manifest, for it has sustained us through excruciating turmoil. The children, too, must see that we belong, and it will give them, eventually, some base of certainty and good health. Tell me you will never allow yourself to be hurt by the talk; a hurt person cannot be whole, and we need to be whole.

I was present at a discussion Nayak,[98] the Secretary, had with Esso, I was struck by the tread and temper of it. There is obviously tension between Esso and the government. I asked Nayak about it after they left and he said Esso particularly (Burmah Shell less so) have never liked the Indianizing of oil control, through imports from Russia, the creation of the IOC. They have a strong lobby with their government and think they can lay down the law to India, in view of our dependence on the US for food.

~

74/Sector 9-A, Chandigarh
September 7, 1967

I arrived at 5:15 am and took in the dark still, a scooter which splashed through water at the depression of the Sukhna Cho, and as I came into town the light was brighter, and I thought of my association with this place. In a way I helped to build it as I dealt with finance then, and many of the projects here were evolved with my association. I don't know why I thought of all this, and then of the solidity of my own house. It is solid, N, it may not be pretty, it may not be remembered, but it will last. It is very middle class. That is what I am when you remove the veneer.

[98]P.R. Nayak, Secretary, Ministry of Petroleum and Chemicals, Government of India.

The registration was over about 5:30 pm. I have felt a bit like a story of Edgar Allan Poe about a man pinned to a bed in the middle of a room, from whose roof a pendulum swings slowly, inexorably from one end to the other, being slowly lowered at every swing, and the hook attached to it scratches and rescratches the man at each swing, going deeper and deeper into his stomach and entrails. Anyway this registration has been a nightmare and it is finished. The moral challenge has been faced and now translated into an act of public acceptance. But the law must have its pound of flesh and flesh is always at the cost of human beings. If the law asks me to wait for you five years, I cannot accept that as morally binding on me, or even reasonable. So let us regard ourselves as rid of extraneous considerations. I will regard you as my wife, my friend, my chosen, my loved, my soul. This has been the most difficult period in my life. I have never faced such prolonged strain. I have come through for I have loved you dearly. It cannot be that with the signing of a document all the turmoil is over. It is not. Yet this is an 'outward and visible sign' of faith and dedication, from which this whole thing began, and developed. I have thought at times of both my father and my grandfather setting out on paths of individual, self-chosen belief, and taking the consequences, in acts which must have been difficult, at times almost impossible. Both of them would have repudiated what I set out to do, yet why should not this love of a man for a woman be like the love of man for God?

As I was leaving Chandigarh I felt a separation had been achieved with friendliness and goodwill intact, that I have not abandoned Champa, in fact, re-established myself with her on a basis of freedom and truth, which could be a source of strength, that I would be interested in her welfare and do all I could for it. And you must help me. I ask you particularly, for you are my life, and we will live together and influence each other in a daily way.

My train left at 1 am. And that was goodbye to Chandigarh for the present.

~

23 Safdarjung Road, New Delhi
September 13, 1967

I paid a long visit to A.N. Kirpal[99] last evening to discuss your case. He said the agreement was 'vicious' and was surprised you had agreed to it. He is examining the rather far-fetched idea that the share income could be assessed separately as an 'association of persons'.

You mention 'settling the fee' for my work on your tax problem. I have settled the fee before I took the brief and it is a heavy and continuous fee. It is you. I have settled for you about tax, and everything else. You also thank me for what I did (or do) for the children. But that is also part of the fee, as it were, that I should be allowed to be everywhere around you.

~

E-8 Mafatlal Park, Bombay
November 1, 1967

So C-316 Defence Colony will be where I will live. I wish I had been there and you hadn't had to handle it all on your own.

I did go and see Indi and it was a deadening experience, with as much warmth as an Egyptian mummy's embrace. She was washing her hair when I arrived (9:45 pm) and came out with a towel wrapped round her head and said, 'Yes?' in the tone of someone conducting an inverview that was not in

---

[99]Amar Nath Kirpal, lawyer and specialist on laws relating to income and allied taxes.

the schedule. I said, 'I didn't come to see you *about* anything. I just came to see you.' I told her I was moving to Delhi, and my various difficulties. There was not a flicker from her and I came home thoroughly extinguished.

I'm sorry I have been so afraid of 'one roof', about its effect on the children, and my mother. The time to consider it would be after I have been in Delhi for a bit. I am wretched over this difference between us, and worried about where you will live.

~

23 Safdarjung Road, New Delhi
December 3, 1967

The shadows lengthen to almost dark, and this is, very likely, my last letter to Mafatlal Park. And I have felt, these last few days, sentimental, as if parting from an old and known association. I'm glad I saw Mafatlal Park with you living in it; sorry that I did not have my abode there. Yet in many ways I did—in intense feeling, over a prolonged period; in tenderness, always abundant, sometimes unknowing how to expend itself; in thought about problems and abstractions. What is a home to a person? What is a home to a man? I had a kind of home in Mafatlal Park. My woman was there and I recognized her and all that went on around her as mine, small things and big—a party; where the telephone was kept, the books, the bathroom, I was aware of them all, while in Bombay, and miles away. I noticed the telephone particularly, a line of communication, its resting place beside your bed, which had a peculiar comfort when I was at a distance; its transfer to the dining room, which had a peculiar discomfort, as if alone out on a limb. I rang you up one night, November 12th, when I could not sleep, and was aware of the distance of the telephone from you. No one lifted it. It was after midnight. I was hungry for a word, yet if I had known it was next to your bed, perhaps I would not have telephoned. Odd? I took a chance.

But Mafatlal Park was more than just the knowledge of my woman living there. To it I poured out much thought, much anguish, many views. I made it my testing place for exposure, both personal and impersonal. I wish I had stayed there, at least one night, on this visit. I had an intense desire to do so, to get up with the stretch of one whole day before me, to shave, dress, and to feel the return of life to slept body and mind and being. But perhaps in some ways it was apt that I did not, that this home was not my resting place even for a single night. It was an identification as complete as could be of myself with what I am, what I seek, what life gave me, and yet not a place where I could lay my head in oblivion of the day's discard, its small victories, its many confusions.

~

E-8 Mafatlal Park, Bombay
December 5, 1967

I have been moved by what you have written about your thoughts of this flat. It does seem strange to be leaving. This is where our correspondence began. It seems like yesterday that I walked into the hall and found an envelope in an unfamiliar handwriting waiting on the bookshelf. It was an already stamped envelope. This was unusual as no one else I've known uses these. Then I opened it, and it was from you. And I knew at once all the possibilities that might grow from it. I showed it to Gautam to read, and later gave him my answer to read. And so it all began.

The flat is strewn with trunks and crates. I would have wanted to leave in any case. There is no reason to stay on.

~

23 Safdarjung Road, New Delhi
December 5, 1967

Meanwhile my PS told me yesterday that I am No. 1 for a
lower than my category house on the list circulated by the
House Committee, which means I should be offered one by
mid-December. So events, rather than us, may make us look
at 'one roof' quickly for a decision.

Much love, darling, and a comfortable journey.

~

Delhi, 1972.

Afterword

I underline and emphasize the points Nayantara has made in her introduction.

These events for me, at the time, seemed an indissoluble amalgam of the public issues with which I dealt, albeit only as one of many actors, and the personal problem and situation that surrounded me. 1964 and 1965 were years of crucial crisis for Jammu & Kashmir state where I worked, culminating eventually with the war in Pakistan. For the civilian side of the administration the most difficult times were the months preceding war, with the infiltration of enemy-directed personnel. A degree of apprehension, even terror, stalked the state, in strong contrast to the beauty of its vast variegated valleys, the mountains, and the dazzling streams, waterfalls and rivers that flow through the land. I recalled the partition of the Punjab in 1947, when, too, I was very much on the scene, as an observer necessarily, but also an actor as head of the Food Department, working at Lahore, then Amritsar and the plains of the new East Punjab state. The dimensions and details were, however, quite different from the invasion of Kashmir, for in the Punjab the enemy was within us, in our very bosom, in the fratricidal and cruel mass killings and injuries between families and communities, temporarily driven insane. Yet both in the Punjab (1947) and Kashmir (1965) there was a strong ruling element of fear. In the Punjab, in the spectacle of maimed and mauled men, women and children, and even of individuals dropping dead before one's eyes, it was as if one smelt fear in the air, and constantly saw it among the thousands who fled home, livelihood and security. In those arriving across the border, there was at first the obvious visible relief of safe arrival, and then after but a few hours, often fear and anxiety, gnawing and desperate, to look for and find livelihood and stability. Alas, there were also those on our side of the border who boasted of the numbers they had helped to eliminate or drive out from their homes.

As these letters indicate, my personal predicament seemed in some measure to march in a degree of apprehension with the public situation, and I learned from both my personal and my public experience a great abiding respect for fear, as an overwhelming protective instinct and power which man should not ignore, and which had much to teach. I thought even that here was a principle of conduct, namely to learn, and to accept, that one must not be afraid of being afraid. Indeed one must admit and welcome fear, for only when one recognized it as friend and counsellor, was it reduced to perspective. With that came the ability to assess its genuine proportions, and to achieve the sanity, serenity, speed, and sometimes the means, to meet and combat it.

The amalgam of the personal and the public also seemed to create for me a levitation of mind and feeling, almost as if I were a kite floating in the air, subject to its whims and its many changes of pace and rigour, in all of which I was one of the players, not in command, yet with an inescapable participation. There seemed an inevitability, an uncertain certainty, that somewhere, somehow, a landing of arrival would take place, possibly accompanied by damage. I lived in an aura of near euphoria, believing in this ultimate, destined landing. Its timing and character were mysteries, but its inevitability was clear, with consequences to be reckoned with, and converted to such forms of life and meaning as they may present; and with challenge, defeat or devastation always as possibilities.

I look back on the realization that through this crisis I was associated in my domestic and personal set-up—unlike Nayantara in hers—with persons whose behaviour to me continued invariably affectionate and human, indeed humane. These included my wife, Champa, her relations, headed by a widowed mother living with us, her friends, and our friends and my own friends and relations. Among the latter were my two sisters who often visited and were in touch. This is not to suggest or imply that there was no opposition or criticism or anger. These were manifest in varying degrees. Disagreement about my line of conduct and hostility to it continued throughout this period. At times tempers erupted and were expressed in speech or writing. Indeed I think I would be correct in assessing that I was in a minority of one—and one only—among this group of people. But nonetheless, behaviour remained unchanged in basic decency and action, even when opinions and feelings of categorical hostility were involved. Affection, and where possible, contact, have in fact survived the years.

At the time, and in retrospect, there has been a strong, constant current of regret and sorrow that my feelings and aspirations, and the direction these took caused strain, cracks, and break in the quality of past relationships, especially in the married association and the home. The fact of divorce is common to almost all societies, and even tends to be taken for granted by some. Yet surely a bigger and more intricate question is involved for which we still seek a solution.

On the one hand truth, and personal freedom based on it, are a passionate need, even a right of the individual, and are not only a matter of doing what you value, but also of being what you value. On the other hand, particularly when there is a choice of alternatives, there is sometimes destruction of the human fabric. What then becomes the correct criterion for judgement? I have long believed that the ultimate sanction of truth and value for the individual has to be the aesthetic, the beautiful. Its essence in the last resort is not a matter of reason only, but necessarily of faith. We must seek faith through reason and knowledge, but in its final form it has the texture of a leap in the dark. That is the story of man's endless pursuit of knowledge, his itch for the unknown frontier forever projecting a new thesis on the established thesis, and it cannot but be true of the adventure of human relations. The answer may lie in comprehending that this then is the process of human growth and development, that the question cannot be one of hurting or being hurt, but of learning to cherish the contradictions the process may involve.

E.N. Mangat Rat
Dehra Dun
1994

Chandigarh Diary

Part 1

Anokha, 32/ Sector 5-A, Chandigarh
January 6, 1963

Pen to paper again. What a relief, though not as satisfactory as typewriter, particularly since subject also full of endless annoyances, e.g. sheer impracticality of entire house. What possessed anyone to design or approve it? Obviously both people responsible were men: Jeanneret and Gautam. More and more am of opinion that men least practical creatures on God's earth.

The ramp. It must go. Gives me feeling upon entering house that it is airport—up ramp with luggage, alongside with passport and health papers. Aside from this, aesthetically wrong. No proportion. Too large and space-eating. Quite hideous. Must take it at a run. Walking difficult. Flat shoes liable to skid, while totally unnegotiable with high heels. Joy only to children who stampede up and down—could roller skate too, no doubt.

Each footfall like thunder and echos through house. Each shutting of door like atomic blast with similar after-effect on nerves. This partly because no carpets on floors due to house only being in use one month a year. But difficult, not to say extravagant, to carpet several miles of ramp and corridor at any time. Absurdity of house: (1) Presupposes inherited millions (which, even if existed, highly unlikely to continue in 'socialist pattern of society'). (2) Presupposes vast retinue of servants. In India this never consistent with efficiency. Witness Meghram: vast in himself but would make snail appear jet-propelled. Cook can't cycle, of all things, so must walk miles to bazaar and back. (3) Black floors which love and cherish dust, yards of glass windows and doors which record every touch, stain, fingerprint, Nangal's muzzle.

Difficulties of housekeeping apparent here after smoothness of living in Bombay. Dhobi faithfully promised to appear on Tuesday. Appeared following Sunday. I scolded. He agreed delay very inconvenient to me. Explanation: wasn't well. Tailor said would come in two days' time. Came in seven. Explanation: toothache. I suggested clove oil. He thanked me. Sweeper said he will come in the morning. Appeared at noon when Gautam's beer party in session in sunshine by pool. Explanation: hangdog look. Said he would definitely come in the morning from now on. Next day, came at noon.

The credit side: children ecstatic with freedom, fresh air and cycles. If this were Sahara and they happy, it would suit me. Also, really irreplaceable view of mountains, pale, dusty, coffee colour with dark green patches. My great pleasure: long cross-country walk every afternoon. No walk as lovely or as varied as this. Lake shining, sailboats jaunty with red, yellow, multi-striped sails. Hard yellow berries growing wild on clusters of thorny bushes. Fields freshly ploughed. Ground soft and cracked in parts like giant jigsaw. Tall dry grass in places. And then the lovely miniature forest with bare branches upstretched, ground covered with crackling shining brown leaves.

Garden: we eat own baby carrots, sweet turnips, lettuce and radishes. Roses in full bloom. Other plants and trees growing well. Gautam likes cooking himself to dark mahogany colour in sun every day. I prefer our gay garden umbrella when there's time to sit under it. This rare.

Also on credit side: all bedrooms comfortable, cosy, with mountain view from each.

Kitchen a chaos: gas, electricity or coal? Use little of each. Nothing really organized without a flaw as one would wish. Must get used to degree of chaos, otherwise life very uncomfortable.

No car. Must depend on Kaka for lift to Sector 22 for shopping. This not always satisfactory. Rush, rush with list, eye on watch, things not always available where anticipated, Gautam anxious to get back for beer. Then, everything far more expensive than in Bombay. Groundnut oil 11/75 in Bombay, 16/- here. Butter -/88 a quarter Ib to Re.1/- here. Only thing cheaper, milk, -/62 a seer to 1/- in Bombay, but not nearly as good. However, eggs and bread much better here.

Spoke to Jugal and Eulie about ramp. Jugal said surface needs something to prevent slipping. Eulie said Jeanneret would be very unhappy. Couldn't I chew over decision to remove it? Said I had chewed over it for a year. She said Oh I see. I spoke to Jeanneret who looked stunned. Said impossible remove ramp. Concept of house built round it. I blame Gautam for approving and endorsing concept. Gautam claims he likes ramp. Says that any criticism, any plans regarding removal must come from me, that I must have talk with Jeanneret. Typical of Gautam.

Have been here since December 22nd this time. First few days madly festive at other people's houses. Semi-collapse of self and decision not to dine out any more. Best times of day, afternoon and after dinner when I read in bed. These not to be jeopardized by aimless chatter and drinking which complete waste of time. Another good interlude, quiet drink with Gutam before dinner, but all too infrequent – not drink, but quiet, since invitations to go out abundant.

Myself considered something of a curiosity. (1) live in slacks (2) like privacy and only too happy to be alone (3) have tendency to make remarks such as 'Indians don't hold their liquor well', etc. Have a feeling am not too popular on this score.

Drinking a favourite topic with Kaka who claims it releases inner man. My view: inner man better off unreleased in many cases. Also, if it takes equivalent of knock on head with hammer to effect releases, surely outer man a more practical proposition. I feel Indians terribly inhibited to start with, hence emboldened only with drink inside, and then to behave frequently in asinine fashion, such as pawing nearest female. Convinced this inhibition partly product of too many taboos in Indian life. Prohibition only prolongs disease instead of wiping it out.

~

Booth children (six of them) and Lorraine have arrived for party. Ranjit and Booth kids racing round on cycles. Noni and Lorraine disdain mob, chatting by themselves. Gitu insisted on putting on blue silk party frock, has ventured down to join mob. Feel ideal solution for all as absolves me of responsibility for games. Only worry: Gopal[100], who will not mix. Refuses to join party. Wish I could shake him out of this. Feel he is too timid. Needs more confidence and toughening up.

~

New Year's Eve was spent dining at Sikris', and then here with Jugal, Eulie, Maxwell Fry and Shiv. Opened bottle of champagne, put on tape recorder and did the twist. Max most original, with several variations of drying back with towel. Shiv looked like advertisement for Chandigarh Driving School, Jugal like Bharat Natyam gone wrong.

---

[100]My Sister Rita Dar's son.

Sikris and guests went on to Club which some seventh sense had told me to avoid. Thank heaven, as Club full, and everyone liquored up. Free for all in progress. Balibir Grewal grabbed by tie and given piece of somebody's mind. Barman pushed aside. Drinks poured and not signed for. Many 'inner men' released with dire effect to surroundings. Story round Chandigarh next day. General dismay expressed, among others by Kalwant Singh who renowned for similar behaviour on several occasions. Smug satisfaction on part of those who not present.

Our contribution to general festivities, our January 2nd party. Forty to drinks. Morning discovery by Gautam that our glasses insufficient Remembered Gautam's frequent uncharitable remarks regarding lack of organization on my part. Nobly refrained from launching like attack. However, thought so. Hurried to town to buy two dozen inferior quality. Salesman in no hurry, however, leisurely unpacking glasses, one by one, to show soundness of each. On selection of one design, told only seven of this kind available. Finally two dozen of a kind found. Assistant called to produce carton. Carton produced without undue haste. Each glass unwrapped to exhibit, then wrapped, placed in carton. Taxi fare mounted since Kaka's car not available. Home, to find cook did not know meaning of stuffed eggs. Had ruined several. Gave task to Meghram who set about it with injured dignity. Happily, 'dip' ordered for that evening never produced, since cook had merely set bowl of dahi out as 'dip'. Pretended raw vegetables intended to be eaten without 'dip'. While preparations going ahead, beer session on near pool.

Rover Grover (named by Max because of roving eye and paw) and wife arrived to be neighbourly. Asked Kaka where his wife was. Kaka replied, 'Typical bourgeois question.' Topic turned to the Chinese. Rover, happily stewed by sun and beer, promised Gautam bottle of Scotch. (Black Knight and beer bought up by army for officers, rum for jawans, hence little and highly priced alcohol left in market. Scotch not available at any price.) Passed Rover and wife today on their way to Delhi, Scotch forgotten. Inner man obviously did not want to provide it.

~

Have feeling Gautam prefers house to children. Hollers if speck on chair, spot on floor, feet not scrupulously wiped on doormat, door left open. Fact is, children not perfect. Things will be spilled. Gautam does not accept fact. Has obviously forgotten what dreadful little monster must have been himself.

Lawn lavishly manured few days ago. No one allowed to step on it. Impossible to start garden croquet (set offered by Roma and Prof). my point: lawn could be manured in our absence, which eleven months.

~

Kids' party in noisy progress in garden. Gopal singing sweetly, alone, in next room. Feel I should try and do something about this. Know from experience would be ineffective. Gopal has no desire to play with other children. Wary of any new situation.

~

Saw film 'Cimarron' here some time ago. Clouds of dust, covered wagons, confusion and violence eventually led to State of Oklahoma. Also, oil discovered, hence fabulous fortunes founded out of rags and nothing. Going into Sector 22, with clouds of dust and bullock carts, feel eventual progress therefore possible here, if distant. However, no oil, and the 'desi bhai's' foibles to contend with, which definite drawbacks.

~

Kids' party getting on successfully. Gopal still not 'with them. Gautam who till now asleep in chair in sunshine on lawn, wakes up and sets off for walk with Eulie and Kaka. Am convinced Gautam not keen on children. Think back to his enthusiastic anecdotes of Peter Sachs' darling 4-year-old in Berne, of Clovis Maksoud's 6-year-old Najua in Delhi. Conclude that for Gautam grass is greener elsewhere. Like some men and other people's wives. Such a pity, as our own children do us credit. Enormously nice people.

~

Clovis Maksoud burst in from Delhi just as last two guests, Jeanneret and Prem Thapar, leaving our cocktail party on 2nd. Last two guests stopped leaving. Clovis ravenous, but only two cold cocktail sausages and few raw carrots left. Dinner held up till last two guests departed. They not in a hurry. Clovis ate carrots, leaves and all. Jeanneret eyed Clovis with suspicion, said, 'Nasser don't like de Gaulle.' Prem Thapar, also suspicious, said he believed in 'Socialist pattern of society' but not in communism. Clovis bewildered.

Dinner finally on table. Ate and talked and talked after dinner. Clovis of opinion, like me, that Gautam not suited to be ambassador. Said Tiger good potential ambassador. Gautam felt he himself would do well as ambassador to Switzerland. No one agreed.

Clovis launched long monologue in vindication of non-alignment. This unnecessary as Shiv, Gautam and myself totally committed to non-alignment. Heartily concurred. Then followed somewhat confused discussion about whether Nehru representative of India or not. This capable of several interpretations, all of which launched. Argument a draw. Next the inevitable Krishna Menon who, by now, discussed threadbare, disposed of innumerable times, but like Amber

'Forever More'. So K. Menon once again wrung out, squeezed dry and put away. And then to bed.

Next morning early, Gautam and Clovis went for walk. Breakfast followed by more non-alignment. Shiv convinced that Clovis soon to become unchallenged leader of Arab world; his eloquence, intellect, persona and beliefs all militate towards this. I agree but feel Clovis should use simpler language, less involved sentences. Involved sentences a distinct drawback to leadership.

Tomorrow Gamtam's chiefs' college friend, Harcharan Singh, (now-ex-minister of newly reduced Kairon Cabinet) coming to lunch. Also Kaka, Prem, Eulie. Complication: electric stove out of order. Lunch will take even longer to prepare. Further difficulty: Prem on diet for ulcer. Must have different food. Staff totally unable to cope with this or any crisis. Feel saddled for life with impotent staff. Life spent dashing between cookbook and oven. How different from last year when Buddhi[101] told ten to lunch or dinner, and we sat back and ate like kings.

~

Kids' party ended with music in drawing room. Noni agitated for twist music. Myself in dark regarding intricacies of tape recorder and other modern machinery. Shiv not too helpful. Ranjit strolled in. Got tape working. Twist tape found and put on. Noni refused to do the twist. Everybody sat in circle listening.

Gautam, Kaka, Eulie arrived from walk but unable sit with them as took kids upstairs for baths and bed. Kaka and Eulie gone when I descended. Jeanneret due, to discuss ramp. Interesting point: in what language discussion to take place

---

[101] My mother's cook.

as Jeanneret determinedly non-English speaking. At same time decidedly not French speaking, but given to frequent repetitions of 'You like?' or 'You no like?' and 'Achcha!'

~

January 7, 1963

Whole idea of building this house began after ten years of living in flat, desperate for own home and above all, garden. Bombay would be wonderful if had a house there. Gautam decided to build house, but in Chandigarh where plot existed. This wonderful idea, only several hundred miles from Bombay.

I realize advantage of house in Chandigarh. Apart from holiday home for kids, Gautam renews friendships with old Chief's College colleagues, friends of family, people who have known him since childhood. All this very important and I realize fulfils an inner need for him. Also remember that Gautam has led 'normal' life like other people, unlike mine. That is, one stage of life has prepared him for next stage, and so a continuous pattern formed that has some connection between past and future. My own life in no way resembles this. No stage prepared me for next stage. Childhood and adolescence in India a different world from American life into which launched unawares at tender age of only just sixteen. Life in India on return from college again strange and unrelated both to college years and childhood memories. Marriage plunged me into wholly alien atmosphere where not only knew no one (since had not mixed in this society), but did not recognize types I met. Values wholly alien. Now, at ripe age of thirty-five, am just beginning to understand scene, to have humour and tolerance, also firmness toward it. Hence can understand Gautam's need to re-identify himself with his background. Above all, house here enables Gautam to breathe air of Punjab. This, he claims, makes new man of him. Evidences of new man: early rising, sitting in veranda for morning tea while mali waters roses and lawn, endless interest in garden, and details and finish of house, beer every noon.

The only drawback of house: it is six hundred miles from Bombay where we must live eleven months of year.

~

Jeanneret arrives – small, bald, with fringe of longish white hair at base of skull. Bow tie, bell-bottom trousers. 'You and me combat?' he asks. I assure him no combat. 'Then why this here?' 'This' is Ranjit's chest expander lying on stool, which I assure Jeanneret is not preparation for combat.

We study ramp. Gautam gives alternative solution which he had propounded two nights earlier when he, I, and Shiv returned from Bill Mathula's dinner. Solution: Wall to break up hall. Lower half of ramp to be replaced by staircase. Solution presented by Gautam as mine. Jeanneret aghast. Pronounces it architectural imbecility. 'Le ramp est le ramp! Cannot be half stair, half ramp!' Adds: 'Le ramp est signature of house!' Adds: 'This no bourgeois conception like every other house of staircase.' Says Gautam: 'My wife thinks entrance dominated by ramp resembles airport.' Jeanneret bursts out: 'But airport one very modern building!'

I venture to say airport inside house rather inconvenient. Feel I am culprit as Gautam declares he loves ramp. Argument back where we started. We repair to drawing room to resume drink, then again to corridor to study ramp.

'Le ramp majestique. One beautiful view of whole corridor upon entrance,' says Jeanneret.

Much discussion, at end of which Jeanneret says, 'only for you will think of système. But very difficile. Must keep la verité.' I agree. So grateful that Jeanneret will think of 'système' that I invite him to soup and salad on 9th.

~

January 9, 1963

Letter from Rita[102] with upsetting news. Has finally found house in Washington, not nice as expected. Earlier inspected lovely house. House agent told by owner: 'Mrs Dar looks all right, but I hope Mr Dar isn't dark.' Rita rejected house. Next house: Owner emerged while Rita being shown round. Introduced as Mrs Dar from Indian Embassy. Owner: We don't want Indians, niggers and kykes here.' Shiv interprets this as follows:

(1) most people are evil and corrupt and would do harm to fellow men. (I don't agree.)
(2) This is last stand of reactionary element to Kennedy's enlightened administration. (I agree.)

However, difficult to stay objective, calm, and fair-minded in face of such incidents. Thank God for non-alignment which preserves our integrity and independence. Would rather die, children and all, than surrender any fraction of integrity which is meaning of freedom.

~

To Prem and Kaka's for lunch of makki ki roti and sarson ka saag and dahi. Delicious beyond words. Nice thing about Chandigarh: delight of garden before and after lunch, informality of entertaining, hence no duress.

---

[102]Sister, Rita Dar, married to diplomat A.K. Dar.

Tomorrow we go to Kaku halvai for puris. Kaku now prospering here while son holds fort in Simla.

Gautam had idea in bath today which he will pass on to Morarji Bhai regarding additional money to Defence Fund. Government should issue a 10 naya paisa stamp to be compulsorily used in addition to normal postage. I feel there will be hue and cry about government using compulsion. Gautam says let there be, and that postcards which are poor man's avenue, be exempt.

~

Little joys of Chandigarh: opposite me in drawing room where I sit is empty bottle of Old Parr whisky which I use as vase. Stands against stark white wall – short, squat, square brown bottle with long neck, containing two exquisite roses, one dark crimson, one flaming sunset, their green leaves forming rippled pattern against wall.

~

January 11, 1963

Guests in December. First Gladys and Shori Kapur. Difficult, because it is necessary to entertain them. Gladys unable to walk due to flat feet. Shori determined to walk despite fact he doesn't enjoy cross-country, and pace too fast. Walk disastrous for him. Their main occupation and pleasure: morning beer and evening whisky.

Myself under great strain. Long dreary hours without real conversation. Amazing how few people talk about anything, how few read. Discussed price and shortage of beer and whisky threadbare. Gladys called Shori a rogue. Topic became increasingly personal. Followed good old worn out Gladys-Shori pattern. Fortunately Crays' eggnog party, Grewals' lunch Mahijit's drinks helped get through days.

Gladys and Shori left 31st morning. Shiv arrived same morning 5:30 am and sat and shivered on veranda, waiting for his room. Had travelled without bedding from Delhi. I said there was trouble ahead, chill, fever, etc. Shiv laughed scornfully, said he took cold baths, used cotton shirts, no woolens even in mid-winter. Came out after cold bath, in cotton shirt. Soon had chill and fever. Dosed with Elkosin and sent to bed by Gautam. Bounced out too soon, in cotton shirt. Chill and fever back again. Shiv insisted fever nothing to do with cold bath and cotton shirt, as used to these all his life. Refused to lie down. Fever persisted. Felt ill off and on. Finally realized he could not leave for Delhi with Gautam on 11th as planned. Forced back to bed where he now is.

~

Evening visit of Prem and Kaka. Prem said Chandigarh small suburban-type community where everyone's affairs known and discussed. This suits Kaka but not her. Also, deep undercurrents, the result of closeness of life with everyone, make her even more uncomfortable, eg. Fletcher business; Eulie becoming too reliant on sleeping pills.

~

Gautam left for Delhi this afternoon. Eulie and Jugal dropped in in the evening. Discussed China. I feel strange position of India in history. Always plum to be obtained. First, jewel of the Indies, where staggering wealth made her Britain's prized possession. Now, focal point democratic experiment in Asia. So much depends on it.

Is India really focal point to extent I think it is, or just in my mind? Am thinking of record kids played before supper:

You gotta have a dream,
If you don't have a dream,
How you gonna have a dream come true?

The dream – India. For me, this is everything. Cannot get to the root of this or reason for it. Does it matter?

~

January 13, 1963

Another golden day—clear sweep of hills with smoky line of further range behind. Straight road past back of our house lined with trees. Children's voices, music, noise, reminding me of 'These have I loved…'

This morning's paper carries article on non-alignment by John Mander, ex-assistant editer of *New Statesman*. Back of my mind all the time—what next? Am still in confused state. So many considerations. I utterly reject Swatantra[103] type attitude which despicable in its haste to surrender dignity. But also cannot find consolation in attitudes of other non-aligned states because, for whatever reason, these sway towards China. What alternative?

Military preparation essential. Large Western aid therefore necessary. But then, willy nilly enter arms race if must keep up with China. Then how different are we from other nations whose arms race we deplore? Yet, to live without arms today obviously disastrous. (Here, feel government policy not disastrous so much as where allotted money went. Spend fairly large per cent of fairly small budget on defence, yet money frittered away on percolators, etc. produced by

---

[103] A conservative political party.

ordnance depots, instead of badly needed equipment. Defence Minister's responsibility, not failure of government policy, except inasmuch as did not remove DM.)

But what does defence mean? If purely defence, it is the means to throw back attack, therefore, minimum requirement the means to do this along entire border forever. Includes nuclear weapons if China deploys same? This a crucial question, for where then does defence stop?

West, in outright criticism of non alignment, forgets three essential points:

(1) The attitude of freedom. The only psychological attitude possible on part of people who were slaves till recently.
(2) Will not add to arms hysteria, nor become totally dependent on any single country for arms, even if this possible, which it isn't because then where would self-respect be?
(3) On the other hand, where is self-respect if large-scale war declared by China and we suffer second round of terrible humiliation? Only one avenue possible ultimately:

  (a) maintain sturdy independence of approach.
  (b) Building up defences with help as far as possible, alone rest of the way. Military preparedness not to be confused with military alliances.
  (c) Fight.
  (d) Die.

This last the great test of courage, the true test for India. All these years did what we thought was best. Miscalculated strength and intention of Chinese. But now we are surprisingly one in determination. If really alone, i.e. alone in Asia (due to Chinese propaganda), then alone, and must face fact and face whatever comes along. Thrilling thought that Indian peasant after centuries will fight for his own earth if it comes to this.

And all India will rise for first time in history, unyielding. Thank you China. And thank you Government that had made proud independence possible, and given every Indian opportunity to stand alone and unafraid.

~

January 16, 1963

Days are slipping away too fast. Yesterday was grey, wet, chilly. Today, again sunshine. Gitu's right arm in sling because she fractured collar bone in fall off Ranjit's cycle.

Every night since Gautam left, people in for drinks in Shiv's room. Myself thoroughly unpleasant (when not occupied in household chores) towards Shiv. Have been lecturing, scolding, cold, aloof. I am surprised when he says I am responsible for his 'restoration', his return to world of the living.[104] Do not see how I am responsible, but am glad. Suggest his return be made fuller gradually. Should meet people, go out more, discard a little of his intellectual arrogance and descend to the level of ordinary people. Also should look upon woman as woman, with all the delightful expectations and consequences this implies—not as part of dialectic. Shiv agrees, but feels the latter proposition (woman as woman) difficult because of age, uncertainty regarding future, and own fastidious inclinations. Says he would rather keep me in mind—as symbol, and pay homage. No return expected or demanded.

Am not unwilling to be symbol as it involves no effort on my part, but feel relationship for him thoroughly unsatisfactory and one-sided. Therefore, hope that woman-as-woman idea will materialize for Shiv. Age etc. nonsense. Typically Indian limitation.

---

[104]Shiv was recovering from a divorce.

Shiv writes in my diary: 'Yes, but a limitation which enables a self-contained and undemanding adjustment with life rather than frantic dependence on others. A dependence of the latter kind is unfair since it imposes one's own shortcomings on others and creates emotional expectations which have no basis.

'You are certainly responsible—or my visit here is—for my resurrection. This is the first step. What you say can follow and probably will, is my relationship with women. But since I have already been in such a relationship and been hurt by it, I find it difficult for the moment to think of women in terms of sex. That is why I regard your affection and friendship as a symbol of the kind of relationship which endures because it is not demanding on either side. Thus I can pay you homage as a woman who is always wonderful. In this case the abstraction and the pleasant aspect of the reality are combined. The "unpleasant" aspect may exist but I am not a recipient of it since it is a part which by definition concerns human beings in relations of complete totality.

'It follows that in my present state of development I regard the relationship (partially in operation) as the basis of an intellectual and moral strength which as Hegel said reverses the process of the self-alienation of man.'
(End of Shiv's contribution)

~

Dinner at Eulie's on January 14th. Drinking released Kaka's, Balbir's and Ron Booth's 'inner men' which apparently still adolescent, because Kaka suggested kissing games. Hand-holding and kissing began. Boring, not to say revolting.

~

Part 2

December 23, 1963

Came ahead with four children. Gautam involved in big-deal discussions in Delhi which are endless because Ministry of Finance and Ministry of Commerce & Industry not coordinated and decisions clash. Also the two Ministers don't get on, and one has ulcer, which always detrimental to good cheer. In this case good cheer essential since seven crores in foreign exchange involved – but one would think foreign exchange grew on trees because Finance Ministry utterly unconcerned. Gautam at it hammer and tongs with and without Swiss colleagues. His persistence, thoroughness, competence, continually astonish me. I wish, however, that business discussions did not involve so much alcohol. Leads to nerves, hysteria, quarrelling, exhaustion. Much more work possible without it, but tell that to the marines as far as anybody cares.

~

Children whooped for joy when plane landed in Chandigarh, yelled when Anokha came in sight. So excited and happy to be here. Garden looks beautiful with hedges grown tall and trim, trees and shrubs flourishing. 'My' tree already a good height. Wretched ramp still here. Start trudging up and down with armfuls of warm clothes taken out of trunks in garage. Must dispense with mothball routine and seal clothes in polythene bags so they can be left in cupboards.

Another primitive sight: sweeper on haunches, sullenly dragging filthy wet rag over yards and yards of floor. Impossible at this rate to clean entire floor space in less than a week. Carpets need brushing. Hoovers not yet available in India. But soon will be.

Gautam arrives next day assures me glass cleaning will present no problem as companies will hire out cleaners. This begun in Bombay, but I fear no companies to do this here in my lifetime However, in my lifetime Gainda Mull Hemraj has actually organized itself into tidy shop in Sector 17 (untidy one remains in Sector 22). Here I actually find Saffola, unlike last year, and Indian dried soups. So far no cause for pessimism in food department. Also overjoyed to find cold storage where plump chickens available. No more stringy creatures from bazaar with Kirti Singh wringing scrawny necks behind kitchen.

~

Another year nearly over. Stock-taking finds Gautam at the top. No further to go in office, responsibility-wise and title-wise. Me—ready to conquer quite a few new problems, which may be the result of coping on lecture tour in America.[105] Lecture tour decidedly helpful in preparing one to face almost anything. Everybody ought to go on a lecture tour which if it doesn't drive one mad has character-building possibilities. Grateful my tour over and character built.

Time slipping by too fast. This cause for both challenge and regret. Too much still undone. So much to do. Novel begun in Mahableshwar still hanging suspended.

Dread Gautam's new role in office, as my own precious, beloved incalculably cherished privacy must needs be somewhat invaded. Imagine, any other time or stage of existence, would have been delirious with joy at getting house in town and shack in Juhu. Now terrified at own new role extra entertaining trips to Delhi. How to keep that area of mind quiet and concentrated so that novel can proceed? Feel highly irritable when cannot work.

~

---

[105]To promote Nayantara Sahgal's book, *From Fear Set Free*.

December 24, 1963

Christmas Eve. Sunshine and roses and children on their bicycle. Day began uncertainly with fuse of last night not repaired. But Prem Thapar and Ron Booth both helpful and obliging, so did not feel stranded though Gautam left for Delhi last night. Last bit of big deal to be tied up. All the more urgent to conclude it now since Manubhai Shah has resigned and resignation accepted. Gautam finds Mamu's attitude toward this baffling and feels it is terrible mistake as Manubhai now well-known and widely respected internationally. Gautam feels Manubhai had no choice since two-thirds of his responsibility taken from him and given to Kanungo who is a nitwit. Resignation will be blow to foreign industry which get on well with Manubhai, and for country which he served so well. G. feels TTK's[106] dislike for Manubhai responsible for this impasse and, if so, looks like another Rasputin in our midst. Also, private sector losing its spokesmen one by one.

Fuse finally repaired and lights and geysers finally functioning by 11 o'clock, but too late for bath as thousand other things to do.

Lala Meherchand comes with man to remedy curtain rings so that they won't make an ear-shattering noise when drawn together and apart. Says, naturally rectangular rings will make noise and only round rings will be silent. I feel nothing to do with shape but with size of ring. Point finally made and Meherchand and man repair to bazaar for larger rings.

I run up and down yelling at children for not tidying rooms. Get cheeky reply from Noni, irritation from Ranjit who bent on cycling endless miles before lunch. I tell him cycle is with Gopal Singh who must fetch sugar from ration shop. Ranjit asks why it must be away till 4 pm as Gopal Singh claims. I explain ration

---

[106]T.T. Krishnamachari

shop in Sector 22, sugar more valuable than diamonds and far rarer, long queue collects for it, hence much time spent. Ranjit tidies room, sobered by realization that otherwise must have afternoon milk without usual two spoons of sugar.

I go into kitchen to see if all well and find Das smoking State Express cigarette. Pretend haven't noticed. Das very useful and the odd cigarette, even if State Express, expendable.

~

Krishna and Choti arrive en route to Simla. Spend pleasant hour in sun having beer. Garden umbrella collapses, just missing Choti and glass of beer. Gita and Manju in hysterics. Krishna and Choti love house and garden and enjoy interlude.

Children are angels and eat good quick lunch to vacate table for us. They have spent morning dancing to tape. After lunch, seeing Krishna and Choti off, I am overjoyed to see Gopal cycling. This comparable to invention of wheel in man's progress. Great stride forward, pregnant with untold possibilities for Gopal. I go in filled with subdued excitement. Go out in a few minutes and Gopal is on bar as usual with Das doing the cycling. Feel greatest benefit of all bicycles has been to Das.

~

Gopal is too quiet this time. School has squashed something in him. Hates it. Says so repeatedly. Also, though never mentions it, misses home and parents and Jyoti. At breakfast this morning I tell him of his Mummy's frequent enforced absences from her parents, of every diplomat's child's absence from his parents. He laughs at my anecdotes and face lights up but soon becomes sombre again. I ask him if he is sad, medium, or happy. He says, sad in school, medium otherwise. I tell him to try and make it medium in school, happy otherwise, as little children are meant to laugh and have fun, and never, never be sad. He jumps up, hugs me in usual clinging, affectionate way, and renders long solemn monologue about hating school, but says will try and be happy outside it.

~

December 25, 1963

Asked for guest house car at 10 am to go to Sector 22 for cake and tonight's chicken. At 11 still no car. Sent Das on cycle with instructions to fetch chicken and cake. We trooped over to Booths' where Christmas cheer celebrated with community dropping in for eggnog. Met couple who belong to Peace Corps, another who working in education here under British Council, and Kittu Riddle and husband. Kittu very touched at my references to Mr Parker in book. Talk about old days and changing world. If only felt it was changing for better. Life finds me, even on Christmas Day, uncertain about most values. I feel uncertainty—along with kindness, consideration, and a love of beauty thrown in—the only course.

~

Part 3

January 7, 1965

The terror and sorrow of trying to live as a whole person, revealed, oneself, true. The ugly face of anger, the distortions of jealousy, the floodtide of passion let loose, all because of this.

Don't live like that then. Bury yourself in part, let only a little show, the rest lie hidden, festering. Only you can't. Because you were not born to lie half-buried, not born to live half-alive. You were born to a vivid awareness of the hazy purple hills, the starry sky, the evening light on the lake, the forest where nude branches create a delicate tracery against the winter air.

It is a beautiful world this morning after the third night of the new moon. It must have been the third, last night, for the virginal curve had thickened and the red new-born glow had changed to calm silver. This morning the wind is cold but not sharp. It is fresh and clean, like belief that comes unbidden because it is natural, like hope because it is instinctive. And somewhere in consciousness is 'the soul's invincible surmise' that you will not only survive, but live, with all you have; the struggle will continue and with it the hurt and the bruises and the bleeding, but not for nothing— for in the process a human being will have been born, rich in faith, blessed by belief, dauntless in courage.

So much to think about: Tradition—how much of it should we carry on our backs like beasts of burden? Convention—where in all these tortuous pathways does choice lie, choice of belief and choice of action? Where does freedom lie, and integrity, and duty?

So the New Year begins with much to think about, and against this background life goes on. And I have been strangely blank and neglectful of its needs – the children needing me, the household not quite efficiently run, Mummie's visit over without my having flavoured it at all. Above all, not being in touch with the children. Have they missed it, thought me far away, cut off? Have I hurt them, upset them?

Ranjit, I think, has been most aware, because Noni has been deeply involved with new friends and activities, and Gitu absorbed in Manju. Ranjit, always clinging, affectionate, uncertain, has lingered uneasily on the fringes of each outburst. What has that done to him? No harm, I think. For why should

Charcoal sketch of Nayantara Sahgal and
Gautam Sahgal by Elizabeth Brunner, 1949.

children be protected, isolated, shielded from the impact of adult emotions and reactions? Why should they be shut out? They must know that adults quarrel, that their own small world is full of fierce emotions, capable of fury, of hate, as much as of love and peace: that a small world is part of a larger world; that no corner of it is exempt from suffering, as none is exempt from hope and love; that all these things make life; that living is acceptance of them, but that it is also the struggle against them; that it is always the whole self reacting to whatever situation arises, with confidence and courage.

~

January 22, 1965

Time to go again, tomorrow morning. This evening on our walk through fields and woods the sky looked immense, the green and brown and blue of earth and hills vivid, and I thought, 'look thy last on all things lovely every hour....'

At last the roses have burst into bloom, into exquisite, unbearably lovely bloom. The peach-coloured ones look almost sculptured, still and perfect, flawless in cut. Nothing in the garden affects me as much as these roses do. And I am filled with sadness at parting from them, from all this—and am I actually looking my last upon it?

~

Appendix 1

An article by Nayantara Sahgal, published under a different title in *Indian Express* August 29, 1964.

No Shadows in Kashmir

Sultry August weather augmented and intensified every aspect of the beauty of Srinagar. It had not rained for several days and the lull had produced a shimmering heat. We noticed with a heightened clarity the full-blown roses and giant dahlias in the hotel garden, the brilliant green of the fields, a sky like buttermilk, feathery poplars skirting a lake like glass. People said it was the prelude to a storm and that a good shower would soon cool the Valley again, but meanwhile the sun was strong, the air warm, and there were no shadows over Kashmir.

The people, as lovely as the land, went about their business with a typical serenity and naturalness, two qualities notably absent from much of the rest of India. This would seem a paradox in what has been a storm centre for so long, but as with so many storms, the centre of this one has remained still. The Kashmiris have lived with insecurity for seventeen years and insecurity makes a people both sensible and practical. There are fewer flights of fancy among them, more earthy common sense than among the rest of us. When they take flight in fancy it is towards the things for which fancy was intended, poetry, love and the appreciation of beauty, not politics, commerce or the conduct of daily affairs. We had a fresh glimpse of their approach to life during a recent trip to Srinagar.

We drive to Dachigam with a friend. Here the rest house is set in a garden against a backdrop of steep mountainside. Beyond the wire fencing that surrounds the garden are tall grass, brooks and the thick woods of the game sanctuary. On arrival we found that a minister of the state government was already there, a fact which in any other part of India would have made a picnic uncomfortable, if not impossible. We did wonder for a moment whether we should stay. But the minister came forward to greet us and apologized for his presence. He said he would sit under the furthest tree to finish his work and hoped he would not disturb us. We chose a walnut tree across the lawn from beds of riotous pink roses and opened our beer and apple juice while the chowkidar brought us green walnuts off the tree. After the minister had finished dictating we asked him to join us while his speech was typed. We discovered he was eloquent in two languages, Urdu and English, besides his own Kashmiri, and well-versed in Persian poetry and the culture that goes with Hafiz. Conversation ranged over politics, poetry and wine with the rhythm and nuance of a musical composition. It was hard to believe we were with a minister of a state government, discussing different facets of our national life on a level far above detail and routine. Two things stood out—the quality of the conversation which had freedom and range and was lit with a brimming intelligence, and the total absence of constraint. We might in any other part of India have been uncomfortably conscious that we were with a VIP, if indeed a VIP had consented to share a bottle of beer with anyone without compromising his reputation. Here we were only aware we were with a gentleman, one who possessed all the worthwhile attributes of that much-maligned word. It is a hallmark of Kashmir that there are gentlemen in politics, men of education, breeding and culture, and that politics can still attract such men.

After ten years of rigid personal rule there is an atmosphere of relaxation, a huge sigh of relief, as it were. And this is the achievement of those in power today. The release of Sheikh Abdullah was an act of faith and faith is the foundation supremely necessary to the building of a free society. In Kashmir today there is a strong base for a free society. It is also the only truly emotionally integrated society in India, for there is no communal feeling at any level, a fact brought into sharp focus after the theft of the sacred relic. Srinagar remained calm and the only damage done was to the property of those, both Muslim and Hindu, whom the people felt had caged them and violated their rights. The incidents following the theft were in a very real sense the assertion of outraged feeling against an unpopular regime. Today no part of India can claim the complete absence of communal feeling that Kashmir enjoys, and this is another hallmark of this state. Men who dislike each other's politics meet each other socially and are friends. There are few inhibitions about food. Even the Dachigam bear, unlike bears elsewhere, is supposed to eat meat, and we were warned by the chowkidar not to venture too far into the woods. During the upheaval of the partition that rocked the subcontinent and through all the tension that followed, leaders of every opinion in the Valley were able to ensure that there was no communal killing and serenity reigned.

Lying under the walnut tree at Dachigam, listening to my companions, a new awareness and appreciation of Kashmir dawned on me. I left them to their talk and going to the far end of the garden picked the most perfect pink rose I could find for the minister in gratitude for the uniquely civilized approach to living he and his state embodied. Our friend, who is chief secretary to the state government, invited us to a dinner where the Prime Minister of Kashmir was present. There was no reserve or constraint because he was there. Conversation did not revolve around him and nobody deferred to him in any way. He was a guest like any other and he injected the discussion with his own frequent humorous observations. We ate and drank and talked in an atmosphere of relaxation and intimacy. I felt that this man's personality contrasted strangely with the idea, current in parts of India, that stern leadership is the answer to our problems. For this is a man who believes that the human equation does not blossom under sternness, and his tolerance and humanity could be cultivated with impunity in other states. It has been amply demonstrated that Indians are a people who respond to gentleness and reason. Our troubled states today are those where the proverbial strong men are in power and ruthlessness the guide. There has been no room for the individual in their approach, no exercise of compassion or tolerance without which there will never be a strengthening of the democratic processes. We can learn a lesson from Kashmir today where confidence and hope exist because a prime minister rules with tranquil assurance and faith in the future. I did not have the feeling that there was a problem in Kashmir. I felt there were problems elsewhere in India and that we had much to learn from Kashmir about the manner in which they ought to be tackled. So many of our problems are magnified because of our pathetically limited approach to them. In Kashmir today there is no such narrowness or limitation. If the Nehru approach to politics is reflected anywhere in India, it is Kashmir that now exemplifies it, and Kashmiri leadership alone that projects its grace, its generosity and humanity.

Our friend has served the Government of Jammu and Kashmir just six months and we asked him his impression of it. It was the only state, he told us, that he would now willingly serve, not only because of the generally high standard of intelligence and appealing practicality of its people, but because of the enlightenment of its leaders and the manner of their response to the challenges ahead of them. There is clear thinking in Kashmir and no cobwebs of humbug to cloud it.

Kashmir has much to give the rest of India. What have we to offer Kashmir? First, the simple direct and final assurance that it is a living part of us and there can be no discussion at any level about this. Second, all that we can contribute in the way of help and advice toward better crops, greater industry and richer opportunities for its people. It showed a cowardly lack of faith in us that the tourist trade was so severely hit this year. The tourist can never in any circumstances come to harm in Kashmir for the Kashmiri needs him and well understands that the politics of the Valley are his own. He has never attempted to inflict them on the visitor unless the visitor himself is a politician. Nor has there ever been such a propitious year as this for tourists. It is our shame that we did not recognize this, and our loss that we deprived ourselves of the joys that only a holiday in Kashmir can provide. And finally, we can offer Kashmir the homage all civilized people owe to unique beauty and the free spirit, and the pledge that these gifts will freely flourish in their closer association with us.

Appendix 2

A letter to the press written (but not sent) by E.N. Mangat Rai on the occasion of Pratap Singh Kairon's death.

February 6, 1965
Jammu-Tawi

Sir

As a man of sorts—a civil servant who worked with Sardar Pratap Singh Kairon for several years, you will permit me to express my horror at the way he has been killed. I am shocked, though not surprised, as I thought such reprisal may, in fact, come much earlier than it has. It is an indication not merely—as I have no doubt many will interpret it—of the inherent violence latent in the Punjab, but perhaps more so of our lack of effective and reasonably quick institutional and conventional arrangements for grievance and insult, which no doubt several persons felt had been inflicted on them, to seek enquiry, and where justified, redress. And yet the murder is wholly wrong, a disgraceful crime. For Pratap Singh Kairon represented a principle and need in Indian life—no humbug—you are what you are—you do what you can—a principle we must respect if we are to succeed, which often seems doubtful.

To kill such a man is to kill yourself—that part, perhaps the most valuable, that rebels, that will not accept the half-baked paraphernalia of sighs and aspirations which frequently masquerades as policy. As for example prohibition as it is practised, or the trappings of khadi in an independent, textile-producing and exporting India. Kairon was real-politik. Whatever his faults and deviations, he was real and that's why he lasted.

Let's take our hats off to him—so easy when a man is dead—for he did represent and light up a principle in Indian public life—that we shall live and square our account with reality, however distasteful, however corrupt. That he should have been displaced from power goes without saying. That he should be respected and loved for realism goes without saying, as that we should learn to be idealistic and yet practical. Have we learned? When will we? Pratap Singh Kairon helped. Will we help ourselves? To the extent that we do, we shall pay homage to a great, and deluded, and much misled, Punjabi—nevertheless, a MAN.

Appendix 3

Transmission from D.P. Dhar, Home Minister, Jammu & Kashmir, to Prime Minister regarding Pakistan's intentions.

Srinagar August 8, 1965
Transmitted 4.30 p.m.

From D.P. Dhar, Home Minister J & K, for L.P. Singh, Home Secretary, for immediate attention of Prime Minister Stop We have assessed situation in Kashmir in detailed consultation with local army authorities including Corps Commander, civil administration, and amongst ourselves at political level under guidance of Chief Minister Stop It is our unanimous view that this is an invasion planned and directed by Pakistan and cannot be considered a mere border incident or violation of the ceasefire line Stop This is evident from the fact that trained well-armed and ration-supplied men have entered behind our defence line in considerable depth, even up to 40 miles and within 3-4 miles of Srinagar, and are engaged in attacking army positions, civilian objectives and persons in an organized planned manner Stop It is my view that at least 6-7 battalions must be earmarked for this manoeuvre, and that entry will continue Stop It is our assessment that Pakistan aims at tempting us to a dispersal of our forces in a terrain where we will lose the initiative and men, and that more immediately she intends to create large-scale internal dislocation and disorder to convince the world that Kashmir is in revolt and is held by sheer force and violence Stop Our conclusion is that we must consider that the ceasefire agreement has been violated and ceases to operate Stop India is therefore now in the position of being driven to defend its territorial integrity in the most advantageous way and place it can Stop In this situation we are categorically of the view that an announcement of policy, backed by suitable action, should be taken in hand immediately Stop We consider the policy announcement should be made by this evening, preferably appearing in the evening news today Stop Our reasons for this urgency are both internal and external Stop There is evidence that Pakistan has synchronized action with August 9th the anniversay of Abdullah's arrest in 1953 which was to be observed in hartals and the like locally by anti-India political parties Stop It is likely therefore that on this date Pakistan will attempt internal disorder and take the initiative in its propaganda to the world that Kashmir is in revolt Stop We will then be in the position of having to give a rejoinder to world opinion, which is a defensive and weak posture, which should be avoided and the initiative retained by us Stop If in fact there is disorder internally this will lend credence to Pakistan's case, and we will not at that stage be believed in our invasion facts Stop From the internal point of view the most effective strength and determination will be given to the morale of pro-India elements and the most effective deterrent to those who are anti-India or doubtful if a clear announcement is available from Delhi before August 9th that it regards this as an invasion of India to be resisted by all means necessary and available Stop We would therefore pray that you consider the subject in this background and do not delay the policy announcement till our preparations for action are complete Stop We recognize the need for action backing up policy but in the present circumstances we see overwhelming advantage in an announcement of policy today backed up by appropriate action as soon as practical.

Responses to *Relationship*

From Professor Granville Austin, author of *The Indian Constitution*

Dear Tara and Nirmal

I am reading your *Relationship*. Much as I liked you both before reading it, I like you more now. Thank you for the opportunity to share your tenderness and passion and steadfastness—attributes I find so lacking in much of life, and others' relationships today. I am taking the book home to Nancy who, predictably, will share my reaction.

I have booked a seat home to her on 20th June. Research has to be concluded sometime, no matter the need felt to learn more. This work is like an onion: peel away one skin and many more remain. My ignorance increases daily, not decreases. There is so much I want to know. 'God willing and the rivers don't rise', I shall return, with Nancy, to India in the autumn of 1995 with a nearly completed manuscript. I may ask you—each of you—then to read parts of it for 'howlers' and for points that badly need to be included. Whether or not you are able to do this is, of course, up to you.

All good wishes and very warm regards to you both. Be well and happy.

Yours sincerely,
Red Austin
June 5, 1994 – India International Centre, New Delhi

~

From Lakshman Menon, nephew of Gautam Sahgal

Dear Tara Mami,

Thankyou for your letter and birthday wishes. Men seem to have a rougher time growing older—burgeoning middles or falling hair or both! I envy you for looking as matchlessly lovely as you did when I was fourteen!

I haven't seen a copy of *Relationship* yet. But I did come across horrid old Khushwant Singh's review of it in the *Sunday Observer* and I must confess I was horrified and angry at his casual, dismissive portrayal of Mamu as some kind of lout with fists for a brain. I wrote a letter in protest (which was duly published after some heavy editing) in which I said you had the right to your perspective of your relationship with Mamu, and the privilege to write about that particular period in your life, but that Khushwant's crude characterization of Mamu was grotesque.

I suppose the fact is that I never knew Mamu and you as a 'couple'. I was far too young when we all did meet occasionally in Simla—the graveyard of many a Sahgal relationship—and it was only much later—sometime after your divorce—that I came to know you, and later still when I came to know Mamu. With both of you I felt unfettered by the usual 'Sahgal relation'—who's in, who's out, who's rowing—and in time I got to know each of you independent of my mother and the family, and as people rather than as my relations. I don't have to tell you how much I value knowing you and how much I love you both, and with that, I guess, comes a sense of protectiveness towards each of you.

At a time when I was emotionally spotty and adolescent you treated me as an adult with valid adult views, and I felt then as I do now that we could meet and talk together as such. And with Mamu—I can never forget his hospitality and great generosity of spirit to me. It was not just that he started me on my career, but that he found the time and took the trouble to get to know me and to build an equation with me which I greatly cherish. And so, to end this ramble, I don't know how I will react to *Relationship*—possibly I will be rather torn by it, but there it is!

Lots of love as always,
Lakshman
May 19, 1994 – Dubai, UAE

~

From Stephen Espie, former editor of Span magazine

Dear Tara and Nirmal

You have written a very moving and powerful book. It has a special meaning for me since I met you both only five years after the last letter in this book was written. Do you remember the occasion of our meeting? I had just arrived in India, June 1972, and Tom Dove hosted a 'champagne cocktail party' (in Dan Oleksiw's house) for me to meet some people he said would be worthwhile meeting.

It took courage for the two of you to publish these letters. And it took even more courage to do what you two did in 1964-67, the 'house you built'… One phrase of Nirmal's describes Tara with powerfully poignant words: '…too many people see only the façade, and you have learned to control the effervescence within.'…

Nirmal's letter of 3/1/66 quoted from one of my favourite poems, a poem I read again and again, Wordsworth's great 'Ode on the Intimations of Immortality from Recollections of Early Childhood'. What the two of you did—the 'house' you created—was and is 'apparelled in celestial light'.

The book is bathed in that same light.

Congratulations – Love, Steve
November 18, 1994 – Shakti Kutir Farm, Patinan Village,
West Bengal

~

From Ratna Ramchandani, wife of Gulab Ramchandani,
Headmaster, the Doon School

Dear Tara,

I have just finished reading *Relationship* and I want you to
know that I almost suffered with you and Nirmal through
your ordeal by fire. Providentially there is a happy ending
and all is well.

You have been extremely courageous to expose yourselves
to public view and I salute your total honesty. We have met
often but hardly know each other. Now I feel I understand you
so much better. Hopefully we will have other opportunities
to really talk.

With warm good wishes to you and Nirmal – Yours
sincerely, Ratna
July 27, 1994 – Shamrock Cottage, Landour, Mussoorie

~

From Khushwant Singh, writer

Dear Tara,

Altaf Gauhar reviewed *Relationship* for *Nation of Pakistan*. He had many nasty things to say about me—a cuckold who was Master Tara Singh's secretary and advisor about ethnic cleansing of Muslims from East Punjab. I don't know where he got that garbage from. I was in London 1947-51 and met Tara Singh three times in mid-1950's on the Punjabi Suba resolution. He claims to know all about our little circle in Lahore. Neither Mangat Rai nor Champa were in the circle. Reviewing the book gave the fellow an excuse to libel everyone. I was very upset.

Love,
Khushwant
July 22, 1994—New Delhi

~

From Nonika Sahgal, my daughter (on a birthday card)

Your new book *Relationship* seems to have made a hit with my friends. I hope to borrow it from them sometime. They say it is exquisitely written. I didn't like Khushwant's (*Sunday Observer*) or Kamath's (*Pioneer*) reviews very much as they were one-sided and heavily in your favour. All the best, Noni

May 10, 1994 – New Delhi

~

From Sumanta Banerjee, author of *Crime and Urbanization: Calcutta in the 19th Century and Dangerous Outcast: the Prostitute in 19th Century Bengal.*

Dear Nayantara,

Just finished reading *Relationship*. Heart-wrenching! Amazing—the way both of you fought it out—you especially. I met E.N. Mangat Rai once for a brief while at Sarvat's place (was it some time in the early 2000's when we had just shifted to Dehra Dun?) As we sat in a corner, I remember him recalling his Bengali ancestry when he heard my surname. And then, at the end of the party, as we rose to depart – and there were you emerging from the crowd—and he said, 'She's my wife'. Being an ingenue in Dehra Dun circles, and not knowing either of you, I passed over the remark as a mere introduction. Only after reading your letters that I discover that those words of his carried a long history of struggle, pain, anguish and courage.

To add a personal note, the letters reminded me of the terrible agony that Bizeth and I suffered in the 1980's when we parted—a strange co-existence of a life of love and passion with another partner on the one hand, and a peculiar nostalgic pain at the end of a marital relationship on the other! It's another matter that we've come back together. It's a different story.

Shall return the book when you're back—Wishing you a very happy New Year—Sumanta

December 30, 2006 – Dehra Dun